Wasting a Crisis

Wasting a Crisis

Why Securities Regulation Fails

PAUL G. MAHONEY

THE UNIVERSITY OF CHICAGO PRESS CHICAGO AND LONDON

The University of Chicago Press, Chicago, 60637
The University of Chicago Press, Ltd., London

Paperback edition 2016
Printed in the United States of America

24 23 22 21 20 19 18 17 16 2 3 4 5 6

ISBN-13: 978-0-226-23651-3 (cloth)
ISBN-13: 978-0-226-42099-8 (paper)
ISBN-13: 978-0-226-23665-0 (e-book)
DOI: 10.7208/chicago/9780226236650.001.0001

Library of Congress Cataloguing-in-Publicatioon Data

Mahoney, Paul G. (Paul Gerard), 1959– author.
Wasting a crisis : why securities regulation fails / Paul G. Mahoney.
pages cm
Includes bibliographical references and index.
ISBN 978-0-226-23651-3 (cloth : alkaline paper) —ISBN 978-0-226-23665-0 (e-book)
1. Securities industry—Law and legislation—United States. 2. Securities industry—Law and legislation—United States—History—20th century. I. Title.
KF1070.M34 2015
346.73'0926—dc23
2014031054

♾ This paper meets the requirements of ANSI/NISO Z39.48-1992 (Permanence of Paper).

TO MY PARENTS, MARY AND BERTRAND MAHONEY;
MY UNCLE, JOHN L. GUBSER;
AND MY GRANDMOTHER, THE LATE MRS. JOHN H. GUBSER

Contents

Acknowledgments ix

Introduction 1

CHAPTER 1. Long before the New Deal 9

CHAPTER 2. The Blue Sky Laws: A Tale of Progressives and Interest Groups 20

CHAPTER 3. What the Securities Act Got Right 37

CHAPTER 4. What the Securities Act Got Wrong 49

CHAPTER 5. Did the SEC Improve Disclosure Practices? 77

CHAPTER 6. Was Market Manipulation Common in the Pre-SEC Era? 100

CHAPTER 7. Regulation of Specific Industries 118

CHAPTER 8. The Old Is New Again: Securities Reform in the Twenty-First Century 149

Appendix A 171

Appendix B 173

Notes 179

Bibliography 185

Index 197

Acknowledgments

I owe many intellectual debts. George Priest first exposed me to law and economics as a student during the early 1980s, a time of great ferment in the field, and encouraged me to think about an academic career. I had the extraordinary privilege of clerking for Judge Ralph Winter, one of the pioneers of the economic analysis of corporate law. Ralph's example and our many deeply substantive conversations convinced me to focus on corporate and securities law. He is everything one could ask for in a teacher, employer, friend, mentor, and role model.

Also in the early 1980s, Frank Easterbrook and Dan Fischel wrote a series of articles that set the agenda for corporate and securities law scholarship for that decade and beyond. Those articles formed the basis for their book *The Economic Structure of Corporate Law* (1991), published just as I began my academic career. At about the same time, Roberta Romano pioneered the use of empirical methods in the legal literature on corporate and securities law, bringing legal scholars into conversations that had previously taken place almost exclusively among financial economists. These three scholars had a deep influence on my own agenda and methodology. I've been fortunate to get to know each, and each commented on parts of this book. Roberta read the entire manuscript and has my particular thanks.

Parts of chapters 5 and 6 represent joint work with Jianping Mei and, in the case of chapter 6, Guolin Jiang. These chapters contain what I regard as some of the most important empirical results in the book. Jianping and Guolin deserve an equal part of any credit that is due. I'm grateful to them for allowing me to include our joint work here.

I've been fortunate to have an extraordinarily supportive and intellectually demanding group of colleagues at the University of Virginia, where

I've spent my entire academic career. Countless conversations with current and former corporate and securities law colleagues Barry Adler, Ian Ayres, Michal Barzuza, Albert Choi, Quinn Curtis, Mike Dooley, George Geis, John Harrison, Ed Kitch, Kevin Kordana, Saul Levmore, John Morley, George Triantis, and Andy Vollmer shaped the ideas contained in the book, and most of them commented extensively on one or more parts of it. My three most recent predecessors as dean, Tom Jackson, Bob Scott, and John Jeffries, were unfailingly helpful and encouraging.

Colleagues from other disciplines, some within the Law School and many in other parts of the University of Virginia, helped me anticipate substantive or methodological criticisms from their fields. Historians Barry Cushman, Chuck McCurdy, and Ted White, economists Yiorgos Allayannis, Bob Bruner, Robert Conroy, Ken Eades, Leora Friedberg, Bob Harris, and John James, and John O'Brien, an expert in eighteenth-century British literature, all gave generously of their time.

The University of Virginia Law Library was a partner throughout, doggedly tracking down sources and in general upholding its reputation as the best law school library in the nation. Special thanks go to Cathy Palombi, who spent many hours on the telephone persuading other libraries to lend us archival material and carefully tending it while in our custody, and to Kent Olson, who helped me navigate the early twentieth-century financial press.

An army of research assistants worked on the various parts of the book, often meticulously entering or verifying data from microfilmed newspapers or, in more recent years, from online archives. They also carefully read contemporary accounts of market, legislative, and regulatory developments. I'm very grateful to Kelly Baker, Daniel Barden, Travis Batty, Julie Bentz, Katherine Beury, Lindsay Bird, Nick Bluhm, Federico Botta, Rebecca Brown, Andrew Brownstein, Theresa Clark, Adrienne Davis, Ryan Davis, Matt Einbinder, Padraic Fennelly, Will Gould, Sangyean Hwang, Kelly King, David Luce, Matt Middleton, Jennifer Mink, Noah Mink, Kimberly Paschall, Thomas Pearce, Anna Shearer, Kris Shepard, Angela Sinkovits, and Jacky Werman for all their help.

I received incisive and helpful comments on parts of the book from Franklin Allen, George Benston, Mary Anne Case, Jill Fisch, Stuart Gilson, Bruce Johnsen, Reinier Kraakman, Randall Kroszner, Ed McCaffery, Alan Meese, Geoff Miller, Eric Orts, Eric Posner, Bill Schwert, Andrei Shleifer, Jeff Strnad, Steve Thel, Bill Williams, Guojun Wu, Chunsheng Zhou, and several anonymous referees. Mark Weinstein went far beyond the call of duty, not only commenting extensively on the chapter relating to market manipulation in the 1920s, but spending many hours helping me think through the data and methodological challenges that the work raised. The individual chapters also benefited greatly from comments received at workshops and seminars at the law and/or business schools at the University of California at Berkeley, the University of Chicago, George Mason University, Harvard University, New York University, the University of Pennsylvania, the University of Southern California, Stanford University, the University of Toronto, Vanderbilt University, the College of William & Mary, and Yale University, and the economic history seminar at the University of Virginia.

My editors at the University of Chicago Press made a new experience entirely enjoyable. I'm very grateful to Chris Rhodes and Jillian Tsui for their advice, encouragement, and assistance.

My greatest debt is to my colleague and spouse, Julia Mahoney, who read the manuscript in multiple incarnations and provided patient guidance throughout.

Introduction

The 2007–8 financial crisis and its aftermath inspired countless references to the Great Depression, the New Deal financial reforms, and the collapse in equity prices of 1929–32. News coverage of the Dodd-Frank Wall Street Reform and Consumer Protection Act of 2010 routinely referred to it as the most sweeping financial reform since the Great Depression.

Dodd-Frank was as extensive and complex as the entire package of New Deal financial reforms, so in that sense the analogy is appropriate. But the references to the New Deal financial reforms were also intended to suggest that both addressed a common set of underlying problems. Many analysts argue that misbehavior by financial market participants was a strong underlying cause of both financial crises, that lax regulatory oversight facilitated the misbehavior, and that new regulations adopted after the crisis made a repetition of the problems less likely. Throughout this book, I refer to a description of a financial crisis incorporating these three claims as a "market failure narrative."

My purpose is to examine the evidence behind market failure narratives and the efficacy of the resulting reforms, focusing principally on securities laws. As I write this in 2014, much of Dodd-Frank has not yet been fully implemented and it is accordingly too soon to measure its effects reliably.[1] We are better positioned to analyze the role of regulation and securities market practices in the Depression-era financial meltdown and the subsequent recovery. The individual chapters aim to do so, thereby helping us predict the likely effects of the current reforms.

My conclusion is at odds with the conventional wisdom. The analysis in this book—which ties together twenty years of research on US securities markets around the time of the New Deal—suggests that "lax" regulation was not a substantial cause of the financial problems accompanying the Great Depression and that most (although not all) of the subsequent regulatory changes were largely ineffective and in some cases counterproductive. In short, it argues that the market failure narrative of the Great Depression is mostly incorrect.

I expect the reader to approach this claim skeptically. Generations of law, history, economics, and political science students have learned that the New Deal securities reforms "saved capitalism from itself" by ushering in a new era of transparency and ethical conduct. If I am right, many experts have been wrong. How could that be?

The reason has to do with the process by which policymakers create and justify financial reforms. Typically, market failure narratives compete with alternative explanations that blame government policies. In the case of the Great Depression, these include monetary and trade policies in the United States and Europe. In the more recent crisis, they again include monetary policy as well as government housing and bank regulatory policies. For the sake of simplicity, we can call these "government failure" narratives.

Policymakers are not indifferent to which explanation the public believes, which helps to explain the dominance of market failure narratives. Admitting error, even well-intentioned error, is not a good career move for an elected or appointed official. Weaver (1986, 371) contends that politicians "are motivated primarily by the desire to avoid blame." A common strategy for avoiding blame for bad outcomes is to find a scapegoat. For reasons I will examine in more detail, securities markets are unusually good scapegoats. As a result, in the aftermath of a financial crisis, policy makers routinely formulate and promote a story of misbehavior by securities issuers, intermediaries, and traders in order to protect or gain power or influence. Those stories then form the basis for regulatory reforms described as a solution to the identified problems. Because the market failure narrative is created for reasons of political expediency, there is no reason to believe it will produce useful regulatory solutions.

In the case of the New Deal, President Franklin D. Roosevelt and his allies were stunningly successful in creating and selling a market failure narrative of the late 1920s that is now almost universally accepted. The New Dealers were articulate and self-confident and wrote extensively about the problems they confronted and the brilliance of their solutions. Secondary sources describing the New Deal era can be remarkably uncritical in repeating these self-assessments.

The result is that very intelligent people often suspend their natural skepticism where the Great Depression and the New Deal reforms are concerned. In 1995 I sat in Thomas Jefferson's Rotunda on the grounds of the University of Virginia, where I teach, and listened to a speech by Arthur Levitt, then chairman of the Securities and Exchange Commission. He gave a standard SEC-chairman stump speech, reminding us why we need the SEC:

> The need for disclosure was a very painful lesson for the United States to learn. Sixty-six years ago, the machinery of American finance stopped on a dime. In the span of a few months, the value of all stocks listed on the New York Stock Exchange plunged from nearly 90 billion dollars to around 16 billion, and bonds from 49 billion dollars to 31.
>
> Scholars often disagree about the causes of the Great Depression—but they rarely disagree about the marketplace anarchy that preceded it. . . . Before the crash, stock prices often had little to do with the fundamentals, because most of the fundamentals were never disclosed. . . . Investors were sold securities without benefit of a prospectus or offering circular; without ever seeing a balance sheet; without knowing the first thing about a company beyond its name and share price.[2]

The familiarity of this recitation should not blind us to the fact that each of its factual assertions is demonstrably wrong. American finance did not "stop on a dime" in the fall of 1929, nor did NYSE stocks shed more than 80 percent of their value in "the span of a few months." From the peak month of September 1929 to the trough of November 1929, the Cowles index of all New York Stock Exchange stocks declined by 33 percent. Beginning in mid-November, stocks began a sustained rally that brought the index back to 80 percent of its peak value by April 1930. Contemporaneous accounts of the October 1929 crash identify a sense of panic, but it is associated primarily with the unprecedented trading volumes that swamped the paper-based trading and settlement systems. The price declines themselves, although certainly unwelcome, were not unprecedented.

Another way to look at the Great Crash is this: Over a six-month period comprising the last quarter of 1929 and the first quarter of 1930, stocks gave up their gains from the summer of 1929. In early April 1930, broad stock indexes such as the Cowles index and the Dow Jones Industrial Average stood about where they had been at the end of May 1929. In that respect, the October 1929 crash is similar to the October 1987 market crash, as Temin (1992, 43–45) has noted. From the perspective of someone watching only the stock ticker, there would have been no more cause for alarm in the spring of 1930 than in the spring of 1988. The stock market did indeed suffer catastrophic losses during the Depression, but these came gradually as the magnitude of commodity price deflation and problems in the banking and industrial sectors revealed themselves. The market hit bottom in summer 1932, nearly three years after the Great Crash.

There is also virtually no evidence connecting the stock price declines to fraud by listed companies. One can, of course, identify companies in the 1920s, as in every era, that used misleading or incomplete disclosures to attract credulous investors. Taken at face value as a statement about common market practices, however, Levitt's statements about marketplace "anarchy" are unfounded. As I describe in more detail in later chapters, the major exchanges enforced a serious and effective set of disclosure rules. Knowledgeable contemporaries observed that traders could draw on voluminous information about the companies traded on organized markets (Berle and Means 1932). Prospectuses and annual reports of the pre-SEC era were skimpy by today's standards but contained financial statements and other key information. The SEC paid existing market practices the compliment of largely reproducing them in its initial disclosure forms.

Standard analyses of the effects of securities reforms are as flawed as the analyses of their origins, and for similar reasons. Banner (1998) and Romano (2005, 2012) note that nearly all significant financial reform legislation in England and America has been enacted in the aftermath of a collapse in equity values. This pattern introduces several biases into the creation and evaluation of financial reform legislation. None is difficult to understand and all have been commented on in prior literature, but policymakers and scholars have not recognized their severity or taken them sufficiently into account.

When regulatory overhaul occurs after an extreme event, mean reversion makes it appear effective even if it is nothing more than a placebo. Financial crises causing large and widespread losses to retail investors are rare. The S&P 500 index has fallen by more than 18 percent in a calendar year only three times since World War II (1974, 2002, and 2008). It is therefore likely that there will be no financial crisis during the first few years after a regulatory overhaul, simply because crises are infrequent. The timeline of financial reform almost always consists of a financial crisis, followed by reform legislation, followed by no financial crisis. To the casual observer, then, financial reforms always appear to make things better.

Why are major financial reforms enacted after large declines in equity values? An optimist might argue that these events provide important new information about market failures and regulatory gaps. Unfortunately, this is entirely implausible. The practices that policymakers later seek to curb—external auditors offering consulting services, issuers of mortgage-backed securities shopping for favorable ratings, or banks trading large quantities of over-the-counter derivatives—are invariably hiding in plain sight for years prior to the downturn. A financial crisis does not provide new information about these practices or their associated risks. It provides public anger, which politicians cannot ignore. Financial reforms follow equity market declines because they are intended to deflect public anger from elected and appointed officials to the securities industry.

This point is particularly clear in the case of the most recent financial downturn. The financial crisis began in 2007 in the credit markets. However, most voters do not have their 401(k) plans invested in mortgage-backed securities. Only in late 2008, when equity prices tumbled, did Congress become interested in securitization and over-the-counter credit derivatives. As was the case in the Depression, government officials created a market failure narrative and used it as the basis for financial reform legislation.

This might not be a bad thing if financial reforms, although prompted by politicians' self-interested desire to avoid blame, generally fire at the correct targets. Unfortunately, there is no guarantee that this is the case. Economists, political scientists, and journalists have long understood that regulation frequently benefits the regulated industry or some portion of it (Stigler 1971). Regulation can raise barriers to entry that give incumbent firms a built-in advantage over new entrants. It will routinely create winners and losers because compliance costs are not uniform across firms. If potential winners and losers can be identified in advance and potential winners are sufficiently cohesive, legislators may prefer to play the role of auctioneer of beneficial rules rather than protector of the public.

Although it is perhaps counterintuitive, public anger at an industry may facilitate rather than impede the process of "selling" regulation. Public anger gives the government and the affected firms cover as they bargain. In the aftermath of a financial crisis, politicians and the press speak of new regulation as a form of punishment for the wayward financial industry. Congress and the president pledge to "get tough" and "crack down" on Wall Street. Press accounts intone that the industry's image is too damaged for it to "resist" new regulation.

Such statements are nonsensical. Regulation is not a bill of attainder aimed only at identified wrongdoers; nor can it retroactively criminalize the activities that politicians blame for a crisis. Regulatory reforms are forward-looking and apply to everyone engaged in the relevant activities, the honest and dishonest alike. Fundamentally, they change the relative costs of different business practices.

Experience demonstrates that the press and public do not look beneath the ritual shows of outrage and condemnation to ask how the differential costs imposed by new regulations affect competition within the regulated industry. Whether intentionally or unintentionally, then, these rituals deflect attention from the reforms' counterproductive features.

Policymakers frequently respond to their own limited knowledge by using regulation to mandate "best practices." Whether the topic is disclosure, sales practices, or conflicts of interest, policymakers ask how "high-quality" firms behave and require that all firms do the same. This provides leading firms with a substantial structural and informational advantage in the policy process. Diversity in business practices among firms often reflects comparative cost advantages. Imagine, for example, that there are two ways to perform a particular task, which we can call A and B. Some firms can do A at lower cost and therefore do so, whereas for others B is the less costly practice. If the firms that use practice A can convince policymakers that it is the "best" practice and should be mandated for all firms, they gain an automatic cost advantage over their competitors who use practice B. Thus a best practices mandate can give one segment of an industry the upper hand over its competitors.

Regardless of the influence of the regulated industry in the reform process, financial regulation often increases industry concentration, as we will see in the chapters to come. Because regulatory compliance has large fixed costs, it tends to burden large firms less, relatively speaking, than small firms. Sometimes this makes large firms allies (if only behind the scenes) of reformers. The reverse may also be true; regulators may do the bidding of larger firms, even if unintentionally. Large firms can more easily bear the fixed costs of compliance staffs and regular consultation with outside counsel, both of which leverage the regulators' limited resources and supplement their enforcement efforts. Regulators thereby become dependent on the compliance efforts of large firms and suspicious of the less extensive efforts that smaller firms can afford. Thus regulatory mandates can drive smaller firms out of an industry even if their larger competitors do not actively seek out the new regulations—indeed, even if they oppose them.

Logically, regulation can have three different effects in varying combinations. It can benefit society by solving informational or incentive problems that keep markets from functioning effectively. It creates social costs because complying with regulations takes money and effort. Finally, it creates private benefits because compliance costs are not uniform across firms. Some firms can comply at lower cost; they profit relative to the rest. The resulting private benefits give the winners an incentive to support socially detrimental legislation or shape regulations in ways that harm society. Whether the public or just certain segments of the regulated industry are net beneficiaries in any given situation must be determined empirically.

That is the purpose of this book. I survey evidence of the effects of the New Deal securities laws on the functioning of securities markets. When useful, I turn to other financial crises and their aftermath to illustrate a point. I then provide a brief overview of the two major securities reforms of the twenty-first century, the Sarbanes-Oxley and Dodd-Frank acts, to show that they follow a similar script and will therefore likely result in further financial industry concentration but little benefit to investors.

The fundamental methodological assumption throughout is that to understand a financial crisis and its aftermath we must look at objective measures of the market's performance. Polemical writings are not a reliable guide because they often reflect ideology or self-interest. Many contemporaneous accounts of past crises were written by people who had an axe to grind. To understand financial reform legislation, we should look at objective measures of its effects, not at its supporters' stated intentions. Accordingly, whenever possible I try to test the received history of the New Deal and other eras against whatever data are available.

I wish to emphasize that the message of the book is not that the market is always right or that regulation is never effective. Rather, it is that the aftermath of a financial crisis is a bad time to redesign the regulatory framework. It is politically useful to argue that a major event requires a major response. But what is usually needed is incremental change incorporating standard tools from the legal toolkit. The most successful reform discussed in the chapters to come did just that. Broader, inventive reforms were counterproductive, in part because they offered too many opportunities for interested parties to seek advantage. Regulatory improvement should be an ongoing process, not a periodic fit of crisis management.

As we will see, the Securities Act of 1933 incorporated useful disclosure standards that built incrementally on common law rules governing agents dealing adversely with their principals. But this seemed too modest a fix to its drafters, who added on novel and pervasive regulation of the offering process to the ultimate detriment of investors. The Public Utility Holding Company Act could have focused attention on transfer pricing and intercompany transactions, which are ubiquitous issues within business groups. Instead, the statute required the dismantling of utility holding companies, causing investor losses. Dodd-Frank could have focused on making capital requirements more effective. Instead, its proponents had the grandiose wish to be the authors of a new New Deal with consequences that remain to be seen but that I predict will be harmful. In the closing chapter, I make a few suggestions about how policy makers should approach their task in the future. But the primary focus is on demonstrating how regulatory reform goes wrong.

Most of the data analysis is drawn from papers I have published over the past two decades. Those papers often rely on data my research assistants and I gathered by hand from a variety of published sources, including stock quotes from the *Wall Street Journal* and *New York Times* from the 1920s and 1930s, regulatory filings, reports of regulatory bodies, data assembled for litigation, and other sources. Since these papers were written, however, the Center for Research in Security Prices (CRSP) at the University of Chicago's Booth School of Business has extended its database of daily securities prices back to 1926, thus making the same stock price data generally available to scholars.

CHAPTER ONE

Long before the New Deal

The introduction presents two basic ideas about the regulatory response to financial crises. The extreme rarity of crises and the fact that reforms are enacted hastily after a crisis ensures that all reforms appear to make things better. This fact gives a surface plausibility to market failure narratives in which a corrupt and lightly regulated financial system brought misery and ruin to unsophisticated investors until intrepid reformers stepped in to restore order. Those narratives, formulated by government officials and "policy entrepreneurs" (Romano 2005) often become the main sources on which later historians and journalists rely.

The second key point is that financial firms are adept at using the legislative and regulatory processes to disadvantage their existing or potential rivals even when the financial industry's public standing is at a temporary low point. This is easy to see when legislators care primarily about mollifying an angry public. But it is true even when legislators or regulators try in good faith to cure market failures that they necessarily understand less well than the regulated industry.

Subsequent chapters describe in detail how these phenomena played out during the New Deal era. But I hope to persuade the reader that both points are of more general applicability. One way to see this is to look at the earliest, most comprehensive, and most influential treatise on the federal securities laws, Louis Loss's *Securities Regulation* (Loss, Seligman, and Paredes 2014). The treatise opens with a chapter on the historical antecedents of the New Deal securities laws. These include a pair of English statutes: a 1697 statute regulating stockbrokers and the Bubble Act of 1720. Both are described as reactions to chicanery—by stockbrokers and corporate promoters, respectively. The treatise discusses at greater length the "blue sky" or state securities laws of the early twentieth century, which it also describes as a response to fraud in the sale of new issues of securities.

As I will show, the market failure narrative of each of these three incidents is incorrect. Each episode does, however, fit nicely into the analytical framework of this book. This chapter takes up the first two incidents briefly in order to illustrate the broad applicability of my framework and the remarkable inaccuracy of the histories on which most lawyers have been raised. The analysis here is qualitative. The blue sky laws, which we can analyze quantitatively to a limited extent, are the subject of chapter 2. Subsequent chapters will provide qualitative and empirical assessments of the New Deal financial reforms.

A Modern Financial Crisis in the 1690s

The London securities market grew up in the late seventeenth and early eighteenth centuries. Following the Glorious Revolution of 1688, England shifted from haphazard short-term borrowing by the Crown to a more organized national debt authorized by Parliament and issued with longer maturities. Secondary trading in the shares of financial and overseas trading companies increased during the same period. London merchants began to act as securities brokers and some specialized in this new form of intermediation. Initially, they met at the Royal Exchange or in nearby coffee houses to buy and sell; the creation of a dedicated facility would not come until the late eighteenth century.

Dickson (1967) describes the regularization of public finance after the Glorious Revolution as a "financial revolution" that increased the government's credibility and therefore creditworthiness. North and Weingast (1989) focus on a broader set of institutional changes, such as the growth of parliamentary government and an independent judiciary, as a central reason for England's increased capacity to borrow to finance its late seventeenth- and early eighteenth-century wars.

Neither the development of an organized securities market nor the improvement in public finance, however, was a guarantee against financial crisis. In 1689 England's new king, William of Orange, brought it into the Grand Alliance fighting France in the Nine Years' War (1688–97). Government spending increased substantially during England's participation in the war, resulting in large shipments of specie overseas. Money was therefore in short supply at home.

The government responded in part by creating the Bank of England, chartered in 1694 expressly to lend money to the government. The Bank would later also purchase government debt in the secondary market and present it to the government to be refinanced. The creation of the Bank was also a response to the shortage of specie; as a fractional reserve bank, it issued banknotes in excess of its gold and silver reserves, thus expanding the money supply.

The government's shipment of money overseas was not the only reason for money scarcity. Given the market price of silver, the English mint created relatively too few coins from an ounce of silver. This created an additional incentive to export silver coins to the continent where they could be sold at market prices, exacerbating the shortage of silver coins in England. The English mint also minted gold coins, but these were imperfect substitutes for lower-value silver coins for everyday transactions.

The practice of "clipping" silver coins, or shaving off small amounts of metal, was also common. The shavings from many such operations could be collected and melted into bullion (Kleer 2004). Clipping became endemic in the 1690s. By 1696, contemporaries reported that the average coin in circulation was less than half its original weight (Li 1963, 56–57). The government accordingly announced and implemented the "Great Recoinage," calling in all underweight coins to be melted down and recast as full-weight, milled coins (that is, coins with a serrated edge that deterred clipping by making it obvious). Legislation implementing the Great Recoinage provided that unmilled coins would be accepted in payment of taxes until May 4, 1696. Any remaining unmilled coins could be taken to the mint to be weighed and sold to the government on the basis of their silver content.

Contemporary and modern accounts agree that the Great Recoinage was badly mismanaged. Individuals who owed money to the government could rid themselves of clipped coins by the deadline, but others were not so lucky and stood to suffer significant losses. The process of minting milled coins and calling in unmilled coins was more cumbersome than expected. As May 4, 1696 approached there were not enough milled coins in circulation to meet demand. Moreover, the new milled coins were still undervalued and therefore could be profitably exported, so insufficient money entered circulation.

The shortage of money in early 1696 touched off a rush to liquidity. Consequently, holders of Bank of England notes sought to redeem them for specie. By May 6 the redemptions had turned into a full-fledged run on the Bank, which had to suspend payment of its notes temporarily. As in the early 1930s and late 2000s, the banking crisis was accompanied by declines in asset prices and an economic downturn.

Not surprisingly, merchants criticized the government for this state of affairs. In late 1696 petitions poured in to Parliament from around the kingdom asking that the old coins be once again accepted for government payments. The criticism clearly stung. Parliament took the trouble to denounce one pamphlet arguing that the silver content of coinage had been mismanaged. Not stopping there, Parliament ordered the pamphlet burned and petitioned the king to offer a reward to anyone who would expose the anonymous author and publisher.[1]

Like Congress in 1933–34 or 2009–10, Parliament in late 1696 and early 1697 hastily considered and enacted a number of bills in response to the crisis. One new act empowered fiduciaries acting on behalf of creditors to settle with debtors for less than the full value of a debt. There is an interesting parallel here to recent events. As mortgaged homes fell in value after 2006, doubts were raised whether the servicers of securitized mortgages had the authority to restructure those mortgages without the consent of all holders of the mortgage-backed securities. Similarly, Parliament in 1696 worried that trustees, guardians, and others acting in a fiduciary capacity did not have clear authority to settle debts owed to their beneficiaries at below face value. Parliament acted to provide that authority.

One act offered a temporary premium price on clipped silver coins delivered to the mint. Other acts extended the period in which clipped coins would be accepted at face value for payment of taxes and debts to the Crown and imposed new taxes to make up for the decrease in revenue occasioned by the government's acceptance of clipped coins at face value.

Parliament also appointed various committees to investigate allegations of abuse and incompetence in the receipt of old coins and minting of new. Of particular interest for our purposes, a committee was asked to consider the broader question of the health of the economy. This committee would provide the market failure narrative on which Loss and other modern authors have relied.

The committee reported back to Parliament in November 1696.[2] Its report said nothing about deflation or the effects of exchange rates on exports, both of which would have laid blame in part at Parliament's own door. Instead, it identified two purported causes of the downturn in economic activity. The first was outsourcing (although of course not referred to as such). Rather than manufacture woolen cloth in England, the producers of raw wool were increasingly exporting it to take advantage of cheaper foreign labor. The committee strongly condemned this practice.

The second was "the pernicious Art of Stock-jobbing," or, in other words, misconduct by securities brokers and traders. According to the parliamentary committee, securities professionals purchased newly issued securities and sold them to "ignorant Men, drawn in by the Reputation, falsely raised, and artfully spread, concerning the thriving state" of the business. By this means, the legislators argued, the management of businesses "comes to fall into unskillful Hands" to the detriment of the economy as a whole. Parliament thus argued that the fall in asset values accompanying the run on the Bank of England was actually orchestrated by securities traders.

Parliament responded with "An Act to restraine the Number and ill Practice of Brokers and Stock-Jobbers," which took effect on May 1, 1697.[3] The act required licensing of stockbrokers and limited the number of licensed brokers to 100. It also included provisions for the stated purpose of eliminating unfair or fraudulent practices, including a cap on brokerage fees and a ban on the growing trade in time bargains (essentially futures and options contracts in which the purchaser had either the right or the right and obligation to acquire shares of stock at a future date).

This episode may seem remote and irrelevant to present-day concerns, but it nicely illustrates several common features of financial crises and the political and regulatory response. They are worth our careful attention because they will reappear in connection with other financial downturns discussed in this book.

The Role of Monetary Policy

Monetary policy frequently plays a key role in a financial crisis. With the benefit of hindsight, we can identify decisions by the monetary authority that set the stage for the crisis. To be clear, this is only to say that after the fact, with the benefit of additional information and the absence of time pressure, we can identify policy mistakes. It is not to say that policymakers at the time should have been expected to know more and act differently to avoid the crisis that later unfolded. We can only answer that question on a case-by-case basis and it is beyond the scope of this book to do so.

Failed monetary policy necessarily brings criticism to bear on the government. Policymakers have a strong interest in deflecting blame and criticism. It is not politically feasible to respond by saying "it is hard to get monetary policy right all the time and we did our best but failed." The universal response, therefore, has been to argue that the fault really lies with nongovernmental actors. Certain targets of this redirected blame occur almost inevitably—foreign trade and securities markets being especially popular.

Blaming the Messenger

Securities markets are an ideal target to which policymakers can redirect public anger after a financial crisis. A stock market crash is typically the clearest signal to the general public that a crisis is underway. A market crash is both visible and painful to voters who have money invested in equities. The stock market is therefore a tempting target for blame, even when it is just the messenger. Stock price declines also raise the cost of capital for the affected businesses, opening the door for politicians to play a "Main Street versus Wall Street" theme that is evident in the November 1696 parliamentary committee report.

Even in the best of times, the public views securities markets with suspicion. Securities markets involve middlemen who trade assets with volatile prices, which throughout history has been a recipe for unpopularity. The public sees middlemen and price volatility and concludes that the former cause the latter, rather than volatility attracting traders who attempt to profit from differences in price across time and space. Banner (1998) notes the traditional suspicion of "speculators" in agricultural commodities and identifies the many ways English law and policy attempted to regulate them. He then observes that the English public took a similar attitude toward the new securities market and surveys literary works from the late seventeenth and early eighteenth centuries that portrayed securities trading as a type of alchemy practiced by the dishonest. When governments attempt to blame securities markets for financial crises, then, their work is half done before it begins.

The first part of the standard market failure narrative is the claim that a financial crisis was the work of unscrupulous financiers who tricked investors out of their money and destroyed the underlying businesses or asset markets. While this is not a book on psychology, we can imagine that this claim resonates with investors who have lost money and are themselves looking for someone to blame. This was no less true in the seventeenth century than today. One of Daniel Defoe's first published works, *An Essay on Projects* (1697), surveyed the growing diversity of business ventures in England and offered policy suggestions. His contemptuous descriptions of the role of financial intermediaries could have been published after the dot-com collapse of 2000–2002 with remarkably little updating:

> There are, and that too many, fair pretences of fine discoveries, new inventions, engines, and I know not what, which—being advanced in notion, and talked up to great things to be performed when such and such sums of money shall be advanced, and such and such engines are made—have raised the fancies of credulous people to such a height that, merely on the shadow of expectation, they have formed companies, chose committees, appointed officers, shares, and books, raised great stocks, and cried up an empty notion to that degree that people have been betrayed to part with their money for shares in a new nothing; and when the inventors have carried on the jest till they have sold all their own interest, they leave the cloud to vanish of itself.

Defoe himself had invested large sums in ventures that ultimately failed, including a diving-bell company, no doubt enhancing the bitterness of his commentary (West 1998).

Parliament in 1697, like the US Congress in 1933–34, 2002, and 2010, blamed the messenger. Nevertheless, I am aware of no objective evidence supporting the proposition that misbehavior by participants in the new and small securities market contributed to the run on the Bank of England, declines in asset prices, and economic slowdown of the mid-1690s. By contrast, there is substantial evidence to support a different explanation: The government's insistence on maintaining a mint price of silver that encouraged its shipment abroad, the Crown's own shipments of specie abroad to finance a war, and a badly designed and implemented recoinage did considerable harm to the Bank of England, financial markets, and the economy.

Losing the Battle but Winning the War

The most important and enduring lesson from the 1690s, however, is that financial regulation created in the immediate aftermath of a crisis for the principal purpose of deflecting public anger often ends up benefiting the largest and most politically connected financial intermediaries. This is not to say that new regulations never benefit investors, but any benefits frequently come at the expense of reduced competition.

That this was true in 1697 is obvious from the title of the act "to restraine the *Number* and ill Practice" of stock brokers. As the title suggests, it limited the right to act as a stockbroker to people licensed by the Lord Mayor of London and limited the number of licenses to 100. The act, therefore, not only curtailed competition, but gave a leg up in the competition to the best-connected brokers, whom the Lord Mayor would presumably favor. Indeed, the Lord Mayor promptly limited the number of licenses available to foreigners and Jews (Dickson 1967).

Like public utility regulation in later centuries, the act also regulated the price of the service, in this case the brokerage fees. Both theory and experience show that price regulation is less effective than competition in maximizing consumer welfare and is therefore typically justified only when the service is a natural monopoly. Stockbroking is not a natural monopoly, so the argument for regulating prices does not hold.

This combination of limits on competition and the partial substitution of political clout for customer service as the key to success in the financial industry is a common feature of financial regulation. While we lack sufficient information to estimate the net effect of the 1697 securities law on investors, I will show that later financial reforms often benefited the favored financial firms at the expense of their competitors and customers.

The South Sea Bubble

Between March and July 1720, shares of the South Sea Company roughly quintupled in value. Starting in late August, however, they fell back to their prior level in roughly a month's time. There is an ongoing and heated debate over whether the high mid-July valuation was justified by fundamentals or was an episode of investor irrationality. The various perspectives can be found in Neal (1990), Garber (1990), Dale (2004) and Kindleberger and Aliber (2005). The rapid decline, however, is easy to understand after some additional background.

While the South Sea Company's name and the fact that it was awarded a monopoly on English trade with Spain's South American colonies suggest that it was an overseas trading company, its actual business was quite different. As any English merchant or investor knew, English companies could trade in the South Sea only by Spanish sufferance. From 1714 to 1718 the English government was able to negotiate limited rights for the company to transport slaves to the Spanish colonies, but these were clearly subject to diplomatic developments outside the company's control.

With England and Spain at war from 1718 to 1720, the South Sea Company's access to the Spanish Main was again limited. Even the eponymous narrator of *Robinson Crusoe*, first published in 1719, is well aware of Spain's tight control over trade in the South Sea.

Modern critics are so eager to conclude that the company was engaged in fraud from the start, however, that commentators like Galbraith (1990) suggest that the company duped investors into believing it would bring back gold and silver from the New World. But the idea that the South Sea Company's investors, many of whom were members of Parliament or London merchants, did not understand the constraints on the company's overseas trading activities is not merely implausible, but absurd.

Pending the day when English vessels could trade freely in South America, the company's actual business—about which it made no secret—was financial services. Following the Bank of England model, the company purchased outstanding government debt and refinanced it pursuant to an agreement negotiated in advance with Parliament. Quinn (2008) describes the company's business as the securitization of long-term sovereign debt, or the conversion of nonstandardized and therefore relatively illiquid claims on the government into liquid shares of stock.

Most modern analysts conclude that South Sea Company investors were irrational and the company's management deceitful based on a comparison of the company's stock price to the income it could expect on its holdings of government debt (Dale 2004). If we take the company to be a simple pass-through securitization vehicle, then the return to investors would consist entirely of a fixed stream of interest payments equal, roughly, to 4 percent of invested capital. That income would be insufficient to justify the high price of South Sea Company shares in the summer of 1720 at any reasonable discount rate.

However, the company did not intend to use its political clout, purchased with hard cash, simply to buy government debt and pass the income through to investors. The company's plan, as described by Scott (1910) and Garber (1990), was to use the steady stream of income from its holdings of government debt to invest in new commercial ventures, becoming an early example of a venture capital fund. In keeping with the mercantilist political economy of the period, it also hoped to use its political influence to gain monopolies or other special privileges for those new ventures. It is on the soundness of this plan, and not the value of the company's government debt holdings, that one must judge the company's July 1720 share price.

In the event, the company's plans were threatened by the rapid emergence of competing businesses that challenged its hoped-for monopolies. In principle, this should not have occurred. The government asserted the sole right to create business corporations and used its power sparingly and only for its supporters. However, as I have described elsewhere, entrepreneurs and lawyers devised ways of creating the advantages of the corporate form without formal charters (Mahoney 2000). Other entrepreneurs obtained obsolete charters and used them to enter into new businesses. By the summer of 1720, a number of new firms had been established and sold shares to the public without government involvement. The South Sea Company was alarmed by the prospect of competition from entities it neither owned nor financed.

To thwart that competition, the company persuaded Parliament to pass a bill to outlaw the creation of new businesses in corporate-like forms except by royal or parliamentary assent and to ban the use of existing corporate charters to engage in unauthorized businesses. The bill, which became known as the Bubble Act, was enacted and swiftly enforced against some of the new businesses in August 1720. The South Sea Company presumably intended to purchase or simply displace the outlawed businesses. It is indisputable, in any event, that the Bubble Act was enacted and enforced at the South Sea Company's urging and while the company's share price was near its peak.

The company's strategy backfired. Perhaps it failed to consider that enactment and enforcement of the Bubble Act could lead to a general flight from (political) risk. That is precisely what happened. Holders of shares in all companies began to sell and move into less risky assets. The South Sea Company was caught in the de-risking and its shares quickly gave up all their recent gains and retreated to a level consonant with the value of the company's debt holdings. The government's solicitude first created and then inadvertently destroyed option value for the company.

It took only a generation, however, before the South Sea episode was inaccurately recast into a market failure narrative in which the Bubble Act was a stern government reaction to the depredations of the South Sea Company and its fraudulent imitators. This new narrative begins with Blackstone's *Commentaries on the Laws of England*, first published in installments between 1765 and 1769. Blackstone (2001, 4:117) describes the Bubble Act as "enacted in the year after the infamous south-sea project had beggared half the nation." Similarly, standard histories declare that many fraudulent new enterprises sprang up in 1720. The evidence that they were fraudulent is that they failed—but the histories omit the fact that they failed because they were outlawed and then suppressed.

Harris (1994) carefully documents the inaccuracy of Blackstone's account. As noted above, the Bubble Act was enacted and enforced *before*, not after, the collapse of the South Sea Company's share price, at the company's instigation, to protect the company's hoped-for monopolies. Harris graciously attributes Blackstone's error to his confusion about the Old Style dating system, which was still in use in England in 1720 but had been abandoned by the time Blackstone wrote. Blackstone's error was carried forward into the twentieth century by the legal historian Frederick Maitland, writing in 1904 (Maitland 2005, 119) then by Plumb (1950, 26) and Pawson (1979, 89). Interestingly, the first edition of Loss's treatise, published in 1951, repeats the error, stating that the Bubble Act was the "legislative result" of the bursting of the South Sea Bubble. Subsequent editions, written after modern historians had uncovered more of the facts of the South Sea episode, drop the causal claim.

The South Sea episode is a vivid illustration of how commentators' desire to believe (or at least advocate) a market failure narrative can lead them to distort the facts beyond recognition. Many lawyers and policymakers have heard a version of the story of the South Sea Bubble in which gullible investors bought shares of a company that offered fraudulent visions of New World gold and silver and then, their greed unsatisfied, purchased shares of other companies with even more dubious stories. After the whole mess imploded, Parliament stepped in to take more control of the creation of new companies. This narrative is wrong in every particular.

CHAPTER TWO

The Blue Sky Laws

A Tale of Progressives and Interest Groups

The Securities Act of 1933 was not the first significant effort to regulate primary securities markets in the United States. Between 1911 and 1931, forty-seven of the forty-eight states adopted statutes regulating the sale of securities. The market failure narrative of the blue sky laws is well established: there was a "fraud wave" in early twentieth-century America in which corporate promoters sold worthless shares to small investors (Seligman 1983). In order to protect investors from buying "building lots in the blue sky," state legislatures enacted statutes regulating the new-issues market.

As is often the case, the contemporary evidence of a "fraud wave" consists entirely of assertions by supporters of the blue sky laws. Those assertions are quite general and therefore not easily verifiable. However, unlike federal legislation, the blue sky laws varied from state to state in substance and in the timing of adoption. They ranged from "merit review" statutes that gave state officials substantial discretion to ban the sale of a newly issued security in the state to simple antifraud provisions. We can exploit that variation to try to explain the reasons for their enactment as well as their effects.

While the paucity of evidence from the early twentieth century argues for caution in interpretation, the best available evidence supports a plausible theory of the blue sky laws' origins that has nothing to do with a

This chapter was initially published in modified form as Paul G. Mahoney, "The Origins of the Blue-Sky Laws: A Test of Competing Hypotheses," *Journal of Law and Economics* 46 (2003): 229–51. Reprinted with permission of the University of Chicago Press.

fraud wave. Variations in timing and substance across states suggest that the blue sky laws reflect a successful attempt by small banks to exploit progressive politics to fend off competition from stockbrokers. Calomaris and Haber (2014) note that a coalition of agrarian populists and small banks influenced bank regulatory policy for much of the nineteenth and twentieth centuries. My analysis of the blue sky laws shows that a similar coalition made inroads into securities regulation.

We can examine the factors associated with states' adoption of blue sky laws through event history analysis. The analysis employs proxies for the extent of securities fraud, the lobbying strength of progressive and populist political groups, and the prevalence of small banks and asks whether variation in these variables from one state-year to another is associated with differences among states in the timing and substance of blue sky laws.

The picture that emerges is both subtle and fascinating. The factor that best explains the *timing* of a blue sky law is the strength of progressive political forces within that state—the more progressive the state, the earlier it adopted a blue sky law. But the factor that best explains the *type* of blue sky law is the relative importance of small banks. States in which the average bank was relatively small tended to adopt the strictest blue sky laws. This makes sense when we recognize that small banks faced dangerous competition from stockbrokers for depositors' funds but, unlike larger banks, did not have the means to set up their own brokerage and investment banking operations. Thus for small banks the winning political strategy was to try to drive as much brokerage and investment banking business as possible out of state.

Description of the Blue Sky Laws

The first blue sky law was adopted in Kansas in 1911, in significant part through the efforts of the state's banking commissioner, J. N. Dolley. Loss and Cowett (1958) describe the legislative process and the resulting statute. The law required registration of securities and securities salesmen. Before selling a security in Kansas, the issuer had to file an application with the banking commissioner containing financial and narrative information about its business. No sales could be made unless the commissioner approved the offering.

The statute gave the commissioner extraordinarily broad discretion. He could reject an offering if he concluded that the issuer "does not intend to do a fair and honest business" or "does not promise a fair return on the stocks, bonds, or other securities by it offered for sale." This broad authority came to be known as "merit review." Dolley was not reluctant to exercise his statutory discretion. His first annual report on the operation of the statute noted that his office approved fewer than 7 percent of applications to sell securities in Kansas.

The Kansas law quickly spread. In 1912 and 1913 eleven states adopted statutes similar to the Kansas law. Other states adopted less stringent statutes that required preclearance of proposed offerings but limited the administrator's discretionary authority to reject them. Typically, the administrator had to conclude that the offering was fraudulent or met other specified criteria in order to deny permission (I call these "ex ante fraud" statutes because the regulator had the authority to stop an offering before it occurred). Others, including important centers of the securities industry such as New York and New Jersey, adopted statutes that prohibited fraud but did not require preclearance of an offering (I call these "ex post fraud" statutes because the regulator could act only after the fact against offerings that proved fraudulent). Table 2.1 provides the year of adoption of each state's blue sky statute and its type.

TABLE 2.1. **Dates of adoption of blue sky laws**

Year	Merit Review	Ex Ante Fraud	Ex Post Fraud
1911	Kansas		
1912	Arizona		Louisiana
1913	Arkansas, Idaho, Michigan, Montana, North Dakota, Ohio, South Dakota, Tennessee, Vermont, West Virginia	California, Florida, Georgia, Iowa, Missouri, Nebraska, North Carolina, Texas, Wisconsin	Maine, Oregon
1915		South Carolina	
1916		Mississippi, Virginia	
1917		Minnesota	New Hampshire
1919		Alabama, Illinois, Oklahoma, Utah, Wyoming	
1920		Indiana, Kentucky	Maryland, New Jersey
1921		Massachusetts, New Mexico, Rhode Island	New York
1923		Colorado, Washington	Pennsylvania
1929			Connecticut
1931			Delaware

Source: State session laws.

The blue sky statutes, on average, put the greatest burdens on offerings of high-risk (and potentially high-return) securities. Many blue sky laws forbade the sale of any security by a company that had previously issued securities in exchange for patents, goodwill, or other intangible assets unless the administrator concluded that the intangibles were "fairly" valued on the company's books. Others, like the North Dakota statute, singled out for greater scrutiny a class of "speculative" securities, including those whose assets consisted in large measure of intangibles, mining claims, or undeveloped real estate. The statutes often treated banks more leniently than other securities issuers and sellers. Many states followed Kansas in appointing the state's banking commissioner as the sole or lead administrator. The statutes typically exempted bank securities from registration, and in some cases exempted any securities sold by a bank. Others exempted banks from registration as brokers or dealers.

The Market Failure Narrative

The leading legal treatise on the blue sky laws (Loss and Cowett 1958) provides the market failure narrative for their adoption. As securities markets developed, it became apparent that securities sales provide exceptional opportunities for fraud. The combination of a growing market for corporate securities and the relaxation of nineteenth-century laissez-faire attitudes set the stage for the adoption of blue sky laws in the early twentieth century. Seligman (1983) provides a more historically detailed market failure narrative. He argues that the early twentieth century witnessed a "fraud wave" in which the proportion of dishonest sellers increased dramatically.

These explanations are economically naïve in the sense that they do not explain why investors would participate in markets rife with fraud. The evidence of widespread fraud is also thin. It consists, first, of the claims of the blue sky laws' proponents that fraud was rampant. As the introduction argues, this is of no weight standing alone. Proponents of regulatory statutes know that they have to offer a public-interest explanation, whatever their actual motivations.

The fact that state officials used the blue sky laws to reject a substantial percentage of proposed offerings is similarly weak evidence. Merit review statutes gave officials almost unlimited discretion to block an offering. The fact that they rejected many applications shows only that they believed it a good idea to do so. What motivated them to believe so—a correct inference of fraud, a misunderstanding of securities markets, an antipathy to certain sellers, or a simple desire to curtail sales of securities—we do not know.

The market failure narrative also cannot account for the pattern of state adoptions of blue sky laws. As Mulligan and Shleifer (2005) observe, there are substantial fixed costs to regulation, making it efficient only when the regulated activity reaches a sufficient scale. This implies that if the blue sky laws were indeed an efficient response to market failure, the states with the largest financial markets should have been the first to adopt blue sky laws. But the opposite occurred. It is not plausible that the social costs of securities fraud were higher in Kansas, Arizona, and Louisiana (the first three states to adopt blue sky laws) than in New York, Pennsylvania, and Connecticut (among the last adopters).

An Interest Group Story

The relatively lenient treatment of banks in the blue sky statutes gives the first hint that competitive issues may have played a role in their enactment. Macey and Miller (1991, 365) argue that small banks and their regulators were the main forces behind the blue sky laws. These banks hoped that the laws would "stifle[] competition for the funds of potential depositors."

Banks are not the only possible beneficiaries of a blue sky law. These laws could raise barriers to entry that would benefit the securities industry. The investment bankers' trade group, the Investment Bankers Association of America (IBAA), appreciated this possibility and supported legislation to keep "unscrupulous" investment bankers from entering the business. Investment bankers objected, however, to Kansas-style merit review statutes. The IBAA arranged and financed litigation seeking to have the blue sky laws declared unconstitutional. At the same time, the association and its members lobbied intensively in favor of the ex post fraud type of blue sky law. This effort was partly successful, as a number of states adopted statutes patterned on the IBAA model. On the whole, however, the qualitative evidence shows that securities firms did not desire or lobby in favor of blue sky laws.

By contrast, small banks lobbied aggressively in favor of blue sky laws. Macey and Miller present extensive qualitative evidence showing that rural banks and their regulators worked to secure enactment of these laws. Smaller banks stood to gain for a few reasons. Banking in the early twentieth century was highly fragmented. The dominant model was a "unit banking" system limiting a bank to a single place of business. Branching was permitted in only a handful of states and often within only a limited geographical area. As a result there were a great many banks, but those outside metropolitan areas were often very small.

The more difficult question is whether these many banks competed with one another or whether rural banks had an effective territorial monopoly. State banking laws gave bank regulators broad discretion to reject applications to create new banks, particularly when a community was already served by a bank. Incumbent banks in smaller towns may, therefore, have had the ability to block new entry. Flannery (1984) finds that unit banking restrictions caused operating inefficiencies that increased banks' costs, but the resulting lack of competition more than compensated, increasing bank profitability.

A new entrant could bypass state regulators by seeking a federal charter. A 1900 amendment to the National Bank Act reduced the minimum capital required to charter a national bank in small towns from $50,000 to $25,000. Subsequently, according to the Federal Reserve Board's count, the number of banks in the United States nearly doubled from about 13,000 in 1900 to about 25,000 in 1910. During the same period, new state-chartered institutions, such as trust companies and mutual savings associations, also competed with banks for depositors' funds. The prospect of local stockbrokers also competing for depositors' funds may have been particularly unwelcome in the early decades of the twentieth century.

Politics and the Blue Sky Laws

Blue sky laws were first adopted primarily in midwestern and southern states. Supporters often described themselves as foes of big-city financiers and friends of farmers and other small borrowers who relied on bank credit. Simple antifinancial populism, then, was part of the force behind the blue sky laws. Although William Jennings Bryan's Populist Party was a spent political force by the time of the blue sky laws, antipathy to financiers survived in rural America.

The blue sky laws are more closely associated with the progressive movement. As described by Fishback and Kantor (1998), in the first two decades of the twentieth century, social reformers enacted state legislation on child labor, compulsory school attendance, workmen's compensation, and electricity rate regulation. They also pursued political reforms such as direct primaries, initiative and referendum procedures, and merit systems for state employees. Theodore Roosevelt left the Republican Party to run for president in 1912 as the Progressive Party's candidate. Opposed by Wilson (Democrat) and Taft (Republican), Roosevelt won 27 percent of the popular vote.

One common feature of progressive thought was distaste for large economic units, which progressives called "monopolies" or "trusts," whether or not these were monopolies in the economist's sense. Although the reasons are debatable, some progressives found in early twentieth-century American finance the seeds of monopoly.

Louis Brandeis's famous call for financial regulation, *Other People's Money and How the Bankers Use It* (1914), argues that the financial industry is an "oligarchy." The book opens with a 1911 quote from Woodrow Wilson that "the great monopoly in this country is the money monopoly." Congress held hearings in 1912, now known as the Pujo hearings, to investigate the "money trust." The blue sky laws were adopted in the middle of a series of attacks on the financial industry as a "monopoly" or "trust," and those concepts were an important part of progressive rhetoric.

Evidence from the Timing of Adoption

Following Stigler (1971) and others, I assume that the timing of adoption of a regulatory statute is a proxy for the intensity of a state's desire to regulate the relevant activity, with earlier adopters being the most eager. The same motivation underlies the use of event history analysis in other regulatory contexts (Pavalko 1989; Fishback and Kantor 1998).

Methodology

Following Allison (1984), I employ an event history model that estimates the effects of a set of (mostly) time-dependent variables on the probability of adoption of a blue sky statute, given that adoption has not already occurred. The model is a discrete-time system and treats a state-year as the unit of analysis.

My sample consists of 237 state-years beginning in 1910 and continuing, for each state, until the adoption of a blue sky law. Only state-years in which the relevant state's legislature was in session, and therefore in which a law could be adopted, are included. Two states, Delaware and Nevada, had not yet adopted a blue sky law by 1930. Observations on those states are included up to 1930. Event history analysis is designed to deal successfully with right-truncated cases such as these.

The dependent variable is coded as zero for each state-year in which a law was not adopted and as one for each state-year in which a law was adopted. Dates of adoption are determined from state session laws. The effect of the independent variables on the log-odds of adoption is analyzed using a logistic regression. The model assumes that we can express the probability that a state will adopt a blue sky law in a given year, given that it has not already done so (P_{BS}), as a function of the following form:

$$\log\left(\frac{P_{BS}}{1-P_{BS}}\right) = \alpha + \boldsymbol{\beta}_1 X_1 + \boldsymbol{\beta}_2 X_2 + \boldsymbol{\beta}_3 X_3$$

where X_1 is a vector of variables measuring the incidence of fraud and X_2 and X_3 are vectors of variables measuring the influence of small banks and the prevalence of populist and progressive political groups, respectively.

Independent Variables

The source for all variables is described in appendix A at the end of the book. My measure of fraud incidence is the number of securities fraud cases in each state per million of economically active population during the decade ending on January 1, 1911. This variable is time invariant to avoid the possibility of reverse causation—that is, that adoption of a blue sky law could increase the number of litigated fraud cases. My source for securities fraud cases is the LEXIS/NEXIS state securities law database. I exclude cases involving face-to-face commercial transactions. There are also a number of cases involving contractual disputes between a customer and a broker or bank involving, for example, whether the broker has the right to sell securities held for the customer's account when the customer fails to meet a margin call. Although they are presented as contract or fiduciary duty claims, one might argue that they involve claims of securities fraud as we interpret that term today. I accordingly define the fraud variable in two ways, a "narrow" variable that excludes these contract disputes and a "broad" one that includes them. None of the results described below is sensitive to the difference.

The number of litigated cases is, of course, an imperfect measure of the underlying incidence of fraud. Differences among states may also be a function of the quality of the court system and the strictness with which particular states applied the doctrinal limitations on fraud claims. It is, however, the only objective measure available.

My proxy for the influence of small banks is the log of average assets per bank. The proportion of banking assets held by small banks, which Kroszner and Strahan (2001) use as a proxy for the lobbying strength of small banks, would be a preferable measure, but it is unavailable for the period of interest. I re-estimate all regressions using the proportion of state-chartered banks in a given state as the proxy for small banks, with consistent results. Smaller banks were more likely to operate under a state than a federal charter.

I use the fraction of the economically active population engaged in agriculture as a proxy for populism. My first proxy for the strength of the progressive movement is the percentage of a state's popular vote that went to Roosevelt in 1912. I also use a "progressive index" developed by Fishback and Kantor (1998) that measures the number of specified progressive statutes adopted by the relevant state (including, among others, compulsory school attendance, welfare laws, and civil service reform). I also include more comprehensive measures of the party composition of the state legislature and executive for each state-year. I define a dummy variable that takes the value one if the state had a Democratic governor and zero otherwise. Two additional variables measure the percentage of Democrats and third-party candidates, respectively, in the state's legislature (averaging the percentage in the upper and lower houses).

Whatever the reasons behind a legislature's decision to adopt a blue sky law—whether they reflect primarily the public interest, the lobbying efforts of small banks, or political ideology—we would expect adversely affected industries to oppose those laws. The securities industry was most directly affected and, as described above, it opposed blue sky laws other than the ex post fraud variety. The reports of the annual convention of the IBAA provide the number of IBAA member offices in each state for each year in the sample following the IBAA's creation in 1912. I take that number and divide it by the number (in millions) of persons employed for each state-year to create a rough measure of the relative importance of investment banking. The number is extrapolated for 1911 and 1910. Census data also provide the number of stockbrokers in each state for 1910, 1920, and 1930. I calculate that number as a fraction of the total employed population for those years and interpolate for the intervening years.

TABLE 2.2. **Descriptive statistics**

Variable	Minimum	Maximum	Mean	Standard Deviation
Number of securities fraud cases, 1901–10, per million employed	.00	9.38	1.15	2.31
Log of average assets ($ millions) per bank	−2.10	2.50	.09	1.08
Agricultural employment as percentage of total	3.00	77.20	28.18	19.76
Roosevelt's share of popular vote in 1912 (%)	.00	50.60	24.03	9.45
Progressive laws index	.00	8.00	5.05	1.74
Democratic governor (0 = no, 1 = yes)	.00	1.00	.49	.50
Democrats as percentage of legislature	1.71	100.00	46.50	27.85
Other parties as percentage of legislature	.00	25.74	2.15	4.14
IBAA[a] member offices per million employed	.00	64.05	10.60	14.51
Stockbrokers as percentage of employed	.00	.23	.06	.05
Mining employment as percentage of total	.00	21.35	3.23	4.51

[a] Investment Bankers Association of America.

The mining industry was also disproportionately and adversely affected. Many blue sky laws divided companies into classes according to the perceived amount of risk and subjected high-risk firms to greater scrutiny. Newly formed mining companies typically had a large amount of intangible assets (mining claims) and would therefore fall in the high-risk category. Indeed, some blue sky statutes explicitly assigned all mining companies to the highest-scrutiny category. Accordingly, I include a variable that measures the percentage of the state's population employed in mining.

It seems clear from table 2.1 that there are both geographical and temporal trends in the adoption of the blue sky laws. I therefore include dummy variables for year and region. I assign states to regions using the US Office of the Comptroller of the Currency's division of the country into six regions (New England, East, South, Midwest, West, and Pacific). A list of variables (omitting the regional and year dummies) with descriptive statistics appears in table 2.2.

Results

The effects of the fraud, ideology, and lobbying strength measures on the adoption of a blue sky law are shown in table 2.3. The second column contains estimated coefficients of the logistic regression model, which show the effects of the independent variables on the log-odds of adoption. The

TABLE 2.3. **Effect of explanatory variables on the adoption of a blue sky law**

Variable	Coefficient	Standard Error	*p*-Value	Marginal Probability
Baseline probability				.039
Securities fraud cases	−.198	.188	.294	−.016
Log of average bank assets	.551	1.099	.616	.024
Agricultural employment as percentage of total	.064	.052	.219	.078
Roosevelt's share of popular vote in 1912	.109	.046	.018	.056
Progressive laws index	.999	.284	.000	.136
Democratic governor	−1.476	.797	.064	−.021
Democratic share of legislature	.039	.020	.055	.059
Other parties' share of legislature	.035	.059	.557	.003
IBAA member offices	.011	.024	.643	.003
Stockbrokers as percentage of employed	−23.566	10.283	.022	−.028
Mining employment as percentage of total	−.059	.077	.443	−.011
New England states	1.265	1.699	.456	.019
Eastern states	−.732	1.471	.619	−.012
Southern states	2.320	1.580	.142	.045
Midwestern states	.535	1.079	.620	.004
Western states	1.183	1.076	.272	.015

Note: The table does not report estimated coefficients for included year dummy variables. Log likelihood = −60.7. McFadden pseudo-R^2 = 0.48.

fifth column provides a more intuitive measure by showing the marginal probabilities—that is, the change in probability of adoption resulting from a one standard-deviation increase in the independent variable, holding all other independent variables constant at their sample means, calculated as described by Caudill and Jackson (1989). The baseline probability reported in the first line is the probability of adoption when all variables are set at their sample means. I also calculate a pseudo-R^2 for the regression using McFadden's (1974) procedure.

It is first worth noting that the number of securities fraud cases does not explain the timing of adoption. The estimated coefficient has the wrong sign (a negative coefficient predicts a lower probability of adoption) and it is not statistically significant. The table reports the result using the "narrow" fraud variable described above; results with the "broad" definition are similar. Given the limitations of this measure of fraud, we cannot rule out the possibility that an unobservable "fraud wave" caused the blue sky laws. Nevertheless, the best available data do not support the market failure narrative.

Of the political and public choice variables, the one with by far the greatest explanatory power is the progressive laws index. That index counts the number of progressive laws adopted out of a set of eight. Increasing that number from its sample mean of 5 to 6.7, an increase of one standard deviation, raises the estimated probability of adopting a blue sky law in a given state-year by almost 14 percent. This suggests that some of the same political coalitions active in the adoption of progressive legislation also worked to enact blue sky laws. Further support is provided by the fact that greater support for Roosevelt in 1912 is associated with a positive, statistically and practically significant increase in probability. The negative and marginally significant coefficient on the dummy variable for Democratic governors is also suggestive, as many staunchly progressive states had Republican governors.

Neither the agriculture variable nor the average bank size variable is associated with a higher probability of adopting a blue sky law. We must be careful in interpreting these results, however, because the two variables are highly correlated. I therefore re-estimate the model excluding one variable, then the other. Neither has a statistically significant estimated coefficient when the other is excluded. The two variables are also not jointly significant when both are included in the model.

Finally, a stronger securities industry presence, as measured by the number of stockbrokers as a percentage of total employment, tended to delay enactment of a blue sky law. Both the IBAA membership variable and the mining employment variable, however, have small and statistically insignificant effects. None of the regional dummy variables has a statistically significant estimated coefficient.

To determine the sensitivity of these results to the event history methodology, I counted the number of years (ignoring those in which the legislature did not sit) from 1910 until the date of adoption of a blue sky law for each state. I then used that count as the dependent variable in an ordinary least-squares regression using the starting values of the independent variables on the right-hand side. The results were consistent with those from the event history analysis. In particular, the progressive index variable and the percentage vote for Roosevelt predict more rapid adoption and the stockbroker variable predicts slower adoption; in each case, the result is statistically significant.

The data thus suggest that progressive ideology was a strong factor behind adoption of blue sky laws. Neither the incidence of securities fraud nor the lobbying power of small banks is associated with early adoption of a blue sky law. In the next section, I consider whether those factors influenced the type of blue sky law a state chose to adopt.

Evidence from the Type of Blue Sky Law

The decision to adopt a particular type of law may be different from the decision to adopt a law or not. Legislators motivated to avoid blame and ideologically motivated voters may be more interested in the "statement" made by legislation and less in its details. By contrast, the affected industry may be willing to accept the "punishment" of new regulations so long as it can shape the details. In the case of the blue sky laws, a bank wishing to suppress competition would favor a merit review statute giving the administering official (often a bank commissioner, who might be sympathetic to the banks' point of view) maximum authority to prevent securities offerings. A securities firm would prefer an ex post fraud law putting minimal restrictions on offerings but deterring unscrupulous sellers.

I therefore examine the choice among the three types of blue sky law. First, I restrict the sample to the state-years in which blue sky laws were adopted. I then employ a multinomial logit model to estimate the effects of the independent variables on the choice among an ex post fraud, ex ante fraud, or merit review statute. One issue in doing so is the fact that the merit review statutes are limited to the early part of the sample. This is a particular problem for drawing any inference with respect to the average bank asset variable. Because bank assets generally were increasing over time, the result would be biased in the direction of associating smaller banks with merit review, which is one of the hypotheses to be tested. To avoid this problem, I use for each state the log of average bank assets for the first year of the sample. The limited temporal (and to a lesser extent geographical) variation in the type of statute and the reduced number of degrees of freedom make it impossible to estimate the model with the year and region variables. I discuss these drawbacks in more detail below.

The results of the multinomial logit regression are reported in table 2.4. Compared with table 2.3, there is a shift in the importance of the interest group and ideology variables. The estimated coefficients on the progressive index and political composition variables are in each case insignificant. Bank size, however, is a significant predictor of the type of statute. An increase in average bank size is associated with a reduced probability of a merit review or ex ante fraud statute, compared to an ex post fraud statute. This is consistent with small banks preferring a more stringent blue sky statute. A larger stockbroker presence predicts a lower probability of adopting a merit review statute, although the result is marginally

TABLE 2.4. **Effects of explanatory variables on the type of blue sky law adopted**

Variable	Coefficient	Standard Error	*p*-Value
Impact on log-odds of adopting a merit review statute			
Number of securities fraud cases	.848	1.095	.439
Log of average bank assets	−4.789	2.350	.042
Roosevelt's share of popular vote in 1912	.171	.163	.293
Progressive laws index	.347	.739	.639
Democratic governor	−.961	3.417	.778
Democratic share of legislature	−.011	.056	.846
Other parties' share of legislature	−.137	.300	.649
IBAA member offices	.101	.155	.516
Stockbrokers as percentage of employed	−131.013	71.023	.065
Mining employment as percentage of total	.802	.417	.055
Impact on log-odds of adopting an ex ante fraud statute			
Number of securities fraud cases	1.224	.820	.135
Log of average bank assets	−4.125	1.729	.017
Roosevelt's share of popular vote in 1912	.013	.143	.925
Progressive laws index	−.016	.554	.976
Democratic governor	−.792	2.179	.716
Democratic share of legislature	−.004	.038	.907
Other parties' share of legislature	−.354	.215	.100
IBAA[a] member offices	−.092	.066	.163
Stockbrokers as percentage of employed	25.196	24.905	.312
Mining employment as percentage of total	.395	.337	.241

Note: Log-likelihood = −21.61. McFadden pseudo-R^2 = 0.53.
[a] Investment Bankers Association of America.

significant. Interestingly, a larger mining industry presence predicts a higher likelihood of adopting a merit review statute, although again the result is marginally significant.

This test, like the event history analysis, is complicated by the strong correlation between the average bank asset and agricultural employment variables. The model estimated in table 2.4 does not include the agricultural employment variable. With both variables included, the bank asset variable loses significance in the upper panel, although it retains significance in the lower panel. However, the pseudo-R^2 of the model remains the same, and a likelihood-ratio test shows that the bank asset variable, but not the agriculture variable, improves the predictive power of the model. It therefore appears that the presence of small banks, and not agricultural employment, predicts a more stringent statute.

In order to determine whether these results are a consequence of the lack of controls for year and region, I employ an ordinal regression procedure as described in McCullagh (1980) as an alternative to the multinomial logit procedure. The ordinal regression procedure imposes a restriction that the slopes in the regression equation are the same for the choice between any of the types of statute. The corresponding benefit is that it can accommodate a larger set of independent variables, including year and region dummies. The results closely track those of the multinomial logit model. In particular, smaller average bank size is a significant predictor of a stricter statute (whether or not the agricultural employment variable is included).

The fit of the ordinal regression model, however, is poor in comparison to that of the multinomial logit model, which suggests that the independent variables may affect the choice between an ex ante fraud and ex post fraud statute differently than the choice between an ex ante fraud and a merit review statute. This is not surprising. It seems plausible that interest groups might have viewed a merit review statute to be a dramatic intervention but have been indifferent between ex ante and ex post fraud.

The results are consistent with Macey and Miller's (1991) qualitative discussion. It appears that small banks lobbied in favor of stricter statutes, while stockbrokers opposed merit review. Progressive political coalitions seem to have had little impact on the type of statute even though they strongly influenced the rapidity with which a state adopted a blue sky law.

Effects of the Blue Sky Laws: Evidence from Bank Profitability

Was the enactment of a blue sky law actually beneficial to small banks? The most relevant available data are from the Comptroller of the Currency annual reports. These provide information on the rate of return (profits divided by capital and surplus) for national banks grouped by state. While we do not have comprehensive income data for state-chartered banks, the comptroller's data are fortunately presented separately for city and country banks. I use the latter as a rough proxy for small-bank profitability. The data do not cover the smallest banks (which would have been state chartered), but being able to limit the analysis to national banks outside the main cities is the next best alternative.

I measure average annual profitability of each state's country banks for the five years prior to enactment of a blue sky law and the five years after enactment. I omit Connecticut (adopted in 1929) and Delaware (adopted in 1931) to avoid confounding effects from the Depression. This leaves 460 observations, enough to permit state and year fixed effects. The

TABLE 2.5. **Blue sky laws and rural bank profits**

Type of Statute	Coefficient	Standard Error	p-Value	Adjusted R^2
All	.334	.853	.695	.487
Ex post fraud	−.205	.781	.794	.939
Ex ante fraud	.255	1.033	.828	.471
Merit review	4.987	1.877	.009	.765

Note: The estimated coefficient is in each case on a dummy variable that equals one when a blue sky law is in effect and is measured in units of (percent) rate of return.

independent variable of interest is a dummy variable that switches from zero to one after enactment of a blue sky law. The associated coefficient estimates the effect of a blue sky law on profitability, controlling for the state and year. The average annual rate of profit in the sample is 8.9 percent with a standard deviation of 4.0 percent; the range is from −6.5 to 29.1 percent.

Table 2.5 shows the results of the fixed-effects model. If all blue sky laws are considered as a single group, it appears that the adoption of a statute had no effect on bank profits. The estimated coefficient is positive, but it is not statistically significant. When we break the sample down into three subsamples, one for each of the three types of blue sky law, however, a different picture emerges. Neither an ex post fraud law nor a more stringent ex ante fraud law has a significant effect, although the estimated coefficient increases as we move from the first to the second. A merit review statute, however, has a very large and highly significant effect on profitability. If small banks lobbied for merit review statutes, as the prior analysis suggests, these results indicate that their behavior was rational. The result also fits well with the fact that the Kansas bank commissioner used his state's merit review statute to reject the vast majority of proposed bond and stock offerings in Kansas.

One possible objection to the analysis is that the merit review statutes are all in the early part of the sample. If there was something unique about bank profitability trends in the early part of the sample period, it could bias the result. The year dummies attempt to control for this possibility, but if the slope (and not merely the intercept) of the relation between a blue sky law and bank profits varied over time, the results could remain biased.

To determine whether this is the case, I re-estimate the regressions after limiting the sample to those states that adopted a blue sky law in 1911, 1912, or 1913. Fortunately, there are examples of all three types of

TABLE 2.6. **Blue sky laws and interest rates on rural bank savings accounts**

Type of Statute	Interest Rate Increase, 1909–24
Ex post fraud	9.32%
Ex ante fraud	5.45%
Merit review	4.58%
p-Value	.328

statute during that period. The results remain the same—neither an ex ante nor ex post fraud statute is associated with a change in bank profits, but profits increase by a statistically and economically significant amount after enactment of a merit review statute.

If banks correctly believed that a blue sky law would reduce competition for depositors' funds, then banks should have been able to pay a lower rate of interest on deposits in states with more stringent blue sky laws. Data restrictions make it impossible to carry out a rigorous test of the hypothesis. We can, however, use a pair of surveys of interest rates on savings accounts, one performed by the National Monetary Commission for 1909 and a second by the US Office of the Comptroller of the Currency for 1924. That year is later than the adoption of all but two blue sky laws and 1909 is two years prior to the first adoption. For each state that adopted a blue sky law before 1924, I accordingly measure the difference between the interest rate paid in 1924 and that paid in 1909, limiting myself again to rural banks. Interest rates rose generally during this period. However, as shown in table 2.6, they rose least in states with a merit review statute and most in states with an ex post fraud statute. The test is not very powerful, and using a single-factor analysis of variance test, the differences are not statistically significant. However, with that caveat, the interest rate evidence is consistent with the evidence from small-bank profitability.

In conclusion, the best available data tell a fascinating story about the forces behind blue sky laws. There is no evidence at all to support a market failure narrative in which states reacted to an increase in fraud. There is strong evidence that blue sky laws were part of a general package of progressive reforms and a state's eagerness to adopt a law was a function of the strength of progressive sentiment in that state. Finally, there is strong evidence that small banks successfully shaped the type of statute adopted to their benefit—and to the detriment of their depositors, who were left with fewer options for investing their savings.

CHAPTER THREE

What the Securities Act Got Right

The Securities Act of 1933 was the first major securities reform of the New Deal and the first important reform since the blue sky laws. The Securities Act is a fascinating example of legislation adopted hastily in the wake of a financial crisis in an air of anger and retribution. Parts of the statute responded to a genuine problem and crafted a reasonable solution drawing on existing legal principles. Other, more legally innovative, parts curtailed competition and significantly benefited an important segment of the regulated industry.

The Securities Act dealt successfully with the lack of disclosure of investment bankers' and promoters' compensation in connection with the floatation of new companies. This was a genuine problem—but it was a problem that had existed for over half a century in England and America and had nothing to do with the Great Crash or the Depression. The Securities Act imposed disclosure rules borrowed from case law and British statutes. However, acting with a mandate to "crack down" on the financial industry, the Securities Act's drafters overreached by also comprehensively regulating the process of selling new issues of securities. In so doing, they played directly into the hands of the major investment banks, who were the principal beneficiaries of the detailed regulation of the offering process—an ironic result for a statute described by its supporters as a way to take the bankers down a peg.

Rules mandating disclosure of investment bankers' compensation and insiders' profits were useful and easily designed. They had been devel-

Portions of this chapter were previously published as Paul G. Mahoney, "Mandatory Disclosure as a Solution to Agency Problems," *University of Chicago Law Review* 62 (1995): 1047–1112. Reprinted with permission from the University of Chicago.

oped by courts in England and the United States through their incremental, case-by-case process beginning in the late nineteenth century. The Securities Act could have codified and expanded those duties as had the Companies Act in England and stopped there. But the New Dealers, like the progressives before them, believed that existing legal principles enforced through litigation were insufficient to deal with the new problems generated by an expanding industrial economy. James Landis, the principal draftsman of the Securities Act and one of the first commissioners of the SEC, wrote in his book *The Administrative Process* (Landis 1966) that the public's interest in carrying out social policies could not be sufficiently protected by private litigation. In order to serve the public welfare within an industrialized economy, the government should delegate to experts the tasks of writing and enforcing detailed rules of conduct.

Generations of lawyers, economists and historians have been so thoroughly steeped in the market failure narrative of the New Deal securities laws that they have failed to see the obvious—although described as a "full disclosure" statute, the Securities Act as initially enacted was at least as much a secrecy statute. It suppressed information about a company making a public offering at particular times and through particular media. In so doing, it enshrined in law the offering techniques used by established, top-tier investment banks and outlawed offering techniques used by more recent entrants who had competed successfully for underwriting business in the post–World War I era. The detailed rules of conduct curtailed competition and cemented the leading position of the major investment banks. Thus, contrary to the New Dealers' and progressives' expectations, the most investor-friendly and successful parts of the Securities Act were those that borrowed from existing legal doctrines, not the new and innovative regulatory provisions.

This chapter and the next proceed in three steps. First, I briefly explain why the traditional market failure narrative cannot explain the Securities Act. Following that discussion, the remainder of this chapter describes the genuine problem to which the Securities Act was addressed—the nondisclosure of commissions, profits, and other compensation received by investment bankers, other intermediaries, and insiders in public offerings. Courts in England and America recognized the problem early on and developed doctrines to combat it, as did Parliament. Parts of the Securities Act were borrowed almost in their entirety from the English statute. But this narrow solution to a narrow problem did not appeal to Landis's regulatory mindset. Chapter 4 describes in detail the parts of the statute that were not derived from existing disclosure rules and details their unintended consequence of helping investment banks curtail innovative offering techniques that had cost them business.

The Failure of the Market Failure Narrative

The market failure narrative underlying the Securities Act contends that poor disclosure practices in the new-issue market led investors routinely to buy securities that were either inherently fraudulent or overpriced. A common assertion is that half of the securities sold in the years just prior to the Crash of 1929 were worthless (Badger 2008). This is a post hoc analysis—it infers that securities were worthless when sold in the late 1920s because they performed poorly during the severe economic conditions of 1930–32. That analysis overlooks the more plausible possibility that stocks were just the messenger of a dramatically weakened economy.

Economists have generally recognized that the link between the Great Crash and the Great Depression is tenuous. Supporting their skepticism is the fact that economic output peaked in August 1929 and a downturn was already underway when the October 1929 market break occurred (Gordon 1986). White (1990) accordingly argues that the onset of a recession helped trigger a change in investor expectations that contributed to the Crash. The most prominent alternative explanations for the severity of the Depression focus on monetary policy. Friedman and Schwartz (1965) offer one perspective. They observe that the money supply contracted from 1929 to 1933 and the Federal Reserve not only failed to take available steps to counter the decline, but raised the discount rate in late 1931, contributing to the severity of the downturn. Temin (1992) argues that the re-implementation of the gold standard after World War I created a deflationary bias that explains the severity of the Depression. Either view is consistent with the stock market's role as messenger rather than cause, as was true in London in 1696.

The most plausible link between the Great Crash and the Depression would be reduced household wealth and resulting reductions in consumer demand. However, it is difficult to attribute the decline in output, which hit its low point in 1932, to a 1929 market crash that was partly reversed in early 1930. Commenters who wish to draw a causal connection between the Crash and the Depression therefore often exaggerate the wealth effects of the stock price declines of October and November 1929. As noted in the introduction, Levitt mistakenly accelerates the 80 percent fall in stock prices from 1929 peak to 1932 trough, speaking as if it all occurred during the Crash. Commentators sometimes correctly note that the Dow Jones Industrial Average did not regain its 1929 peak until the early 1950s but then incorrectly infer that a buy-and-hold investor would have been underwater for more than two decades (a claim prominently made, for example, in the Wikipedia entry "Wall Street Crash of 1929").

The two statements are not equivalent because the Dow Jones is an index of prices, not returns. It does not consider dividends and other distributions, which are also part of returns and therefore of investor wealth. The difference is important because many companies, lacking profitable investment opportunities, continued to pay dividends during the Depression. Figure 3.1 illustrates the point. The dashed line represents changes in the Dow Jones Industrial Average during the Depression. By the end of 1939, the Dow was at only 40 percent of its peak value. It would not again reach its August 1929 level until late 1954.

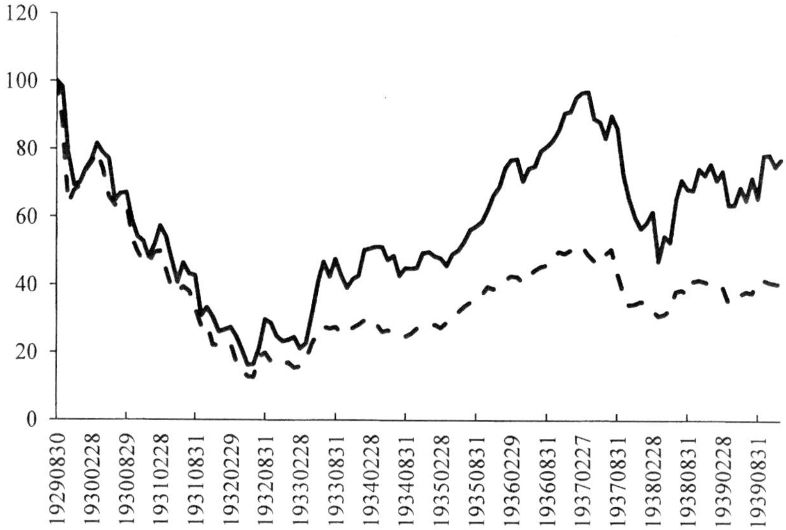

FIGURE 3.1 Dow Jones Average versus investor wealth, 1929–1939. Dashed line: Dow Jones Industrial Average (August 30, 1929 = 100); solid line: Market value of an equally weighted portfolio of all NYSE-listed companies with all dividends and other distributions reinvested (August 30, 1929 = 100).

The solid line depicts the wealth of an investor who did not panic during the Crash and Depression. It assumes that the investor purchased one share of each NYSE stock at the close on August 30, 1929, surely the worst investment decision in the history of US equity investing, and then held onto those shares, reinvesting all dividends in shares of the same stock and reinvesting distributions made upon liquidation of companies into an equally weighted portfolio of all NYSE stocks. This stoic investor's portfolio was almost back to even by early 1937, just before the second wave of the Depression hit. Yet at that same date the economy as a whole was far from healthy; the unemployment rate remained at 12 percent and would soon be back to 20 percent.

Both Temin (1976) and Romer (1990) concede that the wealth effects of the Crash were too modest to account for the collapse of aggregate demand during the Depression. Romer nevertheless finds a link between the two events based not on the net decline in stock prices but on their volatility. This, she argues, led consumers to be more uncertain about future income and to reduce discretionary purchases. Romer's explanation, as she notes, is consistent with the stock market's role as messenger. The message it (accurately) conveyed was one of uncertainty about future output and therefore wages.

Blaming the stock market for the Depression, however, was a clear winner politically and Roosevelt pursued the strategy vigorously. His 1932 campaign was based on the notion that finance was the root of the country's ills. His first inaugural address identified deflation and unemployment as the evils to be conquered and identified their cause as the "practices of the unscrupulous money changers." Faithful to his campaign promises, Roosevelt made enactment of the Securities Act one of his top priorities.

The Securities Act's English Antecedents

Although described as requiring disclosure of "all material information" in connection with a public offering, the Securities Act was actually focused principally on disclosure of investment bankers' compensation and insiders' profits from public offerings. This may seem a jarring assertion given the SEC's longstanding approach to disclosure, but it is the purpose for which the statute's disclosure provisions were originally designed. This is not surprising because Roosevelt had focused on nondisclosure of investment banking compensation as the central problem to which the statute would be addressed.

Nondisclosure of underwriters' compensation lay at the heart of the progressives' critique of Wall Street. Roosevelt himself frequently referred to or quoted Louis Brandeis's classic 1914 book *Other People's Money and How the Bankers Use It.*[1] The book's most famous chapter, "What Publicity Can Do," has come down to us as a cry for "full disclosure" and is the source of the famous reference to sunlight as the best disinfectant. But the chapter is in fact a demand for disclosure of underwriting commissions. Under the heading "Publicity as a Remedy," Brandeis argued

> Compel bankers when issuing securities to make public the commissions or profits they are receiving. Let every circular letter, prospectus or advertisement of a bond or stock show clearly what the banker received for his middleman-services.

The equation of "full disclosure" with disclosure of underwriters' compensation and insiders' profits carried over into the 1932 Democratic Party platform. The Democrats pledged to enact a statute "requiring to be filed with the government and carried in advertisements of all offerings of foreign and domestic stocks and bonds true information *as to bonuses, commissions, principal invested, and interest of the sellers*" (emphasis added).[2]

Recognizing that "full disclosure" meant disclosure of the financial interests of those who acted as agent for or occupied a fiduciary relationship to a company selling shares to the public helps us better understand the Securities Act's disclosure provisions and situate them within a half-century-long debate about a fiduciary's disclosure obligations in connection with securities offerings. This form of "full disclosure" evolved from common law rules applicable to agents dealing adversely with their principals. Initially they did not concern underwriters per se because in the English market in the nineteenth century, the process of going public differed from that in the United States in the post–World War I era.

Companies in England in the late nineteenth century often went public through the following arrangement: a financial intermediary known as a "promoter" identified a privately owned business, created a newly incorporated company that agreed to purchase the business, and then took the newly formed company public, using the proceeds of the offering to complete the purchase. This gave rise to specific conflicts of interest we can call "the promoter problem" for short. They involved the use of funds raised in the initial public offering (IPO) to purchase property or services from the new company's promoter on terms that did not reflect arm's-length bargaining.

When taking a private business public, a promoter commonly created a new shell company that agreed to purchase the assets of the business contingent on a successful public offering of the new company's shares (Jefferys 1977). Until the closing of the offering, title to the business was held by a trustee acting for the shell company. The trustee was typically an associate of the promoter. The promoter identified the business to be acquired, incorporated the shell company, selected an initial board of directors, and circulated a prospectus that described the business and solicited subscriptions for stock. When sufficient subscriptions were obtained, the stock was issued and the transactions described in the prospectus were completed.

These transactions presented numerous opportunities for the promoter to make undisclosed profits. In the simplest case, the promoter charged a commission to the original owner of the business in connection with his sale to the newly formed company and did not disclose the existence of the commission in the prospectus. These commissions could be as much as 50 percent of the purchase price (Cottrell 1980, 131). Shannon (1932, 411–13), Jefferys (1977, 301–2), and Hannah (1983, 19) provide anecdotal evidence that the success rate of IPOs was inversely related to the size of promoters' fees.

A more active form of concealment was for the promoter to arrange an intermediate sale to a nominee who then sold to the trustee at an increased price. This practice became known as "loading" the purchase price. For example, the promoter and vendor (the owner of the business to be taken public) might agree on a price of £50,000 net to the vendor. In order to make the business seem more valuable, the promoter might arrange for an associate to purchase the business for £50,000 and then immediately resell to a second nominee for £100,000, who in turn would agree to sell to the trustee for £105,000. The prospectus could then truthfully but misleadingly state that the business had recently changed hands for £100,000 and was being sold to the investors at a 5 percent markup. In actuality, of course, the investors in this example are paying more than double the actual arms-length (and undisclosed) purchase price.

The practice of loading the purchase price surfaces in evidence presented to Parliament and in court opinions. A House of Lords opinion from 1900 described a fact pattern occurring "over and over again": "[The promoters] issue a prospectus representing that they had agreed to purchase the property for a sum largely in excess of the amount which they had, in fact, to pay. . . . Secretly, and therefore dishonestly, they put into their own pockets the difference between the real and the pretended price."[3]

English law inadvertently facilitated hiding the professional promoter's profit. Courts had called into question whether a company had the power to spend shareholder funds in connection with its own IPO (Palmer 1898, 231). This legal uncertainty created demand for professional promoters because the directors of a newly created company would be wary of offering an underwriting commission or discount. The promoter's contract was with the vendor of the business rather than the company created to purchase it. This facilitated nondisclosure because the prospectus could truthfully state that the company was paying no fees in connection with the offering; when challenged, the vendor and promoter argued that the promoter's compensation was a private matter between them.[4]

Courts responded by concluding that a promoter was a fiduciary for the new corporation and therefore had a duty to disclose his adverse interest.[5] In particular, he had either to disclose his interest to the directors, if they were independent, or to the prospective investors if they were not.[6] The result was that the promoter could not stand on both sides of the transaction; he had to bargain over his compensation with either the independent directors or the investors. Because these were judge-made rules, the details of what exactly the promoter had to disclose and the investors' remedy for nondisclosure were worked out on a case-by-case basis.

In 1900 Parliament stepped in and made disclosure a matter of statutory law. The list of items to be disclosed is of particular interest. It included the names of the vendors of any property to be purchased with the issue proceeds, the price paid for such property, all sums paid to solicit subscriptions for the securities being sold, all amounts paid to promoters, and "full particulars" of every director's financial interest in any property to be acquired or in the offering itself. Companies were also required to disclose all contracts made outside the ordinary course of business within the three years prior to the offering. Both the language and legislative history of the statute make it clear that the purpose was to force disclosure of all commissions and profits earned by any interested party in connection with the offering, regardless of the form of the underlying transactions. These disclosure provisions remained in the revised Companies Act 1929.

The United States: Underwriters Replace Promoters

The promoter problem and judicial attempts to address it did not differ greatly between England and the United States. Reported cases show that American promoters sometimes sought to conceal their interest in property sold to the new corporation.[7] Courts in America, as in England, formulated doctrine to deal with the promoter problem and often cited English cases. However, it was difficult to regulate on a case-by-case basis all the myriad ways in which a promoter might try to hide his financial interest in a corporation. For example, in 1908 the Supreme Court concluded that a promoter's fiduciary obligation ran only to the corporation itself before there were any outside investors. Thus if the promoter created a company and issued all the stock to himself, he could sell property to the corporation after full disclosure to the existing shareholder (that is, himself) and then sell additional shares to the public without disclosing that he was the initial vendor of the company's assets or the profit he stood to make as a consequence.[8]

After World War I, however, the focus shifted to underwriters. By that time, a newly formed company in the United States often went public using the services of an investment bank that underwrote the shares, buying them at a discount and reselling to the public (Carosso 1970). Criticism of financial intermediaries and their compensation thus focused on underwriters rather than promoters.

Roosevelt's invocation of Brandeis (who praised the English disclosure statute) and the focus on sellers' compensation in the 1932 Democratic platform show that the new administration had something like the English statutory approach in mind from the beginning. Both Roosevelt (1972) and Landis (1966) identified the Companies Act 1929 as the model for the Securities Act.

This is particularly evident in schedule A of the Securities Act, Congress's list of the items to be disclosed in a registration statement filed with the government and in the prospectus delivered to investors. Because the SEC has since used its statutory authority to adopt registration forms that supersede schedule A, the latter is of only historical interest. But it provides a useful reminder of the problems to which disclosure was addressed.

Sellers' compensation and financial interests are the core problems addressed in schedule A. Like the disclosure items in the Companies Act, much of schedule A focuses on commissions, discounts, and other compensation paid to underwriters and promoters and on amounts paid to the vendors of any property acquired by the company. Schedule A also requires detailed information about the company's capital structure and the place the offered securities will occupy in that capital structure. This is another means of uncovering any hidden financial interests that would dilute the new shares. By contrast, the disclosure of information about the company's business is limited to the command to identify "the general character of the business actually transacted or to be transacted" by the company.

The paucity of required disclosures about the business itself is in sharp contrast with blue sky laws of the same era, some of which required much more detailed information about the company's plans and operations. Typical disclosure items in the blue sky laws included a business plan, a schedule of the issuer's assets with an appraisal, abstracts of title to real estate and a schedule of insurance policies, and a statement of "all material facts . . . relative to the character or value" of the offered securities.[9] Such information was useful to a state banking commissioner carrying out a "merit review" of the securities to decide whether to permit their sale in the state. But having decisively rejected a merit review approach, Landis did not include such items in schedule A of the Securities Act. Instead, schedule A's disclosure list was focused firmly on uncovering the compensation and financial interests of the underwriters and other offering participants, not on facts about the company's business.

Accounting Disclosures

One apparent departure from the focus on the commissions and financial interests of sellers in schedule A is the requirement to provide audited financial statements of the issuing company. This only seems to be a departure because we are used to financial statements as an aid to valuation. This was not, however, the purpose of the Securities Act's financial statement provisions. The principal architect of those provisions was Robert Healy, a Vermont lawyer and former judge who became the general counsel of the Federal Trade Commission and then one of the first commissioners of the SEC. From a lawyer's perspective, the purpose of accounting was to *account*—that is, to keep track of how an agent had used money and property entrusted to him so as to deter any improper or hidden uses.

Today's accounting scandals typically involve either overstating earnings or using off-balance sheet transactions to hide debts. But to Healy and his contemporaries, the greatest accounting scandal of the age was the valuation of assets on company balance sheets. Subsequent chapters will discuss how this concern affected the design of other New Deal securities reforms. With respect to the Securities Act, the primary worry was that sellers of new businesses overstated their own investments in the business by assigning "inflated" values to intangible assets they contributed to the firm.

The typical problem was as follows: an entrepreneur would convey assets that might include real estate, equipment, patents, mining claims, or other forms of property to the newly formed company in return for its stock. As an accounting matter, the company valued the resulting equity as equivalent in value to the assets received. Critics argued that these assets—particularly intangible assets—were systematically overvalued, leading to stock that was "watered" or issued on terms unfairly favorable to the insiders.

The purpose of the financial statement requirement, in the eyes of the Securities Act's drafters and its enforcers at the Federal Trade Commission and the SEC, was to force disclosure of watered stock. The FTC and SEC did not simply require financial statements—they insisted that those statements conform to historical costs (Zeff 2007). To Healy, historical-cost accounting was a way to force insiders to disclose the prices they had paid for assets that they then contributed to the corporation in return for stock.

The disclosure provisions of the Securities Act, then, were not meant to force disclosure of "all material facts" as we interpret that phrase today. Instead, they were designed to deal with an important but limited problem—hidden compensation received by insiders, underwriters, and other offering participants that would dilute the interest of an incoming shareholder. This was a longstanding problem to which the courts had addressed themselves with considerable, but not complete, success. In England, the Companies Acts 1900 and 1929 contained detailed provisions to force disclosure of hidden compensation and the Securities Act copied the approach while altering it slightly for the American context.

Had Landis stopped here, the Securities Act's effects might have been quite different. But he was committed to the notion that it was not enough to clarify the rights and obligations of parties to a commercial transaction. Instead, he believed that government agencies could and should improve on market-generated arrangements by bringing their disinterested expertise to bear. He therefore added to the statute detailed regulation of the process by which securities were to be offered to the public. These provisions and their consequences are the topic of the next chapter.

CHAPTER FOUR

What the Securities Act Got Wrong

Scholarly analyses of the Securities Act rarely suggest that it could have conferred any benefits on the regulated industry. This may be because the claim would be hard to prove; we have no systematic data on the value or profitability of investment banking firms prior to 1933, as they were mostly private partnerships engaged in a business largely unregulated at the federal level. But this dearth of interest-group analysis also reflects a surprising tendency to ignore the fact that the Securities Act, despite its reputation, is not a "full disclosure" statute. The Securities Act did three distinct things. It required certain disclosures in connection with public offerings. It added a federal ban on fraud to common law doctrines and provided a more generous cause of action for misleading statements in connection with a public offering. Finally, it regulated the process of undertaking a public offering. The third of these made the Securities Act as much an information-suppression as an information-disclosure statute.

As noted in chapter 3, the statute could easily have done only the first two things. The addition of the third reflected James Landis's view that complex economic processes required regulatory oversight by impartial experts (1966). Modern commentators have tended either to overlook the regulation of the offering process or to describe it as a mere administrative detail of the "full disclosure" system. Even Henry Manne (1974), who argues that the Securities Act might have affected competitive conditions in the investment banking industry, describes it as a disclosure statute. Manne suggests that the major investment banks, which underwrote low-

This chapter was first published in modified form as Paul G. Mahoney, "The Political Economy of the Securities Act of 1933," *Journal of Legal Studies* 30 (2001): 1–31. Reprinted with permission of the University of Chicago Press.

risk securities and kept a close eye on the companies whose securities they sponsored, had nothing to lose from a "full disclosure" policy and much to gain from driving out underwriters of high-risk securities.

But scholars have overlooked the fact that in addition to requiring certain disclosures, the Securities Act as initially enacted *forbids* public disclosure of many details of a public offering and the issuing company prior to the filing of a registration statement. The statute also mandated a minimum twenty-day "waiting period" between the filing of the registration statement and the beginning of retail selling. While traditionally described as technical details of the "full disclosure" apparatus, these provisions imposed important limitations on both retail and wholesale competition. These "technical" details can be best understood as means of eliminating several specific competitive techniques that low-status securities dealers used successfully against high-status dealers in the late 1920s and early 1930s.

Until 1996, the SEC lacked general exemptive authority under the Securities Act and thus could not alter these restrictions. In 2005, however, it made use of its exemptive authority to permit certain classes of issuers to use pre-offering publicity and to engage in written solicitation prior to the effective date. In the JOBS Act of 2012, Congress relaxed these provisions further for certain startup companies.

Structural Change in the 1920s

The investment banking industry became substantially more competitive in the 1920s than previously. This section describes the investment banking industry prior to World War I and the changes that occurred during the 1920s. The federal government's antitrust suit against the major investment banks, *United States v. Morgan*, produced considerable information about the history of investment banking practices.[1] I rely on the opinion and trial record from the *Morgan* litigation as well as standard histories of investment banking.

Before World War I

The syndicate system of underwriting and selling new issues of securities evolved in the United States during the late nineteenth and early twentieth centuries. The distinguishing feature of the syndicate system was a coordinated selling effort (Redlich 1968). Under prior practice, investment bankers purchased newly issued securities as a group at a fixed price and sold them individually at times, places, and prices of their choosing. Under the syndicate system, by contrast, the purchasers contractually agreed to sell the securities at a uniform price at such times and places as the syndicate manager specified. Advertising was also organized collectively.

A syndicate was formed by an "originating" or "issuing" investment banking house that performed the functions typical of a managing underwriter today—advising the company, investigating its business, and negotiating the type and terms of the security and the details of the offering. The other syndicate members delegated near-total managerial control to the originating house. I use the terms "originating," "managing," and "lead" underwriter interchangeably to refer to the investment bank that acted as the principal financial advisor to the issuing company.

Underwriters were compensated by purchasing at a discount. The syndicate purchased from the company at a negotiated price. Investors ultimately purchased at a fixed price set by the originating house in consultation with the company. The "gross spread," or difference between the price paid by investors and that received by the company, represented compensation to the underwriters for financial advice, bearing underwriting risk, and finding buyers, and was shared among the investment banks and dealers participating in the offering based on the roles they played. In the pre-1933 era, there might be several syndicates standing between the company and the ultimate investor, with each successive syndicate buying at a slightly smaller discount.

At the top of the pyramid, the managing underwriter received the largest compensation. The syndicate paid it a fee as compensation for managing the issue. The managing underwriter, in consultation with the issuer, chose the other underwriters and distributors of the issue and determined the amount of their underwriting or sales commitments (Galston 1928). The ability to dispense business was a valuable asset to an issuing house.

Prior to World War I, compared to what would follow, the system of distribution and the investment banking hierarchy were static. There was a clear separation between originating houses and distributing houses (Hayes 1979). The former were purely or predominantly wholesalers who negotiated directly with issuing companies and sold to other securities dealers and institutional investors.[2] The originating houses formed the aristocracy of investment banking. Distributors participated in underwriting syndicates at an originator's invitation and sold partly to smaller dealers and partly to investors. For large offerings, the prized position of originating banker would likely be held by one of a few large, New York–based "houses of issue," the most prominent of which were J. P. Morgan & Co. and Kuhn, Loeb & Co. (Edwards 1967). In the years just before the war, William A. Read & Co., which became Dillon, Read & Co. in 1921, joined this exclusive club. Other investment banks carved out competitive niches in selected industries—for example, N. W. Harris (later Harris, Forbes & Co.) and Chicago-based Halsey, Stuart & Co. in public utilities and Lehman Brothers and Goldman, Sachs & Co. in merchandising.

The dominance of the wholesale houses reflected structural features of the new issue market. Institutions and wealthy investors were the principal purchasers; retail investors did not yet participate directly in the securities markets on a large scale (Edwards 1967). The United States was a net importer of investment capital from abroad and underwriters relied in part on access to foreign investors. This tended to channel new issues through the principal financial center, New York, and to underwriters with strong international ties.

J. P. Morgan and Kuhn Loeb had greater access to capital than did other investment bankers. Both were private banks (that is, privately held, unregulated commercial banks that did no business with the general public) that took deposits from their business customers, although their aggregate deposits were small relative to those of ordinary commercial banks. More important, each had extensive European connections and close relationships with large commercial banks. These relationships enabled them to borrow money and place large blocks of securities on short notice.

The distribution process was slow. Syndicate agreements often lasted for a year and the process of distribution usually lasted several months.[3] The new issue market was dominated by bonds. Stock generally reached the market through private sales and insiders' sales through brokers into the secondary market.

From World War I to the Securities Act

The structure of the investment banking business changed substantially after the war. The United States emerged from the war a creditor nation with "the largest stock and flow of broad-based savings in the world" (Friend et al. 1967, 92). Domestic borrowers no longer had to rely on foreign capital. They could also for the first time tap an army of small investors.

INCREASING RELIANCE ON "RETAIL" SELLING. To finance the war effort, the US Treasury sold securities on an unprecedented scale. The four Liberty Loans of 1917–18 and the Victory Loan of 1919 aggregated $21.5 billion (Carosso 1970, 224). To put that number in context, the gross federal debt at the end of 1916 was $1.2 billion and the total amount of corporate securities issued from 1907 through 1916 was $16.7 billion (all figures from Commerce Department publications). To sell bonds on such a scale, the Treasury enlisted the country's commercial and investment banks and brokerage houses in a nationwide sales drive. These institutions sold bonds in small denominations and solicited millions of individuals of modest means who had never before invested in securities. The Treasury Department's 1917 annual report estimated that the noninstitutional bond market prior to 1917 consisted of approximately 350,000 individuals. More than 21 million individuals, however, purchased Liberty Bonds. In the course of tapping this new market, many investment banks got their first taste of what could be accomplished with "high-pressure" selling efforts.

The Liberty Loan drives produced a generation of salesmen who were experienced at contacting hundreds or thousands of retail customers rapidly. After the war, these salesmen created a nationwide network of securities dealers who specialized in selling securities to individual investors. As described in the *Morgan* opinion, these retail dealers formed the bottom rung of the distributional ladder. They purchased new issues for resale and held inventories of securities traded in the secondary markets to meet the growing demand of middle-class households for investments. In many cases it is a stretch to call them "investment bankers" because they served exclusively a distributional function. Thus the term "securities dealer" was used as a broad category to include investment bankers and this new class of retail seller.

Retail selling was not limited to the bottom echelon of the securities industry, however. Three investment banks just below the top tier—Harris, Forbes & Co., Halsey, Stuart & Co. and the National City Company (the underwriting arm of the National City Bank)—developed large, nationwide retail sales forces. Halsey Stuart installed an extensive private wire system to enable it to reach customers all around the country from its Chicago headquarters (Carosso 1970). It used newspaper (and later radio) advertising to reach retail customers and permitted smaller investors to buy securities on an installment plan modeled after the Liberty Loan installment payment plans.

The National City Company built a large retail sales force beginning during the war years. Under the leadership of Charles E. Mitchell, "the greatest bond salesman who ever lived" (Huertas and Silverman 1986, 81), the National City Company purchased several smaller investment dealers and opened branches around the country. National City was at the forefront of high-pressure salesmanship. As a contemporary described it: "Instead of waiting for investors to come, [Mitchell] took young men and women, gave them a course of training on the sale of securities, and sent them out to *find* the investors. Such methods, pursued with such vigor and on such a scale, were revolutionary" (Seligman 2003, 24). Mitchell pioneered door-to-door securities sales and large bonuses for salesmen who successfully moved the bonds the company underwrote. By the end of the 1920s, the National City Company was "the largest agency in the world for distributing securities" (Peach 1983, 87).

MORE RAPID DISTRIBUTION. The growing importance of individual investors and the development of the retail securities dealer as an important class of financial intermediary altered the mechanics of distributing securities. A new layer was added underneath underwriting syndicates, known as a "selling group." The selling group consisted of securities dealers chosen by the originating house that purchased an allotment of underwritten securities at a discount and agreed to sell them to investors at a fixed price.[4] Because they purchased only at the time of retail distribution, selling group members did not "underwrite" in any significant sense; in fact, they often committed to purchase securities only to the extent they could find purchasers. Like the underwriters, the selling group delegated extensive authority to the originating house to control the terms of the distribution. Dealers sold in amounts, at times, at prices, and often in geographical territories specified by the originating house.

The new distribution techniques substantially increased the speed with which a new issue of securities could be sold even though issues were larger on average and many more potential buyers were solicited. More financial institutions were now involved in selling a new issue, and rather than waiting for buyers to come, they actively sought them out. New issues could be sold in a matter of days.

CHANGING MIX OF SECURITIES. Investors' appetite for equity securities grew rapidly at the end of the 1920s. The prewar investment banking industry focused on corporate debt securities and, to a lesser extent, preferred stocks. After the war, investors were increasingly willing to take greater risks in pursuit of higher returns. Businesses responded by selling more equity into the public markets. This increasing tolerance for risk allowed start-up companies to raise capital through public offerings. This in turn created opportunities for smaller, regional investment banks to manage riskier issues. By 1929 investment banks that had little track record as managing underwriters were originating issues of relatively unknown corporations.

Measuring the Growth of Competition

After the war, investment banks could succeed without spending years developing reputation and contacts, and accordingly many new firms entered the business. Established investment bankers soon complained that there were too many firms. By the late 1920s, they also complained of the decreasing profitability of their business. This section attempts to piece together the available information to provide qualitative and quantitative measures of the growth of competition in the industry during the 1920s.

Number and Capital of Investment Banks

The Investment Bankers Association of America's annual reports document the growth in its membership and the organization's response, providing evidence of rapid entry into the investment banking business during the 1920s. After World War I the IBAA began rejecting many membership applications. In 1919 it formally limited consideration for membership to firms that had been in the business for at least two years.[5] Table 4.1 collects quotations from reports of the IBAA's secretary and membership committee. They express dismay about the postwar rate of entry into the investment banking business. These indications of concern subsequently wane during the great boom in new securities issues beginning in the middle of the decade. As a consequence of the IBAA's growing exclusivity after the war, growth in IBAA membership must understate growth in the number of investment banking houses after 1919, perhaps substantially.

Table 4.2 reports estimates of the dollar volume of new domestic corporate securities issues, the number of IBAA members, and the aggregate capital of the investment banking industry for the period 1912–40.[6] The

TABLE 4.1. **IBAA descriptions of membership growth**

Year	Quotation
1919	"The Membership Committee has had before it the largest number of applications in any one year since our organization. . . . The organization of many new houses has occasioned some concern." (p. 20)
1920	". . . it is the opinion of the Secretary that no other Membership Committee ever faced the number of applications as during the past year. New houses have sprung up everywhere, some headed by men of unquestioned ability as bond men; others organized by well meaning but unseasoned young men." (p. 23)
1921	"The large increase in the number of applications filed has caused the Membership Committee considerable concern and has led to the question of limiting membership." (p. 32)
1924	"The Membership Committee is to be congratulated upon the firm stand it has taken in the admission of houses. There has been no side-stepping of responsibility. For the year which closed August 31, 1924, thirty-nine houses were admitted to membership as against forty-five the year previous. Greater stringency caused the decrease." (p. 35)
1926	"I think it is safe to say that with each succeeding year, membership in the Association has become more difficult to secure." (p. 85)

Source: *Proceedings of the Annual Convention of the Investment Bankers Association of America* (Chicago: Lakeside Press, 1919, 1920, 1921, 1924, and 1926).

figures are consistent with Ervin Miller's conclusion that "securities firms increased sharply during the 1920s both in number and in assets" (Friend et al. 1967, 93). During the first half of the 1920s, they also grew faster than the market for new issues. The size of the retail sales force also increased rapidly. According to census data, the number of stock and bond salesmen grew from 6,000 in 1910 to 11,000 in 1920 and 22,000 by 1930, a level that would not be reached again until the 1950s. Table 4.2 also shows the volume of common stock issues as a percentage of the total. Because high-prestige underwriters avoided common stock, its prevalence is also a measure of the penetration of low-prestige firms into the underwriting business.

Industry Profitability

IBAA members complained in the late 1920s that underwriting had become less profitable.[7] It appears that average spreads declined during the 1920s. Dewing (1931, 147–50) estimates that in the early 1920s the gross spread for a typical bond issue was approximately 5 percent of the sales price. By contrast, Haven (1940, 34) found an average spread

TABLE 4.2. **The investment banking industry and the new issue market, 1912–1940**

Year	New Issue Volume ($ Millions)	Common Stock Issues (Percentage of Total)	Number of IBAA Member Firms	Aggregate Capital ($ Millions)
1912	2,254		257	263
1913	1,646		354	
1914	1,437		356	
1915	1,436		340	
1916	2,187		361	
1917	1,531		407	
1918	1,345		399	
1919	2,668	28.2	433	
1920	2,788	19.9	485	
1921	2,270	8.8	552	
1922	2,949	9.8	586	1,053
1923	3,165	10.4	607	
1924	3,521	14.7	617	
1925	4,223	14.4	620	
1926	2,574	14.8	662	
1927	6,507	10.5	676	
1928	6,930	30.2	690	
1929	9,376	54.0	665	2,632
1930	4,957	22.3	626	
1931	2,372	8.2	533	
1932	644	2.0	427	
1933	380	36.1	378	659
1934	397	6.3	495	
1935	2,332	0.9	621	
1936	4,572	5.9	751	
1937	2,310	12.3	796	
1938	2,155	1.2	754	
1939	2,164	4.0	734	526
1940	2,677	4.0	691	

Sources: New issue volume and common stock: *Historical Statistics of the United States.*
IBAA membership: *Proceedings of the Annual Convention of the Investment Bankers Association of America*, various years. Aggregate capital: Friend et al. 1967.

of approximately 3.0 percent for a sample of bond issues from 1926 to 1929. The director of the SEC's Research Division also found an average spread of 3.0 percent on a sample of bond issues from 1927 to 1931 (Gourrich 1937, 69).

The decline in spreads does not prove a decline in profits because the industry's costs were also changing during the 1920s. Some of the expenses of underwriting a new issue—investigating the issuer's business, providing advice, and developing a sales pitch, for example—are fixed costs that lead to economies of scale. As a result, gross spreads are typically smaller on a percentage basis for larger issues, and issue sizes were increasing in the 1920s. An SEC study found that the gross spread on bond issues of less than $5 million during the period 1925–29 was 5.2 percent, suggesting that much of the decline can be attributed to larger average transaction size (Friend et al. 1967, 408–9). Moreover, because the distribution process was more rapid, the cost of financing the securities while in inventory (as well as the associated risk) was decreasing. Other costs, however, were likely increasing. The new selling methods were costlier than the old because they required larger sales forces. Short-term interest rates rose during this period, which would offset some of the decreased financing costs resulting from more rapid distribution.

Absent more information, we cannot determine quantitatively whether underwriting became less profitable in the late 1920s. The strongest available evidence is the bankers' frequent complaints about excess capacity and declining profits. As one investment banker put it, "the big problem is the diminishing ratio of profits."[8]

Concentration in the Underwriting Market

We can calculate market shares among managing underwriters starting in the mid-1920s. The National Statistical Service (NSS) published from 1925 through 1935 a periodical listing all new public offerings of securities grouped by managing underwriter (Schwarzschild 1925–35). I used this information to compile a list of all offerings managed by "major" underwriting houses during that period. I define a "major" house as one that managed at least one public offering of at least $10,000,000 during the period (excluding securities of affiliates or mutual funds). By this definition, there are 105 major underwriting houses that managed 4,344 offerings during the period 1925–35, inclusive.

The NSS data end in 1935; however, additional data on market shares are available from the trial records of the *Morgan* litigation. Using SEC and investment bank records, the parties introduced into evidence data on market shares for a series of three-year periods after enactment of the Securities Act. There are two drawbacks to this data. First, it aggregates market shares over three-year periods rather than year by year. Second, it divides the dollar amount of an issue among all listed co-managers. By contrast, the NSS listings credit the entire amount to the "lead" manager. In order to make the two data sources comparable, I looked at all tombstone advertisements in the *Wall Street Journal* for the years 1936 through 1940 and identified the lead manager for co-managed offerings (the lead

TABLE 4.3. **Concentration in the investment banking industry, 1925–1940**

Year	Concentration	Year	Concentration
1925	37.0%	1933	14.6%
1926	31.2	1934	48.3
1927	29.5	1935	53.6
1928	19.4	1936	54.8
1929	12.9	1937	50.4
1930	34.1	1938	54.1
1931	47.4	1939	46.3
1932	55.3	1940	53.1

Sources: Managing underwriter volumes: National Statistical Service, American Underwriting Houses and Their Issues, vols. 1–6 (1928–35), *United States v. Morgan* trial records.
Total new issue volume: domestic, *Historical Statistics of the United States*; foreign, *Federal Reserve Bulletin*, various issues.
Note: Concentration is the percentage share of the top five managing underwriters of the dollar volume of new domestic and foreign corporate and foreign government securities.

manager appears in the upper left-hand position in a tombstone advertisement). I also looked at the raw data produced by the *Morgan* defendants to produce a year-by-year breakdown of market shares for the same period.

Table 4.3 shows the aggregate market shares of the top five managing underwriters in each year from 1925 through 1940. Based on more limited evidence compiled during the *Morgan* litigation about pre-SEC offerings, it seems clear that the higher level of concentration in 1925 was typical of the period 1918–24. In the increasingly competitive market of the late 1920s, however, concentration fell steadily and substantially, from a high of 37.0 percent in 1925 to 12.9 percent in 1929.

The Crisis of the Syndicate Method

As competition increased at the retail level, sellers began to seek an advantage over their rivals by violating provisions of syndicate agreements that specified the schedule and price of the distribution. The increased speed of distributions and the focus on retail selling during the 1920s made it difficult for managing underwriters to monitor and control hundreds, or occasionally thousands, of securities dealers participating in the sale of a new issue. By the late 1920s, investment bankers perceived threats to the viability of the syndicate system.

Established bankers described the phenomenon as a decline in the professionalism of the investment banking business. Like lawyers or doctors in later decades, many investment bankers of the 1920s viewed themselves as members of a learned profession, the standards of which were being eroded by new entrants who were mere salesmen. A measure of that concern is the creation, at the IBAA's annual convention in the fall of 1926, of a Committee on Business Problems. The bulk of that committee's first report, delivered at the 1927 convention, was prepared by its Subcommittee on Distribution and addressed changes in distribution methods.[9]

The subcommittee's report noted two tactics in particular, "beating the gun," or selling prior to the agreed-upon distribution period, and selling at discounted prices. The report also expressed concern about high-pressure selling efforts and competition from commercial banks. By the time the IBAA convened its 1933 convention, Congress had addressed each of these four problems, the first three in the Securities Act and the fourth in the Glass-Steagall Act.

This section addresses these competitive issues one at a time. It then asks why managing underwriters wanted to uphold the syndicate system. Finally, it notes that the integrated investment banks that combined wholesaling with retailing did not face these problems to the same extent as the separate wholesale and retail firms. This suggests that the integrated firms had a structural advantage in the competitive landscape of the 1920s.

Beating the Gun

In the late 1920s, a practice known as "beating the gun" became common. Under the normal underwriting practice, underwriting and selling syndicate agreements contained an undertaking not to sell securities until they were "released" by the managing underwriter through a telegram or telephone call. To beat the gun was to violate the syndicate agreement by taking orders from customers before the securities had been released for sale.

Beating the gun allowed a distributor to get a head start on the others in the competition for retail customers. It was, however, blatantly inconsistent with the contractual restraints on price, timing, and (sometimes) territory that characterized the syndicate system. Managing underwriters were sensitive to the complaints of retailers who complied with syndicate agreements and in so doing lost customers to others who cheated.

In order to prevent the practice, originating houses tried to keep the timing and price of the issue secret until the last minute. This was not always possible, however, particularly for issues of large companies. These companies were closely followed by the financial press, and newspapers or investment magazines might print the details of a coming large issue of securities before the issuing house had formally released the information to the syndicates. Thus selling group members were able to take orders from customers with reasonable confidence that they could provide the security at the time and price quoted, even though they were contractually obligated to wait.

Contemporary commentators referred to preliminary selling as an "unfair trade practice" (Bates 1937, 212) or "unfair competition" (Gourrich 1937, 44, 65). It caused great consternation. Bates describes investment bankers as "preoccupied" with beating the gun (1937, 212). The IBAA's Committee on Business Problems declared that its aim "has been to establish the principle of 'Fairness of Competition' so that all who are associated in the public offering of an issue of securities should compete on an equitable basis with respect to the time of such offering."[10] The only realistic punishment available, however, was for the managing underwriter to cut the offending dealer out of future deals. A managing underwriter would not want to take such a drastic step unless it was certain that the offender really had cheated. Being sure was easier said than done. Dealers complained to originating houses about other dealers but were generally unwilling to give specifics. A dealer would learn about an infraction when he called a customer on the offering date only to learn that the customer had already agreed to purchase from a rival. The complaining dealer, however, was unwilling to give the customer's name to the originating house for fear that the resulting inquiry would offend the customer and lead to the loss of future business.[11]

The IBAA Subcommittee on Distribution concluded that the root of the problem was excessive pre-offering publicity.[12] Even scrupulous dealers could not avoid beating the gun when both their salesmen and customers could get the details of a pending offering in the morning newspapers. Either the salesmen would find it irresistible to call on customers prior to the offering date or customers would contact the salesmen. The chairman of the subcommittee spoke approvingly of issuing houses that kept a tight lid on information about the timing and price of offerings, but recognized that this "ideal condition" was difficult to achieve. Speaking of the large houses of issue, he noted, "They are doing all they can to get the information to every one of you men at the same time, and what they want is someone to tell them a practical way, someone to also try and keep publicity out of the paper."[13] On the rare occasions when this "ideal condition" was achieved, it led to a different problem—selling group members had to decide how large an allotment to request in a matter of hours. This increased the likelihood of expensive mistakes. The issuing houses wanted to be able to give the details of an upcoming offering to potential selling group members a few days in advance, but nevertheless be confident that those dealers would not take orders until the commencement of the offering. As we will see, the Securities Act made the "ideal condition" feasible and prevented dealers from taking orders before the managing underwriter released the securities for sale.

Discounting

The practice of cutting prices gave rise to even more passionate debate within the IBAA. As described above, underwriters were compensated for their services by purchasing at a price below the fixed offering price. The discount was shared between the house that underwrote a security and the house that sold it. The latter's share was called a "selling concession." The seller could, in turn, "reallow" a specified portion of the selling concession to other securities dealers who purchased for resale to their customers. Thus, for example, in a bond underwriting the gross spread might be $20 per $1000 bond, of which $10 would be retained by the underwriter and $10 would go as a selling concession to a distributor, who could reallow up to $2.50 to any other securities dealer.

Lacking a universally accepted definition of "securities dealer," underwriters and selling group members who wished to compete on the basis of price without blatantly violating their syndicate agreement developed the practice of granting a reallowance to any customer willing and able to negotiate for it. First, all financial institutions, such as banks and trust companies, came to expect a discount.[14] By the late 1920s some dealers were offering concessions to all institutional investors as well as to lawyers and other professionals. The vice president of the IBAA complained at its 1927 convention about "the big giving of concessions which has grown to such an extent now that it is practically a reduction in price to everybody except the few unfortunates" who failed to bargain for it.[15] Like beating the gun, price-cutting was viewed by most members of the association as an unethical practice, but one that was extremely difficult to stop. "Our greatest evil is price-cutting," in the opinion of one member.[16]

IBAA members proposed two solutions. The first was simply to ban all reallowances so that any securities dealer who was not a member of the selling group would have to buy at the same price as the public. The other proposal was for the IBAA's regional groups to draw up lists of "recognized" securities dealers and ban granting a discount to anyone who was not on such a list. The federal securities laws facilitated the latter solution.

Salesmanship

I have already discussed the development of new retail sales techniques—newspaper and radio advertising, door-to-door selling, installment plans, and so on, during the World War I Liberty Bond drives and their spread after the war. Established investment bankers were aghast at the lengths to which their more aggressive competitors would go to solicit potential buyers. As the number of securities dealers grew and those dealers hired more and more salesmen, investors had many sellers to choose from. As one observer noted, "The business is sadly overcrowded and too many salesmen are calling on each customer and prospect. . . . No man who isn't a professional bond buyer needs to have more than four or five bond salesmen calling on him regularly. Most of them have either forty or, finally and in disgust, not any."[17] Thus beating the gun and discounting were important new tactics in the battle to convince an investor to buy a new issue through dealer X rather than dealer Y.

Competition from Commercial Banks

The Treasury relied heavily on commercial banks to sell Liberty Bonds. Accordingly, after the war, many commercial banks created bond departments or securities affiliates to engage in securities underwriting and dealing using the skills they had acquired in the Liberty Bond drives. From 1922 to 1929, the number of commercial banks engaged in the distribution of new issues of securities, through either a separate securities affiliate or a bond department, grew from 277 to 591 (Peach 1983, 83).

The entry of a commercial bank posed a greater competitive threat than the entry of a new investment bank because of the greater capital the former could devote to underwriting if it chose. Rather than lend funds for short periods to investment banking syndicates, banks began to devote those funds to direct competition. Because they combined substantial capital and large sales staffs, commercial banks could easily integrate origination and retail distribution.

Why the Syndicate System?

Why did the IBAA's members want so desperately to retain the syndicate system rather than allow securities dealers to compete on the basis of price? The industrial organization and finance literature each provides a possible explanation.

Fixed-price syndication is a form of resale price maintenance. As in other contexts, issuers and managing underwriters may choose resale price maintenance in order to induce dealers to offer product-specific services (Telser 1960). Consistent with this notion, managing underwriters urged distributors to become familiar with the issuer and the security in order to be able to recommend securities that were suitable for their customers. Telser observes that resale price maintenance is typically observed in highly concentrated markets in which manufacturers have market power. The syndicate system thrived during the early part of the century to the mid-1920s, a period in which a small number of managing underwriters dominated the business. It broke down during the late 1920s, during a large drop in concentration in the market for managing underwriters. It revived after 1933 and survives to the present day, along with a high level of concentration.

A second possibility is that the syndicate system is an efficient solution to the informational asymmetry problems that arise in public offerings, particularly initial public offerings. Issuers are better informed than investors about their own business, but investors in the aggregate are better informed than issuers about systematic factors that influence the price at which a new security will sell (Benveniste and Spindt 1989). Investment banks solve the asymmetry problems by certifying issuer quality to investors and by seeking information from investors about their likely demand prior to actual sale. In order to elicit accurate information from investors, managing underwriters underprice and allocate new issues disproportionately to regular clients who disclose useful information. Retail dealers may have played the role of repeat players in the 1920s just as institutional investors do today.

Either explanation would account for managing underwriters' determination to maintain the syndicate system. As the 1920s progressed, however, they found it increasingly difficult to do so by contract. Investment banks consequently had two alternatives. The first was integration. Firms that combined the wholesale and retail functions could exercise greater control over selling efforts. A second alternative was for a regulator to enforce compliance with the syndicate system. The latter, as we will see, is what the Securities Act and related laws accomplished.

The syndicate system may have been an efficient contractual arrangement given the enforcement costs characteristic of the period from roughly 1900 to the mid-1920s, but by the late 1920s it could survive only with a subsidy (in the form of governmental enforcement). It is possible that the subsidy enhances welfare—that is, the benefits to issuers and investors of more efficient distribution outweigh the cost of the subsidy. The likelihood seems small, however, inasmuch as investment banks successfully used vertical integration as an alternative to government enforcement. More important, the marginal benefits of the syndicate method would have to be implausibly great to outweigh the compliance costs associated with the Act's "gun-jumping" prohibitions and the NASD's "fair practice" rules, discussed below. One may conclude that retail price maintenance is unobjectionable but stop short of concluding that the government should facilitate it by legislation.

The Challenge of Integrated Firms

An alternative to resale price maintenance is integration. Investment banks that had retail outlets all over the country, such as Harris Forbes, Halsey Stuart, and National City, did not have to rely on regional securities dealers to the same extent as the wholesale investment banks. They could control their own firm's retail sales effort. Compared to wholesale-only underwriters, the integrated firms could also have a higher degree of confidence in the information they received about retail demand, as much of it came from their own retail outlets.

The integrated firms were therefore able to seek origination business that would earlier have gone as a matter of course to the high-prestige wholesale firms. In 1927 an integrated firm entered the ranks of the top three originators for the first time, as National City displaced Dillon Read, which fell to number 4. In 1928, Harris Forbes, National City and Halsey Stuart ranked first, second and fourth, respectively. In 1929, Harris Forbes was again the top underwriter, and of the three highest prestige wholesale firms only Dillon Read made it into the top five.

During the years 1925 and 1926, the three top wholesale firms, J. P. Morgan, Kuhn Loeb, and Dillon Read, managed approximately $2.5 billion of securities offerings, double that of the top three integrated firms, Harris Forbes, Halsey Stuart, and National City. In 1927, the gap narrowed, with the wholesalers managing $1.5 billion and the integrated firms $1.2 billion. During 1928 and 1929, the integrated firms turned the tables, managing $1.9 billion to the wholesalers' $1.2 billion. This was an unprecedented challenge to the wholesale firms' decades-long dominance of the new issue market.

How the Securities Act Saved the Wholesale Investment Banks

Leading investment banks and their trade group, the IBAA, were experienced lobbyists. As described in chapter 2 and in Macey and Miller (1991), they successfully influenced the content of state securities, or "blue sky," laws in the 1910s and 1920s. The IBAA supported federal disclosure regulation as a means of improving the ethics of the investment banking industry (Parrish 1970). Industry members supported the proposed Securities Act, although they complained about its liability provisions for underwriters. After a successful lobbying campaign, the liability provisions were amended in 1934 to reduce underwriters' potential exposure.

The wholesale investment banks, whose position was being eroded by integrated firms, favored federal intervention and had substantial access to legislators. J. P. Morgan and Dillon Read, in particular, had numerous partners who split time between finance and government service. John W. Davis, Morgan's lawyer, enjoyed remarkable access to the Senate Banking Committee, even attending several executive sessions to argue against public disclosure of some of his client's financial and business information.[18] Partners of the wholesale firms testified in favor of disclosure regulation at the brief House and Senate hearings on the proposed Securities Act, decrying the decline in the ethics of their business.

The Securities Act and other New Deal financial reforms addressed the specific competitive concerns outlined above. They had, in broad terms, three effects. They provided the government's aid in enforcing the syndicate system by outlawing beating the gun and discounting. They slowed down the distribution process and divided it into distinct wholesale and retail phases. Finally, they removed commercial banks as competitors for underwriting business. The consequence was to neutralize the competitive advantages of integrated firms and return to a system in which wholesale banks originated new issues and sold them through stand-alone distributors. This section shows how the technical details of the Securities Act achieved those results.

Beating the Gun

The Securities Act achieved precisely what the IBAA's Committee on Business Problems wanted to achieve but could not—it made it possible for a lead underwriter to provide distributing houses with detailed information about a pending issue secure in the knowledge that the latter could not agree to sell securities until the official offering date. The Act also assured the absence of retail solicitation prior to the offering date by suppressing pre-offering publicity.

The Securities Act requires that a registration statement be filed and become effective before any person may sell the securities; until a 1954 amendment, the term "sell" included any solicitation efforts. Thus it was illegal to mount a publicity campaign prior to the date of effectiveness. The lead underwriter could control the timing of effectiveness because a registration statement for a fixed-price underwriting could not become effective until it contained the pricing information. Thus the typical practice was to file a registration statement omitting price information, wait the statutorily prescribed twenty days, and near the end of that period file an amendment containing the pricing information. So long as the SEC consented to this amendment, the registration statement would become effective on the twentieth day after the original filing. The mechanics changed over time, but not the prohibition on taking firm orders prior to the SEC declaring the registration statement effective.

Before the registration statement was filed, any "offer" of the securities (defined broadly enough to cover nearly any discussion of the offering) was banned. Securities lawyers today still counsel their clients against premature public statements relating to an offering—to make such a statement is to "jump the gun," although I doubt many securities lawyers know that the phrase antedates the Securities Act.

The statute also directly attacked newspaper and radio advertisements by defining each as a "prospectus," which, with limited exceptions, could not be published prior to effectiveness. The prohibition on newspaper publicity was broad enough to cover a story printed after interviewing a company officer about the pending offering. No longer would detailed information about pending offerings appear in the morning papers prior to the offering date, stimulating customers to call their brokers.

Of course, regulatory restrictions often generate countermoves. In a 1936 bond offering, Halsey Stuart proposed to distribute a "preliminary" version of the prospectus during the twenty-day waiting period notwithstanding the prohibition on "selling" prior to effectiveness. The SEC decided to permit it subject to the inclusion of a legend in red type noting that the registration statement was not yet effective, and thus the "red herring" prospectus was born.[19] Protests soon appeared that investment banks were once again "beating the gun" by soliciting customers during the waiting period (Bates 1937, 73–74). An important difference from pre-1933 practice, however, was that the managing underwriter maintained complete control of the timing of sales through its control of effectiveness. The Securities Act kept securities from being sold until the managing underwriter was ready.

Discounting

The Securities Act made it illegal to grant undisclosed discounts. It required that the registration statement disclose the public offering price of the securities and any deviation from that price by any distributor "to any person or classes of persons, other than the underwriters, naming them and specifying the class."[20] A separate early New Deal reform, however, went much farther and enabled the IBAA to achieve its longstanding goal of limiting discounts to recognized securities dealers.

President Roosevelt signed the National Industrial Recovery Act into law only a few weeks after the Securities Act. The NIRA permitted self-regulatory industry groups to adopt codes of fair practice enforceable by the federal courts. As the only national trade association for the investment banking industry, the IBAA immediately created an Investment Bankers Code Committee and prepared a "Code of Fair Competition for Investment Bankers" and a set of Fair Practice Amendments that were approved by executive order of the president in March 1934.[21]

The code prohibited discounting. It declared that "no participant in a selling syndicate or member of a selling group shall . . . offer the securities being distributed by such syndicate or group at any price below [the] public offering price."[22] Further provisions barred the grant of selling concessions or commissions except to investment bankers registered with the relevant Regional Code Committee and therefore entitled to display the

National Recovery Administration's Blue Eagle.[23] Many of the additional rules relating to selling syndicates were designed to close all loopholes that might permit a discount to anyone not meeting the code's definition of "investment banker."

The Supreme Court declared the NIRA unconstitutional in May 1935, but with the assistance of the SEC the investment banking industry continued "voluntary compliance" with the code.[24] That the code was successful in ending widespread discounting is attested by the complaint of a Firemen's Insurance Company executive in 1937 that dealers ceased giving his company discounts during the NRA period and never resumed (Kuhn 1937, 87–88).

In only a few years the antidiscounting rule was again a formal regulatory requirement. With the SEC's blessing, the Investment Bankers Code Committee reorganized itself into the Investment Bankers Conference, a self-regulatory organization for securities dealers, in 1936. The Conference and the SEC worked with Congress to craft an amendment to the Securities Exchange Act of 1934 authorizing the formation of a self-regulatory organization for securities dealers. Their goal was to "continue the principles of self-regulation under government supervision first tried under the NRA" (Carosso 1970, 390). The amendment, known as the Maloney Act, was enacted in 1938. The Investment Bankers Conference then reorganized itself into the National Association of Securities Dealers, Inc. (NASD). Carosso (1970) notes that while larger, more prestigious investment banks favored the Maloney Act and the Code of Fair Competition, smaller dealers opposed them. This is understandable, as smaller dealers were more likely to need to offer discounts to compete for business.

The Maloney Act explicitly permitted antidiscounting rules.[25] The NASD created a set of "Rules of Fair Practice" modeled on the code. Those rules included (and the rules of the Financial Industry Regulatory Authority, NASD's successor, still include) a ban on discounting as well as a prohibition on giving selling concessions to any person not engaged in the investment banking or securities business.[26]

Separation of Wholesaling and Retailing

The Securities Act's prohibition on solicitation prior to filing and the mandatory "waiting period" between filing and effectiveness create separate wholesale and retail phases of a public offering. Before filing a registration statement, an issuer may freely communicate with potential underwriters and those underwriters may freely communicate with one another. All potential syndicate members, however, are cut off from information about retail demand during this period.

These provisions protected separate wholesale and retail securities dealers from competition by integrated firms. As described above, integrated firms had two important competitive advantages. They could substitute ownership for contract as a means of controlling the timing and price of retail selling activity and had superior access to information about retail demand. The Act provided regulatory enforcement in place of contract, making it possible once again for a combination of wholesale and retail firms to engage in fixed-price underwriting as effectively as integrated firms. The Act also made it easier to gather information about institutional demand than about retail demand. During the waiting period, underwriters may solicit indications of interest using oral communications and roadshows. Prior to the 2005 public offering reforms, however, they could not engage in mass marketing through print, radio, or television. This assured that solicitation during the waiting period was aimed at institutional investors.

Kenneth Haven's (1940) study of the impact of the SEC on investment banking claimed that the distribution of new issues after the Securities Act resembled English practice, under which the initial round of purchasers was largely institutional and the underwriters engaged in minimal retail solicitation. This was precisely the pattern that the wholesalers advocated beginning in the mid-1920s. Wholesale firms had long-established contacts with institutional investors that gave them an advantage in gathering information about institutional demand. The integrated firms had an advantage in gathering information about retail demand. The Securities Act's restrictions on retail solicitation assured that pricing decisions would be made principally on the basis of information about institutional demand. This played directly into the hands of the wholesale houses.

Competition from Banks

I will mention only briefly the issue of competition from banks, which was not addressed by the Securities Act. The Banking Act of 1933 contained provisions popularly known as the Glass-Steagall Act, which separated commercial from investment banking. Macey (1984) argues that

Glass-Steagall was an important victory for the investment banking industry because it removed commercial banks as competitors. Shughart (1988) argues that the Banking Act represented a straightforward division of markets between the investment and commercial banking industries that benefited both.

Glass-Steagall did not dramatically reduce the number of underwriters competing for business. Most of the large bank securities affiliates were spun off from their commercial bank parents, or alternatively their top officers left to form new investment banks. The separation of commercial and investment banking did, however, contribute to the dramatic decline in the capital devoted to securities underwriting in the 1930s. The successors to the bank affiliates' underwriting businesses did not have ready access to loans and capital contributions from a parent bank. The Banking Act therefore removed the principal competitive advantage of the bank securities affiliates. The commercial banks gained something as well, because the private bankers were forced to abandon their deposit banking and stick to securities underwriting (as did Kuhn Loeb) or split themselves into a commercial bank and a separate investment bank (as did J. P. Morgan).

Interestingly, Chernow (1991, 375) notes that until the final days before the Banking Act's passage, Glass's bill did not apply to private banks, meaning that J. P. Morgan and Kuhn Loeb would have been unaffected, while the National City Bank and the Chase Manhattan Bank would have had to jettison their securities affiliates. Both of the latter were integrated firms, and both National City and Harris Forbes (which Chase Manhattan acquired in 1931) had surpassed J. P. Morgan and Kuhn Loeb during the late 1920s. The chairman of Chase Manhattan Bank, however, prevailed upon President Roosevelt to extend the ban on underwriting to private banks over Glass's protest. Morgan's men were not the only skilled lobbyists in town.

Measuring the Impact of the Securities Act

That the Securities Act helped save the syndicate system is clear from the fact that the practices that had threatened syndication during the late 1920s were explicitly outlawed and did not recur. As discussed above, however, it is possible that the syndicate system was an efficient form of organization. If so, the Act may have been benign. This makes it useful to look at the limited evidence we have on the Act's impact on underwriters. I return to the available information on market shares and spreads and argue that the evidence suggests that the Act decreased competition in managing underwriting to the detriment of issuers and investors.

Concentration

Returning to table 4.3, we see that the market share of the top five underwriters was above 50 percent in all but one of the years after 1933. My result is consistent with the Temporary National Economic Committee's estimate of 53 percent as the share of the top five managing underwriters for the period 1934–39. This is not, however, sufficient to show that the Securities Act increased concentration. Concentration increased during the period 1930–32, prior to the Act. An alternative explanation consistent with the data is that concentration fell during a period of increasing new issue volume and greater use of equity (1927–29) and rose again when new issue volume and common stock issuance declined during the Depression. Ervin Miller finds that concentration generally decreases in periods of increasing underwriting volume and that concentration among managing underwriters is substantially higher in bonds than in stock (Friend et al. 1967).

As one way of asking whether the change is most plausibly associated with the Securities Act, I estimate the following ordinary least-squares regression:

$$CON_t = \alpha + \beta_1 STOCK_t + \beta_2 \ln \frac{VOL_t}{VOL_{t-1}} + \beta_3 SECACT_t + \varepsilon_t$$

where *t* indexes years, CON is concentration (the aggregate market share of the top five managing underwriters), STOCK is the percentage of new securities issues consisting of common stock, VOL is new issue volume, and SECACT is a dummy variable that takes the value 1 for the years 1934–40, after passage of the Securities Act, and zero before.

The results are presented in table 4.4. All of the estimated coefficients are of the expected sign—growth in new issue volume and greater relative prevalence of common stock are associated with lower concentration. The estimated coefficient on the Securities Act dummy is positive and significant. It is, of course, important to keep in mind that with only sixteen annual observations, the results are suggestive but not definitive.

TABLE 4.4. **Regression: The Securities Act and concentration**

Variable	Estimated Coefficient	t-statistic	*p*
STOCK	−75.1	−5.29	.000
VOLRT	−4.34	−1.63	.129
SECACT	12.1	3.03	.011
$R^2 = 0.87$, n = 16			

Note: The dependent variable is concentration in managing underwriting for the years 1925–40 (reported in table 4.3). Predictor variables are (1) common stock issues as a percentage of total new issue volume (STOCK), (2) the rate of change of new issue volume (VOLRT), and (3) a dummy variable that takes the value 1 for years 1934–40 and zero for all prior years (SECACT).

The Securities Act dummy effectively bifurcates the sample into pre-1933 and post-1933 periods. A bifurcation at any other year produces a lower *R*-squared and a lower *p*-value on the dummy variable, suggesting that something unusual happened in 1933. The result is consistent with the qualitative evidence that the Act reduced competition in the market for managing underwriters. I estimated alternative specifications substituting gross national product and the number of IBAA members for new issue volume, as well as one including all three as predictors. In each case the estimated coefficients and significance levels on STOCK and SECACT, as well as the *R*-squared of the regression, were very close to those reported in table 4.4.

A few other pieces of information support the analysis. First, the traditionally dominant wholesale underwriters, after losing considerable ground to integrated firms during the late 1920s, returned to the top of the hierarchy after 1933. The average aggregate market share of J. P. Morgan, Kuhn Loeb, and Dillon Read from 1925 through 1933 is 16.1 percent, and from 1934 through 1940 (substituting Morgan Stanley & Co. for J. P. Morgan) it is 31.1 percent. Based on a t-test for equal means, the difference is statistically significant ($p = .008$).

Morgan Stanley's competitive position is particularly noteworthy. J. P. Morgan elected to remain a commercial bank and ceased underwriting from early 1933 until a group of its partners left to form Morgan Stanley & Co. in September 1935. Operating for four months in 1935, Morgan Stanley nevertheless ranked third in managing underwriting for that year and returned to the top spot in 1936. In the six-year period 1935 to 1940, Morgan Stanley managed approximately $3 billion of offerings, nearly double that of its nearest competitor (Kuhn Loeb), and more than J. P. Morgan's total for the boom years 1925–30. By contrast, National City spun off its underwriting arm, but it never regained prominence. Halsey Stuart returned to its original niche in public utility underwriting.

A final avenue of inquiry is to compare investment banks that survived after 1933 with those that did not. Manne (1974), who suggests the comparison, also notes that it is problematic because it is difficult to distinguish the effects of the Depression from those of the Securities Act. To attempt to disentangle the two as much as possible, I limit the analysis to a subset of my list of "major" investment banks consisting of those that survived the Depression. I define a firm as having "survived" the Depression if it is listed as an existing firm in the IBAA's 1933 annual report, is not a commercial bank (which could not underwrite after 1933 because of Glass-Steagall), and engaged in some underwriting business in either 1932 or 1933. The latter is a stringent test because the new issue market was extremely thin in those two years. By this definition, 54 of the 105 major managing underwriters survived the Depression.

Of those 54 firms, 36 managed at least one offering during the period 1934–40 and 18 did not. We can therefore divide the subsample into firms that survived the Depression but not the Securities Act and those that survived both. As table 4.5 shows, there are interesting differences between the two groups. Only 28 percent of the firms that returned to managing underwriting in 1934–40 are based outside New York City, compared to 61 percent of those that did no further managing business. The firms that managed new issues after the Securities Act were more established, as measured by the average number of issues they had managed prior to the Securities Act as well as the average number of large issues (more than $10 million in proceeds). Each of the differences is statistically significant. The result is consistent with the qualitative evidence suggesting that the Securities Act was disproportionately beneficial to large, established, New York–based investment banks.

TABLE 4.5. **Comparison: Firms that did and did not survive the Securities Act**

	Survived (n = 36)	Did Not Survive (n = 18)	*p*
Percent based outside New York City	28	61	.024
Average number of issues managed, 1925–1933	49.9	24.9	.001
Average number of large (≥ $10 million) issues managed, 1925–1933	15.6	4.0	.005

Note: All firms described in the table were in business on the effective date of the Securities Act and participated in an underwriting syndicate during 1932 or 1933. Firms in the "Survived" column managed at least one new issue during the period 1934–40; those in the "Did Not Survive" column managed no issues during that period. The last column reports p-values for a test of equal means.

Profitability

The Securities Act did not stop the decline in spreads. Four separate studies of investment banking compensation before and after the Securities Act each find that spreads decreased after enactment. Haven's data (1940), which are the most complete, show that the average spread on bond issues decreased from 3.0 percent in 1926–29 to 2.2 percent in 1933–37.

Once again, the decline does not tell us directly about industry profitability. Unlike the 1926–29 period, however, we can make an educated guess about the direction of the change. Virtually all components of underwriters' costs must have been lower in 1933–37 than in 1926–29. Issue size continued to increase. Short-term interest rates fell substantially, as did salaries and the number of employees. The only increased costs were the additional accounting, legal, and printing fees generated by the Securities Act itself. Issuers paid most of these costs directly, however, so they had no direct impact on underwriting profits.

Fortunately, we can estimate the most important component of underwriters' costs, which is the cost of retail selling. Recall that selling group members do not underwrite. They perform only a retail distribution function, for which they receive a selling concession paid out of the underwriting spread. Miller's study of bond issues from 1927–31 found that concessions to selling group members averaged 1.65 percent of the proceeds of the issue, or 55 percent of the gross spread (Friend et al. 1967). I calculated the compensation paid to selling group members for all bond offerings underwritten by J. P. Morgan & Co. during the period 1927–31, using data produced by that firm during the stock exchange hearings of 1932–34. The result was 57 percent of the gross spread, closely in line with Miller's data. Both Miller and Haven find for sample periods after the Securities Act that about 44 percent of the gross spread, on average—or about 1 percent of the total proceeds, assuming a gross spread of 2.2 percent—was paid to selling group members. Thus the largest single component of the underwriters' costs declined by 40 percent.

These estimates suggest that net of retail selling costs, underwriting compensation declined by about 10 percent from 1926–29 to 1933–37. Controlling for average issue size (which tends to decrease the spread and which increased after 1933) and average riskiness of the security (which tends to increase the spread and which decreased after 1933), the decline was smaller still. Given the substantially larger declines in the general price, wage, and short-term interest rate levels, it is very likely that underwriters' profits increased after the Securities Act.

The Securities Act is generally regarded as one of the greatest success stories of the New Deal. Unlike many regulatory statutes, it has been largely untouched by claims that it raises entry barriers or enforces cartel agreements among members of the regulated industry. Yet a closer look at the statute, in the light of competitive conditions in the underwriting market in the 1920s, shows that even the Securities Act was a likely source of rents for the firms it subjected to regulation.

CHAPTER FIVE

Did the SEC Improve Disclosure Practices?

The market failure narrative of the 1929 crash, the Great Depression, and the New Deal securities reforms begins with the claim of marketplace anarchy in the years before the crash. Arthur Levitt's quote in the introduction alleges one type of anarchy—issuers' and underwriters' persistent and deliberate failure to disclose material information to investors. The Senate Banking Committee hearings that laid the groundwork for the New Deal securities laws alleged a second type of anarchy—market manipulation by professional traders that created artificial prices. The Securities Exchange Act of 1934, the second key securities market reform, was prompted by the belief that disclosure was inadequate and manipulation rampant on the organized exchanges.

Were these beliefs accurate? This chapter will focus on disclosure rules and the next on market manipulation. Both claims are logically connected to another common feature of the market failure narrative, which is the claim that investors behave irrationally during a bull market. Only an irrationally optimistic or naïve investor would voluntarily purchase securities without knowing "the first thing" about the companies issuing them or voluntarily trade in a market in which manipulators blatantly create artificial prices.

The investor irrationality corollary serves as a bridge between the claims of marketplace anarchy and finance theory. From finance theory we can be confident that disclosure is essential to the health of securities markets. In a low-disclosure environment, some investors will be routinely better informed than others about particular companies. Those informed investors have an incentive to trade whenever their information suggests that the stock price is incorrect. Absent disclosure, then, there is a real danger that most trades an uninformed investor makes will be at an unfavorable price. This is a particular danger when the company is selling its own shares but also true in secondary trading. Rational investors will seek to trade as little as possible and avoid purchasing in public offerings if they think they are at a serious informational disadvantage.

Disclosures can also inform shareholders about private benefits of control (the diversion of assets or cash flows from the firm to its managers). Managers have the opportunity and incentive to use corporate assets for personal gain, put relatives on the company payroll, and so forth. Rational shareholders will reduce what they are willing to pay for shares accordingly, and in that case managers bear the full agency cost, as Jensen and Meckling (1976) observe. But less than fully rational shareholders might bear some of the cost of managerial misbehavior and, indeed, such misbehavior could cause losses in excess of the managers' private benefits. In that case, a disclosure rule that deters managerial extraction of private benefits (by subjecting managers to suit for breach of fiduciary duty) could increase the sum of managers' and shareholders' wealth.

The fact that disclosure is valuable does not imply that all forms of disclosure regulation benefit investors or that there will be no disclosure without regulation. Three different mechanisms can lead companies to disclose information. The first is simple self-interest. Facing rational investors, a company cannot sell its securities for an adequate price unless those investors are convinced that they are not at an informational disadvantage. The second is the rules of an organized exchange, which is just self-interest one degree removed. A stockbroker's living depends on investors' willingness to trade. Stockbrokers therefore have an incentive to create organized securities markets that reduce the cost of trading. They also have an incentive to insist that the companies traded on those markets disclose information so that the brokers and their customers will not routinely be on the losing end of trades. Companies, in turn, have an incentive to agree to the listing requirements in order to increase investors' valuations of the company's shares. The third mechanism is mandatory disclosure rules set by a legislature, a regulatory agency, or both.

That disclosure is good also does not imply that more disclosure is always better. It is costly to disclose information and take care that it is accurate. Those costs may or may not exceed the benefits. The costs and benefits vary from one firm to another and so there is no one optimal level of disclosure for all firms.

With this theoretical background, we can return to the factual claim of marketplace anarchy in the pre-SEC era. The first two disclosure-forcing mechanisms operated in that era, at least to some extent. Publicly traded companies announced earnings, released financial statements to their shareholders, and distributed prospectuses in connection with public offerings. Self-interest induced disclosure.

The level of disclosure was not uniform across firms. As theory suggests, contemporaries believed that the most successful organized market, the New York Stock Exchange (NYSE), had the highest disclosure standards. Fortunately, this allows us to state the "marketplace anarchy" claim more precisely and look for evidence to back or refute it. The Roosevelt administration, Congress, academics, and journalists of the early 1930s argued that the supposed high standards of the NYSE were a sham. NYSE-listed companies, in their view, did not disclose enough and what they did disclose was often inaccurate. Their accounting practices deliberately misled investors about the value of their assets. Subsequent generations of lawyers and historians have generally accepted the claim as true. I will examine the qualitative evidence and then undertake empirical testing.

The NYSE's Listing Standards

From its earliest days, the brokers who owned the New York Stock Exchange spoke and acted, at least formally, as if their livelihoods depended on investor perceptions that the market was honest.[1] In a paper-based securities market, brokers are not merely interested in whether a company's financial statements are accurate. A more basic concern is whether the piece of paper representing a bond or share of stock is authentic and valid. It is a mark of the maturity of modern markets that we rarely think of the forgery or invalidity of shares or bonds as serious regulatory problems. When markets were in their infancy, however, these were very important problems to which the NYSE's brokers paid substantial attention.

The earliest standing committee of the NYSE was a "Committee on Securities" charged with resolving disputes over forgeries and other irregularities in stock and bond certificates (Eames 1968). The exchange also adopted standard rules, applicable to all contracts entered into on the exchange, governing procedures for transfer of title and remedies if either party failed to perform.

A share or bond's validity also depends on the valid existence of the company that issued it. Thus from at least the late nineteenth century, the NYSE's listing committee inquired into the legality of the company's incorporation and the titles to its principal properties. The NYSE's management also recognized that to know what rights a security represents, one must know where that security fits within the issuing company's capital structure. The listing requirements therefore included disclosure of the company's capitalization, or the total of all debt and equity claims on the company. Concern about the basic integrity of the instrument being traded thus opened the door for a more general principle of disclosure of key facts about the company bearing on the value of the security.

In the early twentieth century, the NYSE opened that door ever wider. It required listed companies to provide stockholders with a balance sheet and income statement prior to each annual meeting (Hawkins 1986). By the late 1920s, those financial statements had to be audited by an independent auditor. In the early 1920s the NYSE began to urge companies to report earnings quarterly, and by the late 1920s a clause requiring quarterly reporting was common in NYSE listing agreements.

Critics of the pre-SEC markets recognize, as they must, that there were disclosure rules in place on the NYSE. They were rudimentary by modern standards, but given the technology of the day it is difficult to argue that a regulator could easily have improved on them. Indeed, as I will describe in more detail below, the newly created SEC largely adopted the NYSE's disclosure rules as its own. The critics therefore fall back on the claim that these standards, while fine on paper, were not followed in practice (Twentieth Century Fund 1935).

The empirical basis for that claim has never been entirely clear. Benston (1973, 1976, 1977) found nearly universal compliance with the requirement for an annual balance sheet and income statement and a general tendency to provide more information, or information of a higher quality, than required. For example, most listed companies' annual financial statements were audited by outside auditors before the NYSE's rules required the practice. The next section therefore examines evidence from the initial implementation of the Exchange Act's mandatory disclosure system for NYSE-traded firms.

Evidence from the 1930s

With Jianping Mei

The Exchange Act required listed companies to file periodic disclosures with the newly created SEC. Not surprisingly, the SEC borrowed heavily from the NYSE's own disclosure rules to create a mandatory disclosure system. That fact generates one simple hypothesis about the Exchange Act's effect (and perhaps its real purpose), which may have been to force the smaller exchanges to bring their disclosure standards up to the NYSE's level. In short, the Exchange Act may be an example of a "best practices" command. As described in the introduction, "best" practices often, in reality, mean the practices followed by the largest firms. Mandating them for smaller firms (in this case, smaller exchanges) may burden those firms with a cost structure their size cannot support. If that is the case here, the Exchange Act may have improved disclosure practices, and therefore liquidity, for companies traded on the smaller exchanges, but at a cost that would exceed the benefit (Bushee and Leuz 2005). In that event, the Exchange Act's disclosure provisions could have been on balance detrimental to investors.

We attempt to assess whether the Exchange Act improved the information environment for firms already listed on the New York Stock Exchange. If so, the result would support the market failure narrative holding that the NYSE's rules were toothless in practice. If not, it would support the alternative view that the mandatory disclosure system was a "best practices" mandate that principally imposed costs on the regional exchanges.

Implementation of the Exchange Act began in mid-1935, when companies filed their first disclosure documents with the SEC and the exchanges themselves registered and became subject to SEC oversight. If the Exchange Act's supporters are correct, NYSE firms in mid-1935 switched to a higher-quality disclosure regime, reducing information asymmetry analogously to firms that switch from a lower-quality accounting regime to US generally accepted accounting principles (GAAP) or international accounting standards (IAS) (Leuz and Verrecchia 2000).

We test for improvements in the information environment in two ways. The first is to compare traders' reactions to earnings announcements made in early 1935, before the regime shift, and in early 1936, after the shift. The second is to measure traders' reactions to firms' initial Exchange Act filings, which contained more narrative and financial statement information than prior disclosure documents. The results suggest that the SEC-mandated narrative and financial statement disclosures were no more informative than the NYSE-mandated disclosures, analogously to Leuz's (2003) finding that US GAAP financial statements do not contain higher-quality information than financial statements prepared under IAS.

Implementation of the Exchange Act

The Exchange Act required each company with securities listed on an exchange to file an application (called a registration statement but distinct from a Securities Act registration statement) and then to update the required information annually. The statute also created the SEC and made it the administering agency for both the Securities Act and Exchange Act. The SEC granted temporary Exchange Act registration until June 30, 1935 to companies already listed on an exchange. In December 1934 it adopted Form 10, the primary form for permanent registration.[2] Most NYSE listed companies filed partially complete Form 10s during March through May of 1935 and then amended them to add financial statements and supplemental financial information complying with the SEC's financial disclosure standards in May through July of 1935.

Form 10 was in most respects similar to the NYSE's own disclosure rules. There were, however, a few qualitative differences worth noting. Whether these differences, or their enforcement by the SEC, worked a significant change in the information environment is the central proposition to be tested.

The choice between current market value and cost as the basis for financial accounting was an open question before the SEC resolved it in favor of historical cost-based accounting (Walker 1992; Zeff 2007). In the pre-SEC era, firms revalued assets frequently, which affected reported earnings through its impact on depreciation and reserves. Informed contemporaries questioned whether asset write-ups were a means of engaging in what would today be called earnings management (Dillon 1979; Walker 1992). Robert Healy, whom we met in chapter 3, believed that current-value accounting was inherently misleading and embarked on a crusade to end it (Walker 1992; Mahoney 1995). Healy's appointment as one of the initial commissioners of the SEC ensured that his view would prevail.

Form 10 began the gradual implementation of mandatory cost-based accounting. Item 34 of the form required, as a supplement to the financial statements, disclosure of all asset revaluations since January 1, 1925, including dollar amounts and explanations. The instructions called for any revaluations "made for the purpose of entering in the books current values, reproduction costs, or any values other than original cost." Examining the initial Form 10 filings, Fabricant (1936) found that 75 percent of NYSE companies had engaged in asset revaluations during the relevant period.

The SEC's disclosure rules also required more comprehensive financial statement disclosures than most companies had provided under the NYSE's rules. For example, United States Pipe & Foundry Co.'s published income statement for the year ending December 31, 1933, consisted of four line items: operating earnings, other income, depreciation, and resulting net income.[3] By contrast, Form 10 identified twenty-one separate income statement line items to be disclosed if relevant. The form also required eight financial statement schedules, including a schedule identifying all reserve accounts and changes in their balances.

Pre-SEC annual reports did not typically provide notes or schedules identifying underlying assumptions, conventions, and calculations. As late as 1932, leading figures within the accounting profession viewed such disclosures as unimportant to investors so long as the company followed its accounting principles and conventions consistently (Zeff 1984). Form 10 repudiated that point of view.

Finally, Form 10 required disclosure of nonfinancial statement items that companies had previously viewed as proprietary and confidential, such as management compensation and the identities and holdings of major shareholders. As noted in chapter 3 and by La Porta, Lopez-di-Silanes and Shleifer (2005), such disclosures can inform shareholders about potential sources of misappropriation.

Prior Studies of Mandatory Disclosure

Because of data limitations, there have only been a few attempts to determine the Exchange Act's benefits to investors. The principal attempt is by Benston (1973), who studies the effects of changes in accounting rules. He argues that the most significant difference between pre- and post-SEC financial statements was that the latter had to disclose sales whereas some NYSE firms only disclosed operating profit in the pre-SEC era. He therefore creates a sample of firms and partitions it based on whether the company's pre-SEC income statements disclosed sales. He compares average and cumulative abnormal market- and risk-adjusted returns over an approximately two-year period for firms that voluntarily disclosed sales prior to 1934 with those that did not and finds no significant difference. He therefore concludes that the Exchange Act did not improve the information environment. The analysis in Daines and Jones (2005) is similar in spirit to ours. That paper studies changes in bid-ask spreads after the first half of 1935, when companies made their first Exchange Act filings.

Following Benston (1973), they partition their sample based on whether a company disclosed earnings in its pre-SEC accounting statements and find the difference in differences not significant.

A number of papers test the analytically different question whether, given the existence of a uniform, government-mandated disclosure system, the detailed disclosure document contains value-relevant information that cannot be inferred from a summary statistic such as earnings per share. Companies typically announce earnings before distributing an annual report to shareholders and filing a Form 10-K with the SEC (the 10-K annually updates the information contained in the initial Form 10). The company's announced earnings are derived pursuant to the SEC's accounting rules and are therefore consistent with the 10-K information, although they are obviously only an incomplete summary of that information. Foster, Jenkins, and Vickrey (1983) find no abnormal return on average around the time of a 10-K filing and conclude that the 10-K does not contain incremental information. Other studies, summarized by Asthana and Balsam (2001), reach a similar conclusion.

In 1935, however, the Form 10 did not simply contain incremental information building on an earnings release or annual report compiled in accordance with the SEC's accounting rules. The filing of a Form 10 represented a shift in the entire system of presenting information to the public. An NYSE company operating on a calendar-year basis announced 1934 earnings in early 1935 based on a set of accounting principles determined by market practice and NYSE rules. In mid-1935, that same company filed a Form 10 containing financial statements for the same period based on a new set of SEC-determined accounting principles. Beginning with that filing, the company's disclosure requirements were no longer determined principally by the NYSE, but by the SEC. The SEC also gained oversight of the NYSE and its rules. Thus these initial Form 10 filings are more analogous to changing the company's primary listing to a new exchange, or to shifting from one body of accounting principles to another, than they are to filing a typical 10-K.

Asthana and Balsam (2001) raise the separate question whether SEC-filed information is actually available to investors. They argue that the lack of market reaction to 10-K filings is a consequence of the paper filing system that prevailed before the creation of the SEC's EDGAR electronic-filing system. They find that investors react to 10-K filings on EDGAR, which are available over the Internet within twenty-four hours, although they do not react to paper filings. We discuss this issue in connection with the discussion of traders' (lack of) reaction to Form 10 filings below.

The Exchange Act's Effects on Information Asymmetry in NYSE Firms

The Exchange Act's disclosure requirements applied to all exchange-traded firms at roughly the same point in time, making it challenging to measure their effects. One strategy is to identify a market-wide time series impact that would have occurred, if at all, as a result of the change in disclosure standards. A second is to exploit small differences in the timing of different companies' financial disclosures. We employ both strategies.

MARKET REACTIONS TO EARNINGS ANNOUNCEMENTS. Kim and Verrecchia (1991) model traders' reaction to the information contained in earnings releases. They find that changes in price and trading volume at the time of announcement are decreasing in the quality of the preannouncement information environment. Intuitively, higher-quality information before the announcement leads to lower dispersion in traders' preannouncement private beliefs and therefore less postannouncement reassessment. Beaver (1968) observes that postannouncement trading volumes reflect changes in traders' idiosyncratic beliefs, while price movements reflect changes in traders' aggregate beliefs. Superior preannouncement information dampens both effects. In principle, then, comparing price and volume reactions to earnings announcements before and after implementation of the Exchange Act compares information asymmetry before and after the statute took effect.

Kim and Verrecchia's analysis also raises a potentially confounding factor. In their model, price and volume effects increase with the precision of the earnings announcement. In our setting, if listed companies' public communications were unreliable prior to enactment of the federal securities laws but more reliable thereafter, we could not predict the laws' effect on the market reaction to earnings releases. The securities laws both mandated new disclosures and increased the penalties and enforcement for fraudulent or misleading disclosures. The mandatory disclosure system would improve the preannouncement information environment, implying smaller price and volume reactions to earnings releases. However, the antifraud provisions of the securities laws would improve the precision of the earnings releases themselves, implying larger price and volume reactions. As a possible example of these competing phenomena, Bailey,

Karolyi, and Salva (2006) find larger, rather than smaller, price and volume reactions to earnings announcements in the home market following a cross-listing in the United States, particularly for firms from developing countries. They suggest several possible explanations, including the possibility that reported earnings prior to the cross-listing were less precise.

Fortunately, the timing of the securities laws' implementation substantially eliminates this concern for this study. The Securities Act of 1933 had a broad antifraud provision. The Securities Exchange Act of 1934 created an enforcement agency in the SEC, granted it broad antifraud rulemaking power, and contained several specific antifraud rules. Thus NYSE-traded firms were already subject by late 1934 to both general and specific prohibitions on fraudulent or materially misleading statements and to increased enforcement. However, the mandatory disclosure system under the Exchange Act took longer to implement. NYSE-listed firms had a full set of SEC-mandated financial information on file with the SEC only in mid-1935.

Thus if we compare announcements of 1934 earnings made in early 1935 with announcements of 1935 earnings made in early 1936, both were subject to identical antifraud rules and enforcement mechanisms, but only the latter were made after the Exchange Act's mandatory disclosure system was implemented. This generates a hypothesis that traders' reactions to early 1936 earnings releases should be smaller than their reaction to early 1935 earnings releases, all else equal, if the Exchange Act improved the information environment.

We test this hypothesis by hand-gathering information on earnings announcements made in early 1935 and 1936. Companies commonly issued a press release announcing earnings either before or contemporaneously with the release of an annual report to shareholders. Earnings announcements are taken from the *New York Times*. The sample consists of companies that meet all the following criteria:

The *New York Times* reports an earnings announcement for the company between January 1 and March 15 in both 1935 and 1936. The March 15 cutoff is used because several firms filed Form 10s in late March 1935. Two companies are eliminated because they filed a Form 10 in early March 1935, prior to their earnings announcement, and three because they are described as being in liquidation or reorganization.

The company's fiscal year ends on December 31.

The earnings announcement was not accompanied by a dividend declaration or news of a dividend increase.

Daily price, return, and trading volume information for the company is available in the Center for Research in Security Prices (CRSP) database.

There are 201 companies that meet all four criteria. The companies are identified in appendix B along with earnings announcement dates for 1935 and 1936.

Asthana and Balsam's (2001) standardized absolute abnormal return (SAAR) measure provides a means of quantifying unexpected price changes around the time of earnings announcements. To measure abnormal returns, we first estimate a market model for stock *i*'s return on day *t*, $R_{i,t}$ using the standard event study methodology of Brown and Warner (1985):

$$R_{i,t} = \alpha_i + \beta_i r_{m,t} + u_{i,t}$$

where $r_{m,t}$ is the market return, proxied by the CRSP equally weighted index. We estimate the model for a 100-day period consisting of trading days −110 to −11, inclusive, where day zero is the day the *New York Times* reports earnings or, if that day is not a trading day, the first trading day thereafter. Abnormal return is defined as the regression residual, $u_{i,t}$, during the estimation period and the difference between the actual and forecast return thereafter. We look for abnormal price changes during a five-day event window, days −2 to +2 in event time.

The standardized absolute abnormal return is defined as

$$SAAR_{i,t} = \frac{|AR_{i,t}| - \mu |AR_i|}{s_i}$$

where $AR_{i,t}$ is the abnormal return for stock *i* on date *t* and $\mu|AR_i|$ and s_i are the sample mean and standard deviation, respectively, of the absolute value of stock *i*'s abnormal return during the estimation period.

We estimate an analogous market model for daily share turnover, following Tkac (1999), hand-calculating an equally weighted daily turnover index of all companies in the CRSP data as the proxy for market turnover. Turnover for each firm-day is defined as trading volume divided by the number of shares outstanding. This measure does not require transformation to remove the sign because theory predicts higher trading volumes in response to both positive and negative news. Standardized abnormal turnover (SATO) is calculated analogously to standardized abnormal return. Trading volume is highly right-skewed, producing extreme outliers for the SATO measure; we winsorize at the 99 percent level to reduce the impact of outliers.

SAAR and SATO measure traders' aggregate repricing and individual portfolio rebalancing, respectively, in response to the unanticipated component of earnings. By hypothesis, these should be smaller in 1936 reflecting the superior information environment beginning in mid-1935.

Figures 5.1 and 5.2 show SAAR and SATO, respectively, averaged across the 201 sample companies, for each of the 113 days from the beginning of the estimation period (day −110) to the second trading day after the earnings announcement (day +2) in 1935 and 1936. It is clear from the figures that traders react strongly to earnings announcements in both years and that the magnitudes of the reactions are similar in both years.

Table 5.1 summarizes these measures. In both years there are economically and statistically large abnormal returns and turnover around the time of earnings announcements. However, the year-on-year differences are economically small and insignificant for each day and for the five-day

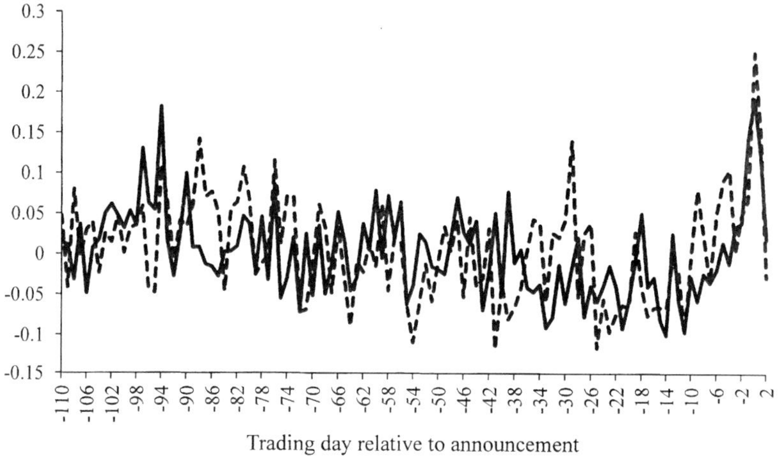

FIGURE 5.1 Standardized absolute abnormal returns around the time of earnings announcements, 1935 and 1936. The average standardized absolute value of abnormal returns for the 201 sample companies is shown around the time of earnings announcements in early 1935 (solid line) and 1936 (dashed line).

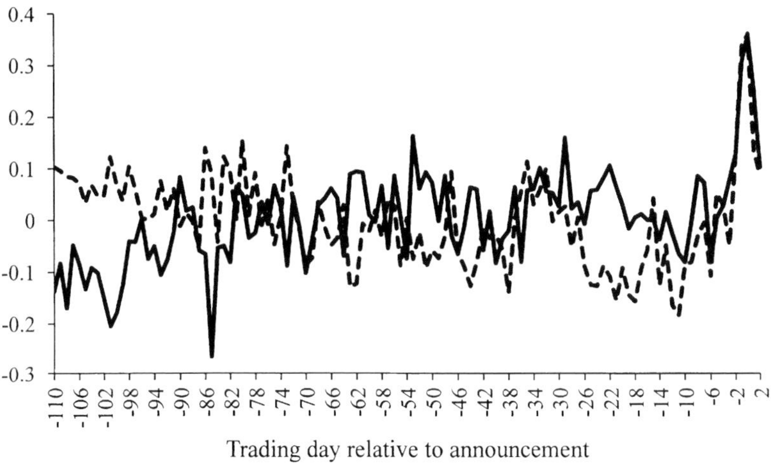

FIGURE 5.2 Standardized abnormal turnover around the time of earnings announcements, 1935 and 1936. The average standardized abnormal turnover (trading volume divided by shares outstanding) for the 201 sample companies is shown around the time of earnings announcements in early 1935 (solid line) and 1936 (dashed line).

average. The entries are in units of standard deviation. The standard deviation of the absolute value of daily return for the sample companies during the mid-1930s is on the order of 2.5 percent. Thus the day zero excess (absolute) returns for 1935 and 1936, averaged across the 201 sample companies, are each on the order of half a percent, while the cumulative five-day difference in absolute abnormal return between 1935 and 1936 is on the order of 8/100ths of 1 percent.

Adjusting for pre-event volatility, then, there is no measurable difference in traders' reactions to earnings announcements after institution of a mandatory disclosure system compared to the prior year. It should be noted, however, that pre-event volatility was higher in 1935. Simple measures of liquidity such as trading volumes and bid-ask spreads improved from early 1935 to 1936. General economic conditions improved over the same period, which may explain the change. However, one might hypothesize that improvements in liquidity and accompanying decreases in volatility resulted from increased investor confidence brought about by the Exchange Act itself. If the latter hypothesis is true, then using price and turnover response measures that control for pre-event volatility, although typical in the literature beginning with Beaver (1968), could underestimate the Exchange Act's effects.

TABLE 5.1. **Measures of price and volume changes around earnings announcements, 1935 and 1936**

	Announcements		
Day Relative to Announcement	Early 1935	Early 1936	Difference
Panel 1: Standardized absolute abnormal return (SAAR)			
−2	.040	.049	−.009
	(.049)	(.052)	(.065)
−1	.143**	.067	.076
	(.052)	(.058)	(.075)
0	.193**	.251**	−.056
	(.064)	(.087)	(.110)
1	.123*	.153	−.030
	(.064)	(.084)	(.104)
2	.019	−.028	.047
	(.049)	(.049)	(.070)
average	.104	.097	.006
	(.126)	(.152)	(.047)
Panel 2: Standardized abnormal turnover (SATO)			
−2	.128	.126	.002
	(.072)	(.086)	(.111)
−1	.306**	.337**	−.030
	(.075)	(.091)	(.109)
0	.360**	.359**	.001
	(.076)	(.089)	(.101)
1	.251**	.133	.119
	(.074)	(.070)	(.100)
2	.101	.084	.017
	(.061)	(.080)	(.099)
average	.229	.206	.024
	(.126)	(.152)	(.068)

Note: Standard errors (in parentheses) are calculated from cross-sectional standard deviations.
* Significant at the 5% level
** Significant at the 1% level

We therefore also analyze the (nonstandardized) absolute value of abnormal returns as in Bamber and Cheon (1995). The results in table 5.1 are not robust to the use of a nonstandardized measure of price movement, although they are to the use of a nonstandardized measure of trading volume. The absolute value of abnormal returns, averaged across the 201 sample firms for each day in the five-day event window and then cumulated over the five days, is higher by 1.3 percent in 1935 compared to 1936 and the difference is significant at the 5 percent level using paired cross-sectional standard deviations. This result supports the hypothesis that the Exchange Act improved the information environment.

To determine whether this result is more plausibly a consequence of changed economic conditions from early 1935 to early 1936 or of the Exchange Act itself, we control for factors identified in the prior literature that affect market reactions to earnings announcements. Beginning with Atiase (1985), researchers find that price reactions to earnings announcements are more pronounced for smaller firms. Hayn (1995) finds different reactions to accounting losses compared to profits.

We therefore estimate the following regression:

$$AAR_{i,t} = \alpha + \beta_1 CAP_{i,t} + \beta_2 LOSS_{i,t} + \gamma YR35_t + \varepsilon_{i,t}$$

where i indexes firms and $t \in \{1935, 1936\}$ indexes years, AAR is the absolute abnormal return, averaged over days −2 to +2, inclusive, CAP is the log of market capitalization measured over the estimation period, $LOSS$ = 1 indicates negative earnings, and $YR35$ = 1 indicates that t = 1935.

Several papers also confirm the intuition that market reactions should be stronger the greater the earnings surprise. We lack reliable data for analyst forecasts for 1935 or 1936, so we use a naïve expectations model in which the prior year's EPS is the expected current-year EPS, following Bamber (1986). We re-estimate the above regression substituting for $LOSS$ a new variable, UE, or unexpected earnings, defined as the (log) absolute value of the difference between EPS in the current year and the prior year divided by the prior year EPS. A drawback of this approach is that the *New York Times* reports an EPS number in 1935 and 1936 only if income was sufficient to cover preferred dividends, which was not true for many firms during the Great Depression. The sample size is thus smaller for this model. In both models, γ is the parameter of interest. Under the hypothesis that the information environment improved between the 1935 and 1936 earnings reports, γ should be positive and significant.

Table 5.2 reports results for both models. The market capitalization, accounting loss, and earnings surprise variables all enter significantly. However, the estimated coefficient on the 1935 year dummy is economically and statistically insignificant. As a robustness check, we re-estimate the model with firm fixed effects with consistent results (not reported). The regression results suggest no change in price reactions to earnings announcements from early 1935 to early 1936, contrary to the prediction if the Exchange Act's mandatory disclosure system improved the information environment.

TABLE 5.2. **Regression: Price reaction to earnings announcements, 1935 and 1936**

Independent Variable	Model 1	Model 2
Constant	6.186**	3.607**
	(.427)	(.387)
Log market cap	−.455**	−.208**
	(.042)	(.379)
Loss	.446*	
	(.200)	
Earnings surprise		.066*
		(.032)
Year = 1935	.053	−.017
	(.129)	(.095)
R^2	.303	.174
Number of firms	201	109

Note: The dependent variable in both models is the average absolute abnormal return (in percent) over the five-day event window comprising days −2 to +2, with day 0 being the announcement date. Standard errors are in parentheses.

* Significant at the 5% level

** Significant at the 1% level

MARKET REACTION TO FORM 10 FILINGS. Did traders react to the Form 10 filings themselves? When firms filed their initial Form 10s in March–June 1935, most were unable to meet the SEC's accounting requirements and so made a partial filing. The SEC indicated that firms could amend their Form 10 filings to include items 34 (revaluations) and 36 (audited financial statements) as soon as they could be prepared, but no later than July 1, 1935. These delays in filing financial statements provide additional evidence that the SEC's accounting requirements were substantially different from the NYSE's.

Although the SEC issued press releases announcing the initial Form 10 filings, it did not do so for the amendments, making it impossible to determine from secondary sources when the financial statements were filed. However, the SEC's records, housed at the National Archives, contain Exchange Act filings. With the help of a research assistant, we examined the paper files. These are unfortunately seriously incomplete for the SEC's early years: of the 712 companies listed on the NYSE at the beginning of 1935 and included in the CRSP dataset, we located an Exchange Act file for 507. Of those, only 94 contain the initial Form 10 filing. Dillon (1979) examined Form 10 filings to study asset revaluations. At the time of his study, the filings were housed at the SEC and he found that some had been destroyed for lack of storage space. Given the modest number we located, many more were presumably destroyed before they were moved to the National Archives.

The sample accordingly consists of those firms for which we could identify a date on which full financial statements were filed and verify that those statements included the required information, including disclosure of sales and of past asset revaluations. Nine of the ninety-four firms were eliminated because we could not find a complete set of financial statements in the files. Another twenty-three firms are eliminated because they sought confidential treatment for all or part of the financial statement information or other financial data contained in the Form 10 filings (typically sales and/or executive compensation). The SEC routinely denied those requests, but typically with some delay, and we cannot be sure when traders gained access to the information. We also eliminate one company whose filing indicated that it was in liquidation and its remaining assets consisted almost entirely of the shares of another publicly traded company. Finally, we eliminate thirteen companies whose filings were not complete by the July 1 deadline. Although those firms later completed their filings, we have no way of knowing whether any market reaction would reflect the information in the filing or the simple fact that the company had avoided delisting. The sample consists of the remaining forty-eight firms, which are listed along with the financial statement filing dates in table 5.3.

We calculate SAAR and SATO around the time of these Form 10 filings consistently with the methodology for earnings announcements. Figures 5.3 and 5.4 show these measures for days −110 to +2 in event time, where day zero is the filing date. Unlike figures 5.1 and 5.2, these do not spike around day zero.

This result is confirmed in table 5.4, which shows both measures along with their (cross-sectional) standard errors for each day in the five-day event window centered on day zero. On the filing date itself there is actually lower than average turnover and almost no price change on average.

This last result may indicate that traders waited to confirm that there were no surprises in the filings before trading. But it may also be a consequence of clustered filing dates. In general, because many of the Form 10s were filed near the July 1 deadline, the clustering of filing dates could produce nonindependent errors and affect inferences. There may have been less trading during the summer months, for example, which we would mistakenly interpret as showing no reaction to Form 10 filings.

We therefore rerun the tests in table 5.4 grouping each firm that filed on the same date into portfolios (twenty-six portfolios in all) and estimating market models for these portfolios rather than individual firms. The results are qualitatively similar; on no date is there a statistically positive

TABLE 5.3. **Form 10 financial statement filing dates**

Company	Form 10 Financial Statement Filing Date
Consolidated Film Inds Inc	2/21/1935
Pittsburgh Utd Corp	3/30/1935
Ulen & Co	4/13/1935
Dominion Stores Ltd	4/22/1935
Reo Mtr Car Co	5/3/1935
Otis Stl Co	5/4/1935
United Drug Inc	5/4/1935
Superior Oil Co Del	5/6/1935
Lima Locomotive Wks Inc	5/7/1935
Chesapeake Corp	5/11/1935
Dresser S R Manufacturing Co	5/13/1935
Belding Heminway Inc	5/14/1935
Standard Oil Co Kans Del	5/14/1935
Intercontinental Rubber Co	5/16/1935
Engineers Pub Svc Co	5/16/1935
Affiliated Prods Inc	5/16/1935
Mother Lode Coalition Mines Co	5/21/1935
Connecticut Ry & Ltg Co	5/22/1935
Timken Detroit Axle Co	5/23/1935
Crosley Radio Corp	5/27/1935
Kaufmann Dept Stores Inc	5/28/1935
Barnsdall Corp	5/31/1935
Public Svc Corp	6/8/1935
Wright Aeronautical Corp	6/13/1935
Western Pac Rr Corp	6/20/1935
Budd Wheel Co	6/20/1935
Wells Fargo & Co	6/22/1935
Colonial Beacon Oil Co	6/27/1935
Associated Oil Co	6/28/1935
Kresge Dept Stores Inc	6/28/1935
Mid Continent Pete Corp	6/28/1935
Pierce Pete Corp	6/28/1935
Tide Wtr Assd Oil Co	6/28/1935
Minneapolis Moline Pwr Implement	6/28/1935
Davega Stores Corp	6/28/1935
American Water Works & Elec Inc	6/29/1935
Atlantic Gulf & West Indies Ss	6/29/1935
Market Str Ry Co	6/29/1935
Pathe Exchange Inc	6/29/1935
United Sts Distrg Corp	6/29/1935
Warner Quinlan Co	6/29/1935
Eitingon Schild Inc	6/29/1935
Truscon Stl Co	6/29/1935
Electric Pwr & Lt Corp	7/1/1935
National Pwr & Lt Co	7/1/1935
Philadelphia & Reading Coal & Ir	7/1/1935
Simms Pete Co	7/1/1935
American Pwr & Lt Co	7/1/1935

Source: Securities and Exchange Commission files in the National Archives.

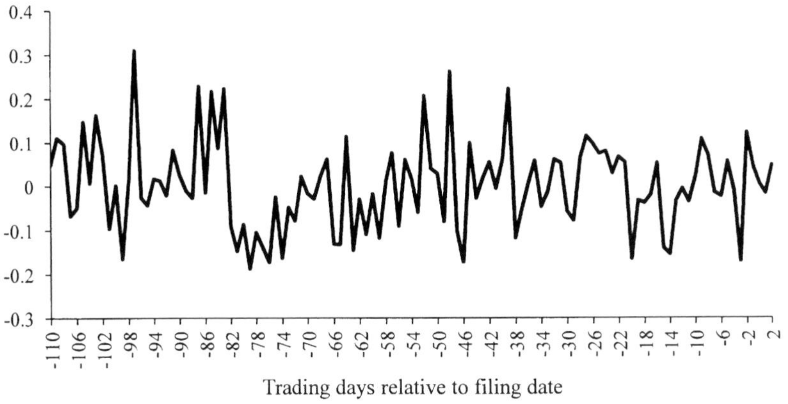

FIGURE 5.3 Standardized absolute abnormal returns around the time of Form 10 filings, mid-1935. The average standardized absolute abnormal return for the 48 sample companies is shown around the time of Form 10 filings or amended filings containing complete financial statements.

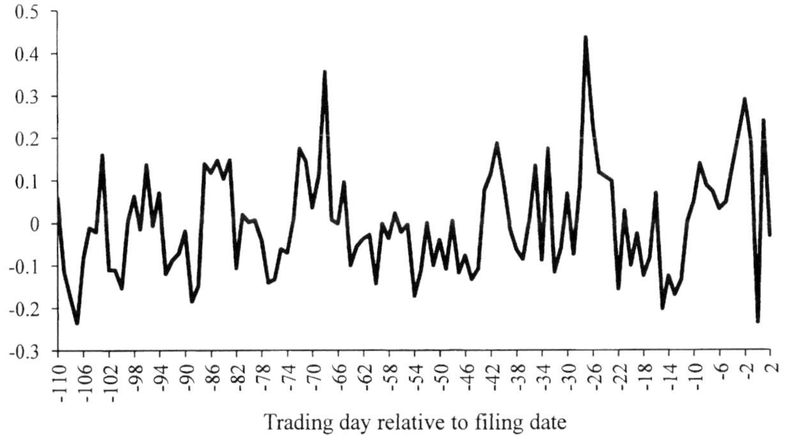

FIGURE 5.4 Standardized abnormal turnover around the time of Form 10 filings, mid-1935. The average standardized abnormal turnover (trading volume divided by shares outstanding) for the 48 sample companies is shown around the time of Form 10 filings or amended filings containing complete financial statements.

TABLE 5.4. **Measures of price and volume changes around Form 10 filings, mid-1935**

Day Relative to Filing	Standardized Absolute Abnormal Return	Standardized Abnormal Turnover
−2	.122	.288
	(.143)	(.221)
−1	.045	.187
	(.101)	(.199)
0	.006	−.235**
	(.097)	(.085)
1	−.016	.237
	(.093)	(.217)
2	.047	−.031
	(.123)	(.156)
average	.041	.089
	(.066)	(.118)

Note: Standard errors (in parentheses) are calculated from the cross-sectional standard deviations.
** Significant at the 1% level

SAAR or SATO averaged across the portfolios. Indeed, the *lower* than average trading volume on day zero persists in this methodology and is accompanied by a (nonstatistically significant) point estimate of lower than average price volatility, again suggesting that traders may have paused at day zero to verify that the Form 10 filings did not contain revelations that would affect valuations.

Interpretation of the Evidence

The study shows no change in traders' reactions to earnings announcements after implementation of the mandatory disclosure system. Although earnings announcements in 1935 and 1936 are promptly accompanied by a sharp increase in price volatility and turnover, there is no analogous response to Form 10 filings.

One might hypothesize that the difference is a result of traders' greater access to earnings announcements in comparison to Form 10 filings. However, qualitative evidence suggests that traders had prompt access to the filings. The SEC's rules required that the Form 10 be provided to each stock exchange on which the firm's shares traded. The SEC's files contain, for nearly all of the sample firms, an acknowledgement that the NYSE received the filing, typically either the same day the SEC received it or the prior day (day −1 in event time). In the 1920s and 1930s, floor traders (NYSE members who maintained a physical presence on the exchange floor and traded for their own account) played an important role in price discovery. Through the NYSE, these traders had access to Form 10 filings in real time and had a strong incentive to look for price-relevant information in them. The press sometimes reported newsworthy information from the filings—typically the salaries of top executives or the holdings of major shareholders. These stories normally appeared in the paper within a day or two of the filing.

For reasons discussed above, whether initial Form 10 filings contained incremental information is an open question even in light of modern findings that 10-K filings do not contain incremental information. These initial Form 10s were the first public disclosures of SEC-mandated financial information, which began the move to a historical-cost accounting system and permitted less managerial discretion in comparison to pre-SEC financial statements contained in annual reports to shareholders. Some traders surely anticipated (correctly) that the SEC would soon go beyond requiring disclosure of asset revaluations and ban such revaluations altogether. This in turn meant that firms' reported earnings could change once their asset values and depreciation charges were calculated on a historical-cost basis. A quick perusal of the response to item 34 of Form 10 would have indicated a company's vulnerability to this coming change.

An important issue to a trader analyzing the new SEC-mandated data was whether companies were using the discretion inherent in asset revaluations to engage in earnings management. Based on review of a sample of the answers to item 34 and the accompanying financial statements in initial Form 10 filings, Dillon (1979) concludes "it seems that corporations were not using asset revaluations as a device for directly manipulating earnings in this period." Our findings suggest that traders reached the same conclusion.

The tests herein should also find no effect if it took time for traders to digest the information contained in the new disclosure documents, in which case the effects on price and trading volume would have unfolded gradually rather than around the time of the filing. By contrast, earnings announcements were a longstanding practice and traders had presumably learned to interpret them quickly. This explanation is doubtful given the steady drumbeat of criticism in the run-up to the Exchange Act about misleading disclosure practices. It is reasonable to assume that a savvy trader who was interested in a specific company would peruse that company's Form 10 filing promptly for evidence of earnings management or other significantly misleading pre-SEC disclosures. Had there been many instances of them, it seems likely that trading and price volatility would have increased within a day or two after the filing reached the NYSE.

That this does not occur is evidence that the SEC's narrative and financial disclosure standards, as of 1935, did not represent an improvement on the NYSE's disclosure standards. The evidence suggests, therefore, that the Exchange Act's mandatory disclosure system was a "best practices" mandate that imposed NYSE-like standards on the smaller, regional exchanges. If so, the system would likely benefit the NYSE relative to the regional exchanges.

The NYSE publicly opposed the Exchange Act and we are unaware of evidence that its private stance was different. Schwert (1977) finds that NYSE seat prices declined substantially around the time of enactment of the Exchange Act and concludes that the statute was harmful to the NYSE. However, the NYSE and other exchanges had good reason to oppose the bill that became the Exchange Act entirely apart from its disclosure provisions. As initially introduced, it would have imposed a single-capacity system, patterned on that of the London Stock Exchange, requiring every member to be either a broker or a dealer, but not both. On an exchange like the NYSE with a fixed commission structure, single capacity would have imposed substantial costs on dealers who would end up paying a (high) brokerage commission on every trade. The regional exchanges also opposed single capacity because regional brokerage houses were a link in the chain by which new securities issues reached individual investors. Forcing those brokers to forego participation as distributing dealers in public offerings would have cut off an important income stream. Sissoko (2013) argues that dual capacity also enabled brokers to exploit customer information through own-account trading.

The Exchange Act as enacted did not mandate single capacity, but like many other controversial issues left it to the SEC to decide. In fact, the SEC never adopted a single capacity rule. However, informed observers would surely have believed at the time of the bill's passage in February 1934 that it might do so, given the strong support for a single capacity rule among the New Dealers. Thus it is not surprising that seat prices declined at the time of enactment.

While the SEC's authority to impose single capacity was a threat to all the exchanges, the mandatory disclosure system in isolation seems likely to have harmed the regional exchanges relative to the NYSE. We know that the regional exchanges opposed the Exchange Act with particular vehemence (Seligman 2003). They were right to do so, as the post-SEC era was not kind to regional exchanges.

In its 1935 annual report, the SEC identifies a total of forty-one stock exchanges operating in states or territories of the United States at the time of enactment of the Exchange Act. Roughly a quarter of these disappeared in the first few years of the SEC's existence after either trying and failing to gain registration or deciding not to make the attempt. Others were acquired by larger exchanges or curtailed their activities so as not to fit within the registration requirement. Only twenty exchanges survived as registered national securities exchanges by 1938.

Remarkably, the Exchange Act did in a few years what wars and depressions could not for the better part of a century. Fietkiewicz and Proffitt (2010) attempt a comprehensive census of every regional stock exchange created in the United States from 1790 to the early twentieth century; they identify thirty. Their list is consistent with the SEC's except that they ignore specialized exchanges in cities that already had a primary exchange, such as the New York Real Estate Securities Exchange and the Seattle Mining Exchange. There is likely some survivorship bias in their list inasmuch as an exchange that did not survive for long might not have generated mention in newspapers and other available sources. Even so, it is remarkable that every exchange in their study was still in existence at the time of enactment of the Exchange Act in early 1934. Six of the thirty did not survive the initial registration process. The Exchange Act set in motion the demise of regional exchanges in the United States.

CHAPTER SIX

Was Market Manipulation Common in the Pre-SEC Era?

Today we view the federal securities reforms as motivated primarily by the desire to improve disclosure standards. However, securities market critics of the 1930s saw market manipulation as the fundamental problem. The preamble to the Exchange Act asserts that "frequently the prices of securities . . . are susceptible to manipulation." That conclusion was based on the Senate Banking Committee's stock market investigation of 1932–34, known as the Pecora Hearings after chief counsel Ferdinand Pecora.

The primary evidence of manipulation from the Pecora Hearings was the existence of so-called stock pools. These were agreements among groups of active traders who combined their funds to purchase and then sell a particular stock. The purpose of the pools, according to the committee report (known as the Fletcher Report), was to buy a specific stock in order to drive up its price, then to sell the overpriced stock to public investors prior to the inevitable price decline.

Galbraith (1979, 79) provides the canonical description of a stock pool:

> The nature of these operations varied somewhat but, in a typical operation, a number of traders pooled their resources to boom a particular stock. They ap-

Parts of this chapter were previously published as Paul G. Mahoney, "The Stock Pools and the Securities Exchange Act," *Journal of Financial Economics* 51 (1999): 343–69, and Guolin Jiang, Paul G. Mahoney, and Jianping Mei, "Market Manipulation: A Comprehensive Study of Stock Pools," *Journal of Financial Economics* 77 (2005): 147–70. Reprinted with permission of Elsevier B.V.

> pointed a pool manager, promised not to double-cross each other by private operations, and the pool manager then took a position in the stock which might also include shares contributed by the participants. This buying would increase prices and attract the interest of people watching the tape across the country. The interest of the latter would then be further stimulated by active selling and buying, all of which gave the impression that something big was afloat. Tip-sheets and market commentators would tell of exciting developments in the offing. If all went well, the public would come in to buy, and prices would rise on their own. The pool manager would then sell out, pay himself a percentage of the profits, and divide the rest with his investors.

There is a longstanding debate within financial economics over whether such "trade-based" manipulation is possible. Fischel and Ross (1991) argue that if prices respond only to information, then large uninformed purchases cannot cause a price rise and manipulation by trading alone is impossible. Other authors argue that there are plausible conditions under which profitable trade-based manipulation can occur. When a trader makes a large purchase of stock, other traders cannot know with certainty whether the purchaser is informed or uninformed and therefore cannot know whether they should revalue the stock. Under appropriate assumptions, large uninformed trades may cause a price increase of sufficient duration to permit the original purchaser to sell at a profit. Allen and Gorton (1992) model successful manipulation when buyers are more likely to be informed than sellers, Allen and Gale (1992) present a model in which informed traders and manipulators are risk-neutral and passive investors are risk-averse, and Jarrow (1992) presents a model in which the price process depends on the history of the large trader's holdings. Both classes of models—those that do and do not permit trade-based manipulation—are based on stringent assumptions about traders' information and reaction to it.

Descriptions of the pools, like Galbraith's above, are often unclear about whether they depict pure trade-based manipulation or fraud. Fischel and Ross (1991), for example, argue that the pools relied on false statements and fictitious trades to create price increases unwarranted by fundamentals. Contemporary commentators claimed that the pools used fictitious trading practices. These included "wash sales" or "matched orders," which lead to reported trades even though there is no actual transfer of risk from one investor to another.

Leffler's (1963, 459) treatise on the stock market relies on both fraud and trade-based manipulation to explain stock pools. It contends that pool operators released "tips and rumors" and engaged in fictitious trades, then states:

> A final device of the pool was artificial market activity. This consisted of a heavy "churning" of the stock in the market; it was bought and sold by the pool in heavy volume. . . . Its purpose was obvious to all familiar with pool operations. The public must be attracted to the stock; few things attract speculators more quickly than a rising volume. The public's attitude became whetted in anticipation of "something big going on." It rushed in to buy before it was "too late." As the stock rose under increased activity, the public entered the market in ever increasing numbers; this was exactly the purpose of the operation.

If NYSE members frequently used fictitious trades and releases of false information to influence stock prices, it would be evidence that the NYSE's rules were indeed paper tigers. At all relevant times the NYSE had rules in place forbidding wash sales, matched orders, or the deliberate release of false information. Critics in the 1930s and since have argued that the NYSE's rules against fraudulent trading, like its disclosure rules, were enforced haphazardly if at all. On the other hand, if traders attempted to manipulate prices solely by trading, they did not violate any explicit stock exchange rules—but there is room for debate about whether the strategy could succeed.

As it did in other regulatory areas, the Exchange Act added an overlay of federal law atop the stock exchanges' own rules. The Exchange Act contains specific prohibitions on wash sales, matched orders, false rumors and other manipulative devices and gives the SEC broad authority to identify and prohibit other forms of manipulation. In a nod to the pools, section 9(a)(2) of the Exchange Act prohibits transactions "creating actual or apparent active trading . . . for the purpose of inducing the purchase or sale of such security by others."

The Senate's conclusion that stock pools successfully manipulated the prices of stocks upward and then dumped the overpriced shares on unsuspecting investors has influenced the SEC's regulatory policies. The SEC has a longstanding concern that an underwriting syndicate could "ramp up" the price of a security in advance of a public offering by making large purchases, thus enabling it to sell the offering to the public at an excessive price. Thus through its "trading practice" rules (currently found in regulation M), the SEC restricts purchases by underwriters and participating dealers of the security they plan to distribute immediately prior to and during a public offering. I have had conversations with SEC staffers who cited the stock pools as evidence that underwriters could in fact price an offering above its fundamental value by making large purchases just in advance of the offering.

As always, however, we should not accept without verification the factual assertions of those who have an ax to grind. President Franklin Roosevelt owed his election in part to his success during the 1932 campaign in channeling public anger about the Depression toward Wall Street and promising to tame it. The purpose of the Pecora Hearings was not objective fact finding but helping to build support for the president's plan to regulate the stock exchanges. The Fletcher Report states candidly that the investigation's "purpose throughout has been to lay the foundation for remedial legislation."

As is true of many other market failure narratives, the notion that manipulation was rampant on the NYSE in the lead-up to the 1929 market crash collapses under careful scrutiny. In the remainder of this chapter I describe a comprehensive study of the stock pools and their effects on stock prices. I begin with qualitative evidence about the pools and then turn to quantitative evidence of their effects.

What Was the Purpose of the Pools?

The principal sources of information about the pools are the 11,000 pages of transcripts of the Pecora Hearings, the answers to a questionnaire that the committee sent to every NYSE member firm, and contemporary press accounts. The questionnaire asked, among other things, whether the firm had managed or participated in any pools trading in excess of 10,000 shares and directed it to attach photocopies of any written agreements relating to them. I examined the 631 questionnaire responses contained in the records of the Pecora Hearings in the National Archives.

The responses show that pools were a common form of proprietary trading. Larger pools typically operated pursuant to written agreements that resemble a modern-day agreement among the members of an underwriting syndicate. Brokerage houses had standard-form agreements that could be filled in. The agreements attached to the questionnaire responses are dated and identify the manager of the pool and its duration; these range from two months to two years. Some are lengthy, detailed, printed documents, while others are informal one-page letters. Some identify all the participants in the body of the agreement, but most do not. The language of the agreements coupled with other information shows that pools often formed in two circumstances. One was when a company or substantial stockholder wished to sell a large block of stock. In that event, the pool served a distribution function. The other was when a group of traders concluded that a stock was illiquid or undervalued and sought to profit from timely trades in the stock. These pools were market-making or informed trading operations. I will briefly describe each.

Distribution

Many of the pools were formed to distribute stock obtained from the issuer (a primary distribution) or from a third party (a secondary distribution). Some of the agreements state this explicitly; in other cases it is the most plausible inference because the pool was formed just before the commencement of a public offering.

It is not surprising that some of the pools are functionally equivalent to underwriting syndicates. In the pre-SEC era, equities often reached the market through secondary distributions in which an insider or institutional investor that had privately purchased a large amount of stock sold through brokers (Carosso 1970). Brokers syndicated these distributions by forming pools, just as investment banks syndicated bond underwritings.

In the 1920s, the NYSE's rules did not yet accommodate block trading in its modern form. Pools, however, were functionally very similar. A pool might begin with an institutional investor or insider who held a large block approaching a broker/dealer, who would then form and manage a syndicate to purchase and resell. The pool manager would find other dealers or traders willing to commit to bear the risk of a decline in the price before agreeing to purchase the block.

Most primary equity offerings of that era were rights offerings, sometimes underwritten on a standby basis. Some of the pools are selling groups formed in connection with these underwritings. Others were formed to distribute newly issued stock obtained from an issuer in transactions that did not trigger pre-emptive rights. The Senate committee regarded distribution syndicates and trading pools as functionally equivalent because distribution syndicates typically engaged in stabilization (Steiner and Lasdon 1934). In the committee's view, stabilization, which might involve active trading in the stock being distributed, was inherently manipulative.

Trading

Most of the pool agreements state simply that their purpose is to trade in a specified stock. It appears that the arrival of information about the company sometimes provided the motivation for trading. Contemporary observers like Huebner (1928) and Pratt (1921) state that pool participants sought out undervalued stocks and purchased them quietly in order to profit from a later price rise. NYSE President Richard Whitney, in his testimony, suggested that some pools were engaged in informed trading (US Senate 1932, 2219): "A group of individuals . . . feel that a stock or a security is selling at a price that is out of line, and they will go and buy that stock or that security up to a price where they think it is in line."

Some of the pools likely crossed the line a modern commentator would draw between informed trading and insider trading. Company insiders participated in some pools. Moreover, because bankers and brokers commonly sat on the boards of industrial companies, a brokerage house that operated a pool might have a partner on the company's board. At the time the pools operated, the line between (legal) informed trading and (illegal) insider trading was not settled. In any event, insider trading and manipulation are two different things, and Congress's concern about the pools had to do with manipulation. Moreover, a would-be informed trader tries to minimize the price impact of his trades, unlike a manipulator who tries to maximize it.

Other trading pools appear to have been market-making operations. In addition to specialists, floor traders who bought and sold actively for their own account provided liquidity on the NYSE. By pooling funds, stock exchange members could provide liquidity and spread risk more effectively. (This was, of course, long before NYSE members were permitted to incorporate and bring in outside capital.) The fact that pools often formed at times when an imbalance of orders was possible, such as after a stock split or stock dividend (when some of the recipients of the additional stock might choose to sell), is consistent with the hypothesis that those pools existed to provide liquidity. A commentator writing as "A New York Stock Exchange Broker" (1930, 298–99) explains that "[a] situation which obviously calls for pool operations occurs when a stock is split up. The same is true when the number of shares of a corporation is increased, or when a block of treasury stock is offered to the public" because "there [is] likely to be heavy [trading] of such stocks; obviously some kind of pool or trading account support is called for." The questionnaire responses make it clear that some pools were formed around the time of a stock split, stock dividend, recapitalization, or stock-for-stock acquisition. These pools were likely formed by floor traders to make a market in the newly listed shares.

Some pool operators who testified at the Pecora Hearings described their activities as market-making. They stated that the purpose of a particular pool was to provide "stability" or counteract an imbalance of orders. For example, Percy Rockefeller (US Senate 1932, 327) testified: "At that time the Air Reduction Co. was not a very active stock, and it had quite wide fluctuations, and we wanted to stabilize it. And of course we also hoped to make a profit in doing it." George F. Breen, when asked if he had been manipulating the market (560), answered, "I am trading in the market. I might be making quarters and half points in there." Similarly, George Whitney of J. P. Morgan described a market-making operation in common and preferred stocks that had previously traded together as a unit, but were then split into two separate issues (US Senate 1933, 509): "I think that we made the gross profit of 2 percent, which is an ordinary merchandizing profit."

Modern economists and lawyers have tended to overlook these less sinister accounts of stock pools and accept Congress's conclusion that pools were manipulative and therefore pernicious. Both Jarrow (1992) and Allen and Gale (1992) motivate models of trade-based manipulation with a discussion of the stock pools. In a discussion of accounting scandals of the early 2000s, Malkiel (2002) analogizes attempts to boost prices through earnings management to the 1920s pools. Loss and Seligman (1989) depict pools as successful manipulations.

These authors rely either directly or indirectly on the Fletcher Report's conclusions, but such reliance is questionable for two reasons. Congress and the Roosevelt administration had strong political reasons to conclude that the NYSE was corrupt and in need of federal supervision. In addition, the hearing transcripts provide substantial evidence that Congress badly misunderstood the mechanisms by which prices are set in a securities market.

Did Congress Understand the Pools?

The political dynamics and lack of financial expertise on display in the Pecora Hearings make the hearing transcripts surprisingly uninformative despite their length. Much of the testimony is a simple standoff, with the witness stating that his purpose was to make money and the questioners contending that if he was making money, he must have been cheating. Representative Fiorello LaGuardia, for example, testified at the hearings based on his own professed knowledge of manipulation, gathered from House hearings on LaGuardia's bill to regulate stock exchanges. He assured the senators that price rises were in themselves adequate evidence of manipulation (US Senate 1932, 463): "It is just like aviation. It is easy to come down. But you do need a motor to go up."

On the whole, the Senate committee displayed an understanding of capital markets that was no advance on the medieval attitudes described in chapter 1. The attention the committee paid to the par values of stocks, the book values of physical assets, and the past history of dividends suggests that committee members believed that those factors were the principal determinants of a company's value. Senator Peter Norbeck expressed irritation that Richard Whitney, the president of the NYSE, refused to endorse this view (US Senate 1932, 280): "But I thought you would admit that one stock that did not pay a dividend, but still getting way up . . . would almost in itself be proof of a pool support; but you won't admit that."

The most striking example of this misunderstanding was Congress's conclusion that movements in the price of Radio Corporation of America—the premier high-tech firm of the early twentieth century—must have been the result of manipulation. At the end of 1925, RCA's stock traded in the low 40s. The price steadily increased thereafter, reaching the mid-50s in late 1926 and the mid-90s in late 1927. It then increased sharply during 1928 to $397 at year's end. In March 1929, the stock split 4-for-1, its roughly $105 post-split price equivalent to $420 pre-split. Not surprisingly, RCA's stock price dropped during the Great Crash, reaching $50 at the end of October 1929. Like the rest of the market, RCA's price recovered partly in the first quarter of 1930 only to decline progressively as the Depression set in, trading below $10 per share during 1932.

The only explanation for the late 1920s price increases, in the view of the Senate Banking Committee, was manipulation. It reached this conclusion by noting that RCA had not acquired any new buildings or physical properties or paid any dividends during that period, but yet its stock had more than quadrupled in price. The price rise was attributed to several pools that operated in RCA stock, the last and best-documented in early 1929. Even the more sober study of the securities markets by the Twentieth Century Fund (1935, 475) describes the 1929 pool as a "spectacular" manipulation.

The conclusion is entirely unsupported by the facts. The 1929 RCA pool operated during the stock split and appears to have engaged in arbitrage between the old and new shares. The Senate Banking Committee compiled a list of the pool's trades. The pool did not engage in massive purchases followed by massive sales, but bought and sold on nearly every day of its brief operations. On average, RCA's stock price fell on days the pool was a net buyer and rose on days it was a net seller, exactly the opposite of Galbraith's description of the effects of a manipulative scheme.

More important, we hardly need a *deus ex machina* explanation for investors' enthusiasm for RCA stock in the late 1920s. During that period, RCA created a national radio broadcast network, the National Broadcasting Corporation, and began to deliver original content to millions of homes, generating revenue both from advertising and sales of new radio sets. RCA's technical expertise made it well placed to exploit the new and exciting technology of talking motion pictures, which began with Warner Brothers' release of *The Jazz Singer* in 1927. Shortly thereafter, RCA acquired a controlling interest in Joseph P. Kennedy's movie studio as well as some of Cecil B. De Mille's production and distribution operations, creating RKO Studios. RKO would produce some of the most successful films of the 1930s, including *King Kong* (1933) and a string of Astaire-Rogers musicals. RCA also acquired the Victor Talking Machine Company, which would produce the RCA-Victor phonograph. It undertook initial experiments in sending photographs by wireless transmission, helping set the stage for the development of television. It is hardly an exaggeration to say that RCA was to the 1920s what Apple was to the 2000s. But all of this was invisible to the Senate Banking Committee, which believed that only factories and machines were sources of value. By contrast, modern observers do not find it perplexing that Apple's stock price rose from the low 30s in 2005 to $200 in late 2009 before dropping to a low of $78 during the 2008–9 market break.

The committee members and their counsel also misunderstood the role of liquidity. They began from the assumption that there is a "natural" level of trading in a stock that is determined by the demands of long-term investors and results in a "natural" price. By contrast, trading by market intermediaries for their own account adds "artificial" demand and/or supply and necessarily results in an "artificial" price. The committee members did not appreciate that the willingness of securities dealers to trade for their own account could increase liquidity without increasing the volatility of prices. Instead, they insisted that any trading by intermediaries must take prices farther away from their "natural" level.

Given those assumptions, it is not surprising that the Senate was deeply hostile toward principal trading by stock exchange members. Like many contemporary commentators, committee members believed that the only appropriate activity for exchange members was acting as agents for customers. They accordingly singled out floor traders for particular criticism. Brokers' attempts to explain their trades as market-making operations therefore did not help their cause. Indeed, the committee and the press interpreted the term "market making" as indicating artificial market conditions (Flynn 1933).

The Fletcher Report's conclusion that pools engaged in fraud through fictitious trades also appears to have been prompted by the committee members' lack of understanding of the underlying concepts. As the following colloquies show, the questioners did not appreciate the distinction between a bona fide purchase followed rapidly by a bona fide sale, where real economic risk is borne for a short time, and a wash sale that transfers no risk at all (US Senate 1932, 277–78, 478; 1933, 2519):

THE CHAIRMAN: Is not the effect [of "churning"] just the same as a wash sale?

MR. WHITNEY: Mr. Chairman, I don't understand you. Churning, by its name, would seem to be buying and selling stock actively. . . .

THE CHAIRMAN: Is it not a fact that churning is a wash sale?

MR. WHITNEY: No, sir.

. . . .

MR. GRAY: Well, buying and selling on the same day is a wash-sale business, isn't it?

MR. BRAGG: No, sir.

. . . .

MR. PECORA: In the case of a trading account buying and selling the same kind of security at the same time, don't you recognize elements which make it similar in its influence on market prices to the wash sale?

MR. WIGGIN: Not at all, Mr. Pecora. Oh, no. One is real and genuine and the other is a fictitious sale.

Although I am only speculating, I suspect that some of the committee members were confused about the different usage of the term "wash sale" for stock exchange regulatory and tax purposes. In the wake of the 1929 crash, many investors would surely have wanted to realize tax losses by selling shares and buying them back soon thereafter. This would create a "wash sale" as it is defined for tax purposes, but would nevertheless constitute a bona fide sale and purchase from the standpoint of stock exchange regulation.

The evidence shows only that pools often bought and sold stock on the same day, and in some instances a pool was buying at the same time that one of its participants was selling, or vice versa. Given their belief that frequent trading by market professionals is inherently manipulative, this evidence seemed quite damning to the committee members, and the Fletcher Report (US Senate 1934, 37–38) complains that the NYSE's rules did not prohibit such trading.

Tests of Market Manipulation

The qualitative evidence suggests legitimate purposes for pools but cannot rule out the possibility that they drove the prices of the targeted stocks above their fundamental value. If so, examining the patterns of stock prices should enable us to identify potential manipulation after the fact. As noted by Pirrong (1995) and Easterbrook (1986), among others, successful manipulation should create a signature price pattern consisting of a sharp rise in price that is sustained for a brief period while the manipulator sells out, then an equally steep fall as investors realize that the initial price rise was the result of manipulation rather than information. By contrast, a price rise that results from information or improved liquidity should be persistent rather than temporary.

The Sample

I accordingly examine returns around the time of the formation of a pool. The Fletcher Report identifies 105 stocks that were the subject of pools during 1929. Of those, six are preferred stocks, one is a closed-end mutual fund, and one is the same as another stock on the list except for differing voting rights. I exclude these from the study. The National Archives contain written agreements relating to seventy-four of the remaining ninety-eight common stocks. Of that seventy-four, the data files of the Center for Research in Security Prices (CRSP) contain daily and monthly stock price data for fifty-five beginning no later than the month in which the pool operated. Those fifty-five stocks constitute my sample. Many of the stocks omitted because of the lack of price data appear to be initial public offerings or initial NYSE listings. They appear in the CRSP data a month or two after the pool was formed but not earlier. The absence of prices before the offering or listing unfortunately makes it impossible to determine what impact the pool had on prices for those stocks.

Although the Senate's questionnaire requested information on pools operating in 1929, several of the pools began during 1928. The pool operators may have included them in the questionnaire responses because those pools continued to operate in 1929 or they may simply have provided more information than requested. Table 6.1 identifies the fifty-five pool stocks and the dates of the pool agreements.

An initial question is whether these stocks have characteristics that would make them particularly good candidates for manipulative trading. Aggarwal and Wu (2006) and Maug (2002) find that manipulators select stocks that are relatively small, illiquid, and volatile. We therefore compare the stocks in table 6.1 to others in the same industries. For each stock in the sample, we create an industry-matched portfolio consisting of every stock in the CRSP data set with the same four-digit SIC code as the sample stock as of the month prior to the commencement of the relevant pool. For one pool stock there is no other company with the same four-digit SIC code, so we create a portfolio of companies with the same two-digit SIC code. We eliminate from the portfolios any stocks identified by the Senate's investigation as the subject of pools but that are not included in our sample. As measures of size we use market capitalization, book value of equity, and market-to-book ratio. For volatility we use the standard deviation of daily return, and for liquidity we use the percentage of trading days in which volume is zero.

Table 6.2 compares the pool and industry-matched portfolios just prior to pool formation. In the case of daily measures (return, turnover, and market capitalization), we calculate a sixty-day time-series average separately for each pool stock and matched portfolio and then calculate descriptive statistics for the cross-section of pools and portfolios. For volatility and liquidity measures, we make the appropriate time-series calculation separately for each stock in the control portfolios, calculate the portfolio average, and then average that measure over the fifty-five portfolios.

Unlike the manipulated stocks in Aggarwal and Wu's sample, the pool stocks are similar to the industry portfolios on size measures,

TABLE 6.1. **Pool stock sample**

Company Name	Pool Formation Date
Bush Terminal	1/17/1928
May Department Stores	1/17/1928
St. Louis & San Francisco R. R. Co.	3/9/1928
Simms Petroleum	3/31/1928
Curtis Aeroplane Co.	4/3/1928
Munsingwear	4/26/1928
South Porto Rico Sugar	5/15/1928
Cerro de Pasco	5/21/1928
Consolidated Cigar	6/4/1928
Pillsbury Flour Mills	6/16/1928
R. H. Macy & Co.	7/17/1928
Childs & Co.	8/18/1928
Continental Can Co.	8/30/1928
Kroger Grocery	10/30/1928
Underwood Elliott Fisher Co.	10/30/1928
American Sugar Refining Co.	11/8/1928
Weber & Heilbroner	11/15/1928
National Dairy Co.	11/19/1928
Mid Continental Petroleum Co.	11/21/1928
Congress Cigar Co.	12/3/1928
R. J. Reynolds Tobacco Co.	12/12/1928
General Cigar Co.	12/17/1928
Lehn & Fink Products	12/21/1928
Cluett Peabody Co.	12/27/1928
Marmon Motor Co.	1/14/1929
Studebaker	1/14/1929
Borden Co.	1/18/1929
Gotham Silk Hosiery	1/30/1929
Gimbel Brothers	2/2/1929
Miami Copper	2/5/1929
General Cable	2/15/1929
Packard Motor Co.	2/15/1929
General Refractories	2/27/1929
Walworth Co.	2/27/1929
Radio Corporation of America	3/7/1929
Bethlehem Steel	3/15/1929
Standard Oil of California	3/15/1929
Purity Bakeries	3/26/1929
Oppenheim Collins Co.	4/12/1929
International Telephone & Telegraph	5/2/1929
A. G. Spalding & Brothers	5/8/1929
Murray Corporation of America	5/26/1929
Pittsburgh & West Virginia R.R.	5/27/1929
Spang Chalfante Co.	7/9/1929
Gold Dust Corp.	7/10/1929
American Ice	8/8/1929
Telautograph	8/12/1929
General American Tank Car Co.	8/20/1929
Campbell Wyant Foundry Co.	8/21/1929
American Commercial Alcohol	8/30/1929
Archer Daniels Midland Corp.	8/30/1929
L.A. Young Spring & Wire Corp.	9/10/1929
Missouri, Kansas & Texas R.R.	9/26/1929
Chrysler Co.	10/17/1929
Columbia Carbon Co.	10/30/1929

Note: The list of pool stocks is from the US Senate, Committee on Banking and Currency (1932–34) (also known as the Pecora Hearings), pt. 17, p. 7949. The formation dates are obtained from the records of the investigation contained in the National Archives.

TABLE 6.2. **Pool stocks and industry-matched portfolios prior to pool formation**

	Pool Stocks	Control Portfolios
Daily return (%)	.081	.151
	(.330)	(.202)
Daily turnover (%)	.767	.841
	(.774)	(.580)
Market capitalization ($ millions)	94.3	92.7
	(156.6)	(184.1)
Book value of equity ($ millions)	48.9	59.1
	(88.5)	(137.5)
Market-to-book ratio	2.43	2.19
	(2.39)	(1.35)
Standard deviation of daily return (%)	2.20*	1.85
	(.891)	(.903)
Trading days with no transactions (%)	6.18**	18.7
	(14.6)	(16.6)

* Pool and control stock portfolio means are different at the 5% level
** Pool and control stock portfolio means are different at the 1% level

although they have slightly higher market-to-book ratios. Interestingly, the pool stocks are more liquid than the average stock in the matching portfolios to a statistically and economically significant extent. The pool stocks, on average, fail to trade on 6.2 percent of the sixty pre-pool trading days, compared to 18.7 percent for the stocks in the control portfolios. This is notable in light of Maug's (2002) conclusion that informed trading is more profitable for more liquid stocks and provides additional reason to suspect that at least some pools were engaged in information-motivated trading. The pool stocks are more volatile on average than the stocks in the control portfolios, which would be conducive to manipulative trading.

Abnormal Returns during Pool Operations

For each of the 55 stocks, I retrieve daily returns for each day from −5 to +50 in event time (with day zero the date of the pool agreement). I subtract the return on the CRSP equally weighted portfolio to generate an abnormal return. (The results are robust to using different methods of calculating expected return, including using the return on the control portfolios or using a market- and risk-adjusted model.) Finally, I average abnormal returns across firms for each event date and cumulate the average abnormal returns beginning on day −5. The resulting cumulative average abnormal returns (CAARs) are plotted by day in figure 6.1.

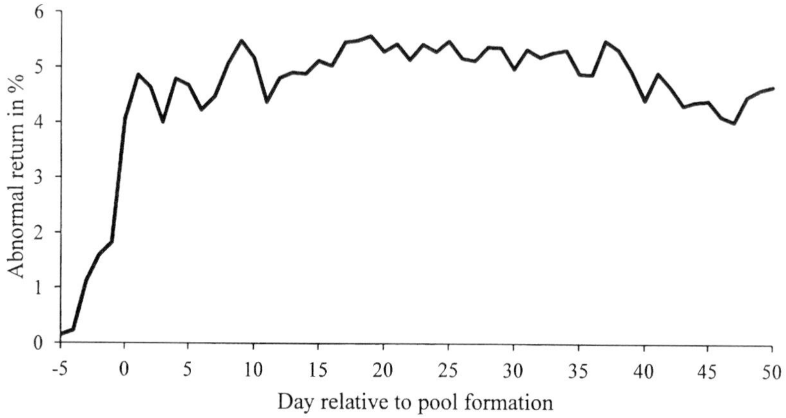

FIGURE 6.1 Cumulative average abnormal returns (CAARs) around the time of pool formation for a sample of 55 stocks (from table 6.1). Day zero is the day on which the pool agreement was signed.

Figure 6.1 shows a sharp increase in market-adjusted return around the time of signing a pool agreement but no subsequent decline. The same pattern holds if we look at monthly returns over a longer time frame. In the month of pool formation, the average pool stock in the sample outperforms the CRSP equally weighted index by 6.4 percent, with a cross-sectional standard deviation of 12.1 percent. The 95 percent confidence interval for the population mean is [4.7%, 8.0%]. Forty-one of the sample stocks (75%) have a positive market-adjusted return in month zero. Over the succeeding twelve months, the mean compounded market-adjusted return for the pool stocks in the sample is −1.5 percent, with a cross-sectional standard deviation of 27.0 percent. The 95 percent confidence interval for the population mean is [−5.1%, 2.1%]. Twenty-five (45%) of the fifty-five pool stocks have a negative market-adjusted compound return over the year following the formation of the pool. In sum, the evidence from stock returns for the fifty-five pool stocks in the sample shows a sharp increase in value around the time of pool formation that is not reversed over the following year. This pattern is inconsistent with manipulation, although it is consistent with informed trading. As discussed above, in the legal environment of the 1930s "informed" trading could include what would today be considered "insider" trading.

I also use a nonparametric runs test to look for evidence of manipulation in individual pool stocks. If the classic pool description is true, we should observe several days of persistently positive returns followed by several days of persistently negative returns, representing the "pump and dump" cycle. We can accordingly ask whether the time series of returns on individual pool stocks exhibits runs (that is, strings of abnormal returns of the same sign) that are longer than expected. If a given pool stock has x days of positive abnormal returns and $(50 - x)$ days of negative abnormal returns during a 50-day period beginning with the pool commencement date and those positive and negative returns are randomly ordered, the expected number of runs, R, for that period is $1 + (2x(50 - x)/50)$. If there is a string of positive returns and a string of negative returns as hypothesized, the observed number of runs over 50 days should be less than the predicted amount. I calculate the expected and actual values of R for each of the pool stocks during the 50-day period beginning with the commencement of the pool. On average, the observed number of runs (27.3) is greater, not less, than the expected number (25.5). Again we fail to observe evidence of manipulation where we would expect to see it.

Abnormal Turnover during Pool Operations

With a small number of exceptions, the Senate's investigators did not gather comprehensive information about the pools' trades. We therefore attempt to infer when the pools were trading by looking at abnormal turnover. We define *turnover* as trading volume divided by shares outstanding. We create an equally weighted index of turnover for all NYSE stocks and define abnormal turnover for stock i on date t as the difference between stock i's turnover on date t and the index for date t.

Inferring the pools' trades from turnover could cause us to overestimate their influence. In some cases, an exogenous event such as a merger rumor may have attracted a pool and simultaneously generated increased trading outside the pool. We assume that the pools either traded on information or to manipulate prices. If the latter, we would expect to find two periods of large abnormal turnover—one during the "pump" phase when the pool buys aggressively and a second during the "dump" phase when the pool sells its holdings to unsophisticated investors, who then learn that the stock is overvalued.

Figure 6.2 shows abnormal turnover, averaged across the pool stocks, for each day from −5 to +50 in event time, with day zero again being the day on which the pool agreement was signed. We observe a sharp increase in trading immediately upon formation of the pool but no subsequent

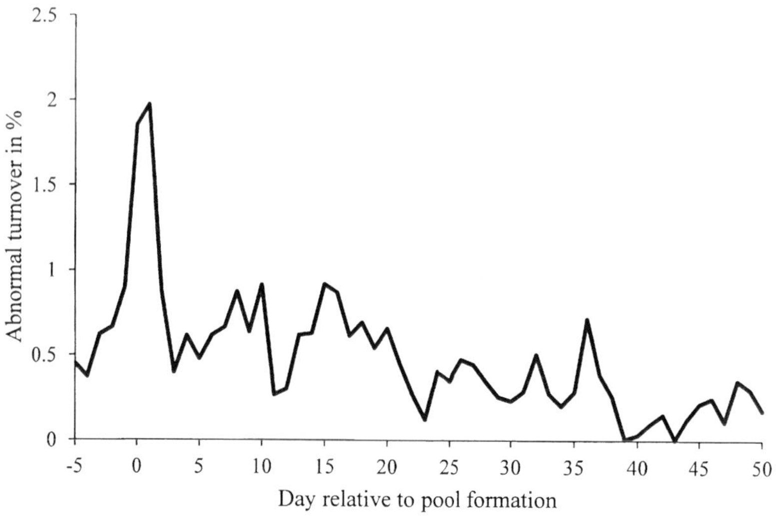

FIGURE 6.2 Abnormal turnover (trading volume divided by shares outstanding) for a sample of 55 pool stocks (from table 6.1) around the time of pool formation. Day zero is the day on which the pool agreement was signed.

period of high abnormal turnover. This result suggests that the pool's trading was concentrated in the first few days of the pool. Because (returning to figure 6.1) we do not see a price fall after those first few days, the pattern is inconsistent with trade-based manipulation but entirely consistent with informed trading.

The design of the federal regulatory scheme for secondary securities markets reflects the view of the 73rd Congress and the Roosevelt administration that manipulation was rampant on the organized exchanges in the late 1920s—a claim echoed by generations of commentators. The evidence for that proposition consists almost entirely of the existence of stock pools. There has been little examination of the canonical claim that pools caused prices to rise and fall by massive purchases and the dissemination of false information.

The evidence in this chapter refutes that claim. Stocks traded by pools do indeed rise in price but do not subsequently fall. This pattern is consistent with informed trading but not with manipulation. Congress had information available to it that would have provided a more complete picture of the pools but chose to ignore it in order to pursue its political objectives. Thus the antimanipulation provisions of the Securities Exchange Act neatly fit this book's claims about the actual purposes of securities regulation. Having decided to use the Great Crash as an excuse for comprehensive regulation of the NYSE, Congress reverse-engineered a market failure narrative to justify the statutory provisions. The facts, however, are sharply at odds with the narrative.

CHAPTER SEVEN

Regulation of Specific Industries

Substantial parts of the Depression-era reforms reflected a desire not to let a good crisis go to waste. Reformers and regulated industries saw in the new political dynamics of the 1930s an opportunity to gain territory that had been denied them in the past. This chapter discusses the two most significant securities reforms after the Exchange Act, the Public Utility Holding Company Act of 1935 (PUHCA) and the Investment Company Act of 1940 (ICA).

PUHCA: Faulty Diagnosis, Faulty Cure

One of Franklin Roosevelt's most creative political achievements was to increase the federal government's role in public utility regulation.[1] States regulated local utility systems and jealously guarded their jurisdiction. Roosevelt argued that through ownership and underwriting of utility securities, Wall Street harmed both utility investors and customers. Therefore, the financing and corporate structure of the utility industry was a proper topic for securities regulation, which was an accepted area of federal responsibility by 1935. Roosevelt was aided by John Bonbright, a Columbia finance professor and policy entrepreneur who made the key conceptual arguments in published writings and as a member of a commission to study utility regulation that FDR created during his time as governor of New York.

Electricity rates were a political issue from the end of World War I to the late 1920s, during which electrical service evolved from a luxury to an expectation in urban areas. Statutes typically called for a public service commission to set rates at a "reasonable" level providing no more than a "fair" rate of return on invested capital. Utility managers argued that this "fair" return should be based on the opportunity cost, or market value, of utility assets, while consumer advocates argued that value should be measured by historical cost (Bauer 1930). The difference mattered because of the substantial post–World War I inflation and the 1920s real estate boom. State utility commissions became referees between utility companies arguing for a market-value rate base and consumer advocates arguing for a lower, historical-cost rate base.

In 1929, then-Governor Roosevelt appointed a commission to study utility regulation. The commission's report (Knight 1930) recommended a middle course between historical cost and market value. It suggested permitting a one-time catch-up in valuation: existing facilities should be appraised and their 1930 market values used thereafter for ratemaking purposes. All subsequently acquired assets should be valued at cost for as long as they remained in service. This was known as the "Bonbright Plan" after its primary proponent.

During the 1932 campaign, Roosevelt took up the cause of basing rate regulation on historical, out-of-pocket cost rather than current market values. There were many acquisitions of utility companies as the industry consolidated, making current market values observable to the public. Not surprisingly, the purchase price of an operating utility was often well in excess of the historical cost of its real estate and physical plant. Roosevelt either confused or pretended to confuse symptom and cause: He argued vigorously that the purchase of operating companies by holding companies drove market values, and therefore rates, higher.

Roosevelt took his script from Bonbright and Means (1932). They condemned utility holding companies for "watering" stock and "writing up" valuations. As discussed in other chapters, these sinister-sounding expressions referred to carrying an asset on a balance sheet at its market value rather than historical cost. In the utility context, the issue became one of acquisition accounting; critics believed that purchasers should value assets for balance sheet purposes at the seller's cost rather than the buyer's purchase price. In the hands of politicians, the accounting question became a substantive criticism—they argued that utility holding companies that acquired operating companies in return for holding company stock had overpaid, to the detriment of holding company shareholders and operating company customers. While the economic substance of the argument was not entirely clear, critics seemed to argue that paying more than book value for an asset was improper. Roosevelt used these themes to bludgeon utility holding companies on the campaign trail. In a September 1932 campaign speech, he argued that because utility holding companies had overpaid for the operating companies in their portfolios, "the people of the United States were called upon to supply profits upon this amount of watered stock. It means that someone was deriving profits from the capitalization into which he had put no substantial capital himself. It means that people had to pay these unjust profits through higher rates."[2] The theme was doubly useful to Roosevelt because it allowed him to remind voters that President Hoover supported state rather than federal regulation of the utility industry.

Roosevelt, following Bonbright and Means, argued that when holding companies issued "watered" stock in connection with acquisitions, they harmed investors and utility customers simultaneously. Having brought investors into the picture, FDR would later claim that the structure, financial policies, and securities issuances of holding companies should be within the control of the newly created SEC. PUHCA achieved that objective. The statute did not merely regulate holding companies' security issues, but also limited them to owning a single, geographically contiguous operating system and prohibited more than a single holding company tier atop any operating company. Over a roughly twenty-year period from its enactment, PUHCA led to a dramatic reorganization of the utility industry, including the complete elimination of pyramid structures, or multiple layers of holding companies.

This raises a simple question that we can answer with available data: did holding companies harm investors? The argument that they did so by paying market prices rather than historical costs for their portfolio companies is too economically naïve to warrant further discussion. However, we can reframe Bonbright's and FDR's arguments in more analytically satisfying terms by tying them to recent work on whether companies with controlling shareholders are worth more or less than those with fully dispersed ownership. The analysis in this chapter will show that the holding companies added value to their subsidiaries, contrary to one of the central claims FDR made on the campaign trail and during the legislative process.

Theoretical Background

A controlling shareholder can be good or bad for the remaining shareholders. Equity ownership aligns a controller's interests with those of the other shareholders, leading it to monitor management (Jensen and Meckling 1976). A controlling shareholder can also add value by reducing financing costs, adding managerial or technical expertise, or providing political connections (Gertner, Scharfstein, and Stein 1994). But the controller may also use its control to channel the subsidiary's cash flows or assets to itself at the expense of other shareholders (Shleifer and Vishny 1997; Djankov et al. 2008).

Evidence on the association between ownership concentration and firm value is accordingly mixed. Some studies find a nonlinear relation between ownership concentration and corporate valuation or performance, while others find no connection or one that depends on the type of controlling shareholder (Demsetz and Lehn 1985; Holderness and Sheehan 1988; Morck, Shleifer, and Vishny 1988; McConnell and Servaes 1990). Gul, Kim, and Qiu (2010) similarly find that the availability of firm-specific information, as proxied by stock price synchronicity, has a nonlinear relation to ownership concentration.

Pyramid structures consisting of multiple layers of holding companies pose a particular risk to noncontrolling shareholders because they permit controlling shareholders to amass votes substantially in excess of cash-flow rights (Morck 2009). Claessens et al. (2002) argue that the positive incentive effects of concentrated ownership are a function of the controller's cash-flow rights while the negative effects are a function of voting rights. They find that increased cash-flow rights of controlling shareholders are associated with higher valuations in a sample of East Asian companies, while increased voting rights are associated with lower valuations. Edwards and Weichenrieder (2004) obtain similar results for a sample of German firms. Faccio, Lang, and Young (2001) find that the misappropriation problem is particularly acute for firms in which the ultimate controller has less than a 20 percent economic stake. Attig et al. (2006) find that a gap between control and cash-flow rights is associated with lower liquidity for the remaining shares.

In order to assess whether utility holding companies extracted value from or added value to their subsidiaries, I study returns of publicly traded holding companies and the publicly traded stock of their partly owned subsidiaries around the time of key events surrounding PUHCA's enactment. I find that both parents and subsidiaries reacted negatively (positively) to events implying a higher (lower) probability that holding companies would be abolished. This implies that being a member of a holding company group was beneficial to lower-tier companies and their shareholders and the prospect of dissolving the group was viewed as bad news.

The result suggests that an entire pyramid structure was worth more than the sum of its parts. The prior literature on utility pyramids suggests several different ways in which the holding companies could have added value. Hyman (1985) emphasizes financing. Individual operating utilities were too small to access financial markets efficiently, but the larger holding companies could raise capital and provide it to subsidiaries. In a similar vein, Schrade and Walls (2008) argue that holding companies reduced financing costs by providing liquidity to utility shares. Bonbright and Means (1932) note that some holding companies provided specialized engineering and construction services to their subsidiaries.

An alternative view is that the holding companies served primarily to help their subsidiaries evade rate regulation and thereby extract wealth from consumers. Under this view, the holding companies sold services at inflated prices to their operating subsidiaries (Bonbright and Means 1932). Coupled with opaque financial accounting and corporate structures, this practice enabled subsidiaries to report artificially inflated operating costs to state regulatory commissions, resulting in higher utility rates to consumers. In this view, the holding companies provided value only through regulatory evasion and the resulting gains were pure transfers from consumers.

There is good reason, however, to doubt that holding companies existed primarily, or even substantially, to inflate the rate base. Kandel et al. (2013, 23) show that a modest portion of a typical operating company's inputs consisted of the output of related companies. They conclude that the use of intragroup transactions to inflate the rate base "is unlikely to have been the main driver for the existence of groups in the United States in the 1930s."

We can try to confirm this by exploiting the fact that the intensity of regulation differed from state to state. I show that PUHCA decreased the value of even the less-regulated systems. In those systems, there was less value to be added by evading rate regulation. The result that these systems too fell in value, and by similar amounts, around the time of important legislative events suggests that the holding companies provided some benefits apart from regulatory evasion. Those benefits were presumably in the form of financial, managerial, or operating efficiencies. I consider other possible explanations, such as investor concern over fire sales of operating subsidiaries, but argue that they are likely less important reasons for the declines in value.

Utility Pyramids

Early utility companies in the United States served individual municipalities or neighborhoods pursuant to a franchise agreement with the municipal government (Priest 1993; Troesken 2006). In the early twentieth century, those franchise agreements were replaced with more detailed municipal-level regulation, and then ultimately by state-level regulation by public utility commissions (Neufeld 2008).

As the utility industry grew, local systems consolidated. However, they faced significant legal and regulatory impediments in doing so. These restrictions often made it too costly to merge two operating companies with one another or into a third company (Bonbright and Means 1932). Thus, the simplest way to control multiple operating companies was for a single holding company to purchase control blocks in each operating company. In other cases, cash-strapped operating companies paid equipment vendors with their own stock and the vendors ultimately acquired control (Schrade and Walls 2008). The holding companies, then, came about through the acquisition of stock in existing operating companies. Kandel et al. (2013) document two waves of consolidation, one at the close of the nineteenth century and another in the late 1920s.

Early holding companies, in turn, were often acquired by larger companies as the industry consolidated geographically. The "super" holding companies at the top of the pyramids often managed construction and financing of new plants for their operating properties and provided centralized management. Some of these holding companies were in turn controlled by construction companies or investment banks. The resulting consolidation, achieved primarily over a twenty-year span, was dramatic. By 1930, the ten largest holding company systems generated approximately 75 percent of the electrical power sold by utilities (Bonbright and Means 1932).

With a few exceptions, the utility pyramids were controlled by firms, not families. The Insull utility group, controlled by Samuel Insull, was a prominent exception. There were often several layers of holding companies between the ultimate controller and the operating companies at the base. The holding company at the top of the pyramid typically had varied levels of cash-flow rights among the subsidiary companies. However, unlike modern-day business groups in some developed and many developing countries, the utility pyramids did not achieve substantial separation between cash-flow rights and control rights. On average, each parent company owned more than half of the equity in its subsidiary companies (Bonbright and Means 1932; Kandel et al. 2013). However, except for the operating companies at the bottom of the pyramid, lower-tier companies often had some amount of stock publicly traded. The utility pyramids were also undiversified, focusing almost entirely on public utilities (electricity, gas, water, and local transportation service).

Group structures may reduce financing costs by raising large sums through substantial debt or equity sales rather than through multiple small offerings. They can also operate an internal capital market. Gopalan, Nanda, and Seru (2007) find that Indian business groups transfer capital to member firms that are in financial difficulty in order to avoid a reputational loss associated with the failure of a group member.

Some commentators therefore see the utility pyramids as a reaction to the industry's massive capital and technical needs. Local utilities were often too small to attract individually the attention of financial intermediaries, but regulatory restrictions made it difficult for them to combine through mergers. A large holding company, by contrast, could borrow large sums at a lower rate than could its individual operating companies (Hausman and Neufeld 2002).

Holding companies provided services to their subsidiaries in addition to financing. Some provided engineering and technical expertise. Still others provided general management services such as accounting, cash management, purchasing, and insurance (Buchanan 1933).

As noted above, however, controlling shareholders can also be detrimental to shareholders. The modern literature focuses on "tunneling," or the use by controlling shareholders of transfer pricing and intragroup loans, guarantees, and asset transfers to exploit other shareholders (Johnson et al. 2000). The problem can be particularly severe in legal systems that lack effective shareholder protections. Jiang, Lee, and Yue (2010) find that controlling shareholders in China use intragroup loans to extract cash from controlled companies. Bertrand, Mehta, and Mullainathan (2002) find strong evidence of tunneling in Indian business groups.

Although holding company critics of the 1930s focused primarily on purported harms to utility customers, they also argued that holding companies were detrimental to shareholders. Their arguments are broadly similar to modern discussions of tunneling (Kandel et al. 2013). They of course used a different vocabulary, arguing that holding companies "defrauded" shareholders (Ripley 1927). As previously noted, they also argued that holding companies issued "watered" stock and revalued assets above their true, or historical-cost, value. To the extent these arguments have any economic substance, it relates to the possibility of tunneling. A controlling shareholder could, for example, overvalue the property and services it contributed to a subsidiary in return for stock, thus obtaining stock at a favorable price in comparison to public shareholders.

Whether the utility pyramids were beneficial to shareholders depends on whether the structure created value and on how that value was distributed among the various tiers. Whether they were *socially* beneficial also depends on whether any value created for shareholders came from efficiencies in financing, management, or operations or was simply a wealth transfer from utility customers.

The Public Utility Holding Company Act of 1935

Critical commentary on utility holding companies began to appear in the popular press by the late 1920s. Articles in the legal literature called for regulation of holding companies or analyzed the feasibility of applying existing public utility regulation to them (Lilienthal 1929). In 1928 the US Senate ordered the Federal Trade Commission to investigate utility holding companies. The investigation lasted until 1935 and generated a report of more than eighty volumes.

The scrutiny and criticism became more intense in the wake of the 1929 market crash, which hit highly leveraged holding companies particularly hard. The Insull utility group, one of the country's largest, was unable to meet its obligations. Its creditors forced it into bankruptcy in 1932, triggering a political reaction similar to Enron's collapse seventy years later. Samuel Insull himself fled the country facing criminal charges of mail fraud, embezzlement, and larceny, of which he was eventually acquitted.

Franklin Roosevelt cited Insull as a symbol of financial fraud during his 1932 campaign. The Democratic platform called for holding company regulation. During the initial months of his presidency, however, Roosevelt chose to make the market for new security issues the focus of financial regulation. The president and his advisers had already determined the basic thrust of the regulatory regime for new issues—mandatory disclosure of basic information about the issuer and the underwriting arrangements—and had a model at hand in the English Companies Act, as described in chapter 3. After enactment of the Securities Act in mid-1933, Roosevelt turned to the task of regulating the stock exchanges, leading to the enactment of the Securities Exchange Act of 1934. Attention then shifted to utility holding companies.

In July 1934 Roosevelt established a National Power Policy Committee to study the public utility industry and propose legislation. Political and market commentators were unsure whether the legislation would seek to regulate or destroy holding companies. The uncertainty persisted up to the introduction of the administration's bill on February 6, 1935. The bill, which major newspapers summarized in detail on February 7, required utility holding companies to register with the SEC and gave the SEC regulatory authority over their financings, acquisitions, and dispositions. The bill also, however, contained what was soon nicknamed the "death sentence" provision, section 11. This gave the SEC the authority, beginning in 1938, to require holding companies to divest any securities and property necessary to reorganize the utility industry into geographically compact systems. After January 1, 1940, the SEC was directed to make every registered holding company engage in such dispositions, reorganizations, or dissolutions as necessary to make it "cease to be a holding company." Section 11 was even more severe than suggested reforms that would have prohibited more than a single layer of holding companies. Section 11 banned *all* holding companies.

Both the *New York Times* and the *Washington Post* referred to the bill as "drastic." It was immediately controversial. Utility CEOs argued that the bill was both unconstitutional and potentially disastrous to investors. The press reported concerns that the bill, if enacted, would force holding companies into fire-sale divestitures of operating companies, causing substantial losses to the holding companies' public investors. Supporters argued that those claims were overblown in light of the fact that the divestitures were not to begin until 1940. However, on March 3, Eugene Lokey reported in the *New York Times* that the bill had provoked "the greatest volume of criticism and objection evoked by any proposed legislation in recent years."

In the House, the bill was assigned to a subcommittee of the Interstate Commerce Committee. Testimony before the subcommittee, including by a commissioner of the SEC, was often skeptical of the death sentence provision. On April 23, the *New York Times* published an article entitled "Utility Companies Show House Gains," reporting that an "informal" vote of the subcommittee the prior day favored removing the death sentence provision by a 14–11 margin. The subcommittee was ultimately unable to report either favorably or unfavorably to the full committee.

The Senate Commerce Committee was also closely divided on the death sentence provision. According to press reports, on May 7 an informal poll of the subcommittee favored removing the death sentence by a 9–6 margin. However, the next day an actual vote to delete the provision failed and the committee adopted a compromise amendment delaying the termination of holding companies from 1940 to 1942.

On June 7, the *New York Times* reported that "informed" sources acknowledged the Roosevelt administration was prepared to compromise on the death sentence provision in the face of "growing opposition" in Congress. On the same day, a column by the *Times*' Washington correspondent Arthur Krock opined that it "seems certain that important modifications" would be made to the bill. Senator Burton Wheeler, however, continued to insist on the death sentence provision, claiming to have received a letter from the president urging passage of the bill with section 11 intact. On June 11, the Senate passed the amended bill including section 11 by a 45–44 vote. The next day, newspapers reported that the Senate action had halted a rally in holding company stocks.

On June 17 the House subcommittee approved the deletion of the death sentence provision and "knowledgeable sources" told the press that the full Interstate Commerce Committee would concur. Newspaper reports suggested that only when the bill went to conference would the issue of the death sentence be resolved. A motion was made on the House floor to reinstate section 11. On July 1 the full House voted to reject the motion, thereby assuring that the bill would pass the House, if at all, without the death sentence. Arthur Krock's July 2 column in the *Times* called the vote a "major defeat" for the president.

By mid-July, the bill went to a House-Senate conference to reconcile the different versions. SEC chairman Joseph Kennedy urged the Senate Commerce Committee to accept the House version. Press accounts, including a July 7 article in the *Washington Post*, stated that fears of declines in utility stock and bond values were behind the House's unusual willingness to defy Roosevelt.

The administration, however, took advantage of the lull leading up to the conference to make its case that opposition to the death sentence provision was actually the work of utility company lobbying. The House Rules Committee announced an investigation of lobbying by the utility industry. In mid-July, its investigation uncovered evidence that a utility executive in Pennsylvania had sent hundreds of telegrams to members of Congress ostensibly in the name of Pennsylvania residents.

This overreaching affected sentiment in Congress. For several days in late July, the Senate heard testimony from residents of York, Pennsylvania, whose names had appeared on telegrams without their knowledge and from employees of the local Western Union office who had transmitted the telegrams at the utility executive's request. Although the Pennsylvania incident may have been isolated, it supported the administration's longstanding position that opposition to its bill was contrived. Turner Catledge opined in a *Times* article on July 28 that the lobbying inquiry had strengthened the president's hand, making passage of the death sentence provision more likely.

On August 1 Representative Sam Rayburn moved to instruct the House conferees to acquiesce in the death sentence provision of the Senate bill. According to press reports, the administration believed that the House would change its stance because of the lobbying revelations. Rayburn and the administration, however, miscalculated; the House voted against the attempt. By mid-August, with the conference committee deadlocked, both legislators and commentators suggested that the bill would have to be held over until the next session.

Finally, in a meeting at the White House on Sunday, August 18, Senator Alben Barkley suggested the compromise language that ultimately resolved the differences among the House, Senate, and administration. The compromise provision permitted only one tier of holding company atop any operating company and required that all of the operating companies under a given holding company be either physically interconnected or capable of such interconnection. The provision also gave the SEC the authority to grant exemptions from this "single integrated system" requirement on a case-by-case basis.

On August 22 the president informed Rayburn of his willingness to accept the compromise and the House approved it. The text of the revised section 11 was reprinted in full in the *New York Times* on August 23. After the close of that day's trading, the conference committee approved the compromise. Passage by the full House and Senate followed on Saturday, August 24, and on Monday, August 26, the president signed PUHCA into law.

Almost immediately, the electric utility industry association brought a test case in federal district court in Baltimore challenging the constitutionality of the statute (Seligman 2003). On November 7, 1935, the district court found that PUHCA exceeded Congress's powers under the federal constitution and declared it "void in its entirety." Although I include the November 7 decision as an event below, two factors likely muted the market reaction to the decision. First, comments from the bench and rulings on preliminary motions led observers to predict that the court would declare the statute unconstitutional, so the November 7 ruling was not wholly unanticipated. In addition, lawyers must surely have believed that the Supreme Court would ultimately decide the act's constitutionality, so the district court ruling was only the first step in a lengthy legal process. In 1938 the Supreme Court upheld the act's registration provisions. In 1946 it found constitutional the geographic integration provisions of section 11(b)(1) and by implication the entirety of the reorganization provisions of section 11.

As this brief history demonstrates, there are several dates on which traders would almost certainly have revised up or down their estimates of the likelihood that holding companies would have to relinquish control of their subsidiaries. I observe returns on both controlling and subsidiary companies on those dates as described in the next section.

One might question whether a breakup of the pyramids that was not even scheduled to begin for several years and was likely to be the subject of court challenges could have a substantial impact on firm values. However, some commentators (and presumably some investors) believed that consolidation in the utility industry was far from over absent legislative action. They anticipated an eventual nationwide monopoly along the lines of the American Telephone and Telegraph system.[3] To the extent that stock prices reflected the expectation of additional consolidation, PUHCA's enactment would have changed those expectations and thereby affected prices.

Study Design

DATA. I begin by identifying every company in the public utility industry (SIC two-digit code 49) in the CRSP data files as of January 1, 1935, a total of twenty-three companies. One of these is a foreign holding company cross-listed on the NYSE, which I omit from the sample because it is doubtful that courts would have given extraterritorial effect to the "death sentence" provision.[4] Another is omitted because it was exclusively in the water utility business and PUHCA affected only electric and gas utilities. Bonbright and Means (1932) identify two other utility holding companies (United Corp. and Stone & Webster) that have two-digit SIC codes other than 49, and I add those to the sample, for a total of twenty-three NYSE-listed companies. To increase the sample size, I also hand-gather return data for an additional fifteen utility companies traded on the New York Curb Exchange. I identify utility companies traded on the Curb based on company names and check that they are listed in the Moody's Public Utilities manual. I omit companies for which return data are unavailable for more than 50 of the 250 days in the estimation period. The final sample consists of thirty-eight utility companies.

Almost all of the sample firms are holding companies rather than operating companies. Very few bottom-tier operating companies had a sufficient public float to be listed on the NYSE or the Curb. Indeed, most of the operating companies were wholly owned or nearly wholly owned by an intermediate-tier holding company. Those intermediate holding companies therefore serve as convenient proxies for their wholly owned operating subsidiaries.

I divide the sample into three categories, consisting of potential "predators," potential "prey," and companies that are neither. I define as predators companies that own a controlling stake, but less than 95 percent, of the common stock of one or more subsidiary companies, as described more fully below. The logic behind the definition is that there is no gain to be had from looting a wholly owned or almost wholly owned subsidiary. The parent could try to extract wealth from bondholders or other contractual creditors, but creditors can protect themselves through their contracts. Potential prey are companies controlled but less than 95 percent owned by a predator.

Some holding companies, primarily large urban public utility systems like Brooklyn Union Gas and Southern California Edison, meet neither definition—they are not controlled by a holding company and their subsidiaries, if any, are wholly owned. Such companies might be pyramids as a structural matter but their subsidiaries did not have public shareholders who could be exploited. The structure could, however, have existed to obscure operating costs and thereby evade rate regulation.

Because of the complex nature of some of the holding company pyramids, these categorizations involve some arbitrary cutoffs. The most obvious is the 95 percent cutoff identified above. Many subsidiaries were almost, but not quite, 100 percent owned. This was often a consequence of state corporate laws that required directors to hold a minimum number of "qualifying shares" of the company. In other cases, at the time of acquisition, the acquirer or target was barred by state law or by bond covenants from engaging in a merger, with the result that the acquirer could only buy shares from willing sellers. Thus, I treat ownership of 95 percent or more of a subsidiary's common stock as functionally equivalent to entire ownership. In addition, some holding companies owned 95 percent or more of nearly all of their subsidiaries, but had a handful of very small partly owned subsidiaries. In many instances, these partly owned subsidiaries were too small to be a realistic source of rents for the holding company. To be categorized as a predator, I therefore require that a holding company have partly owned subsidiaries that constitute in the aggregate at least 10 percent, by book value, of the parent company's consolidated assets. Finally, I define "control" of a company as (1) ownership of more than 10 percent of the company's common stock and (2) being the single largest shareholder. I use Moody's Investors Service (1935), supplemented by Bonbright and Means (1932) and the FTC Utility Report to classify companies. As an additional check, I obtain the names of the directors of all the sample companies from Moody's. All of the "predator" companies in my sample have director overlaps with their "prey."

Some of the holding companies identified as having no parent company were more than 10 percent owned by an investment company. In the pre-SEC era, investment companies could own a large stake in a portfolio company. However, judging from the contemporary and modern literature (Morley 2012), these investment companies were passive investors and therefore not likely "predators," and I do not include them in the sample. I can identify passive investment companies because they are listed only in Moody's Banking and Finance manual and not the Public Utility manual.

Finally, some companies are both "predator" and "prey." They have a holding company that meets the "predator" definition and subsidiaries that meet the "prey" definition. I describe for each test below how those companies are treated.

Figure 7.1 illustrates the categorizations just described by showing the ownership pattern of an important holding company system, the United Corporation system, in 1935. United was formed by J. P. Morgan & Co., its affiliate Drexel & Co., and its ally Bonbright & Co. in 1929 to acquire control of smaller utility holding company systems. In the diagram, United Corp. is a predator only. Although Morgan interests organized it and underwrote all of its securities issues, United Corp. was widely held and the investment banks did not own a control block.

United's partly owned subsidiaries Columbia Gas & Electric Co., Niagara Hudson Power Co., and Public Service Corp. of New Jersey are prey only. They are controlled but less than 95 percent owned by United (including indirect ownership in the case of Public Service Corp.). All of their subsidiaries are either 95 percent owned or too small to constitute a plausible source of rents. United Gas Improvement Corp. (UGI) is both

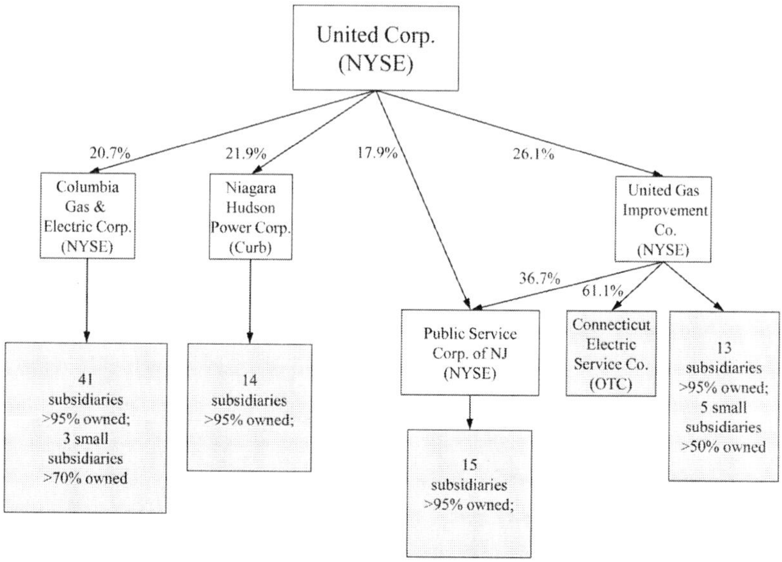

FIGURE 7.1 Structure of the United Corporation utility holding company system. Companies described in the shaded boxes are not contained in the sample. The principal trading market for the common stock of companies in the sample is also shown in parentheses.

predator and prey. United controls UGI through 26 percent stock ownership and interlocking directors. However, UGI itself owns a controlling stake in Public Service Corp. and Connecticut Electric Service Co. The latter company is not in my sample because it is not traded on a major exchange and daily prices are therefore unavailable.

Table 7.1 lists the sample companies and their categorizations. It also identifies the primary market on which the sample company's common stock traded and its parent company, if any. Daily returns for the NYSE-listed companies in the sample are taken from the CRSP data. Daily returns for the Curb companies are calculated using CRSP's procedure—based on closing prices when available and on the midpoint of closing bid and ask quotations when a stock does not trade on the relevant date.

TEST DESIGN. I first create three value-weighted portfolios consisting of predators that are not also prey (n = 7), prey that are not also predators (n = 16), and companies that are neither predator nor prey (n = 9). For purposes of portfolio-level analysis, the six companies that are both predator and prey are excluded from the sample. Alternatively, they could be

TABLE 7.1. **Sample firms**

Name	Market	Parent Company	Type
American & Foreign Power, Inc.	NYSE	Elec. Bond & Shr.	Prey
American Gas & Electric Co.	Curb	Elec. Bond & Shr.	Prey
American Light & Traction Co.	Curb	Unit. L. & Rwys.[a]	Prey
American Power & Light Co.	NYSE	Elec. Bond & Shr.	Prey
American Water Works & Electric Co.	NYSE	Elec. Pwr. & Lt.	Prey
Arkansas Natural Gas Co.	Curb	Cities Service	Prey
Brooklyn Union Gas Co.	NYSE	None	Neither
Cities Service Co.	Curb	None	Predator
Columbia Gas & Electric Co.	NYSE	United Corp.	Prey
Commonwealth & Southern Corp.	NYSE	None	Neither
Commonwealth Edison Co.	Curb	None	Predator
Consolidated Gas, Electric Light & Power Co. of Baltimore	Curb	None	Neither
Consolidated Gas Co. of NY	NYSE	None	Neither
Detroit Edison Co.	NYSE	North American Co.	Prey
Duke Power	Curb	None	Neither
Electric Bond & Share Co.	Curb	None	Predator
Electric Power & Light Corp.	NYSE	Elec. Bond & Shr.	Both
Engineers Public Service Co.	NYSE	Stone & Webster	Prey
Federal Light & Traction Co.	NYSE	Cities Service	Both
Laclede Gas & Light Co.	NYSE	Utilities Pwr. & Lt.	Prey
Long Island Lighting Co.	Curb	None	Neither
Memphis Natural Gas Co.	Curb	Commonwlth Gas[a]	Prey
National Power & Light Co.	NYSE	Elec. Bond & Shr.	Prey
Niagara Hudson Power Corp.	Curb	United Corp.	Prey
North American Co.	NYSE	None	Predator
Pacific Gas & Electric Co.	NYSE	North American Co.	Prey
Pacific Lighting Corp.	NYSE	None	Neither
Peoples Gas Light & Coke Co.	NYSE	None	Neither
Public Service Corp. of NJ	NYSE	United Gas Imprvt.	Prey
Southern California Edison Co.	NYSE	None	Neither
Standard Gas & Electric Co.	NYSE	Standard Pwr. & Lt.	Both
Standard Power & Light Corp.	Curb	U.S. Electric Pwr.[a]	Both
Stone & Webster Inc.	NYSE	None	Predator
Tampa Electric Corp.	Curb	Stone & Webster	Prey
United Corp.	NYSE	None	Predator
United Gas Corp.	Curb	Elec. Pwr. & Lt.	Both
United Gas Improvement Co.	NYSE	United Corp.	Both
Utilities Power & Light Co.	Curb	None	Predator

[a] Parent companies that are not traded on the NYSE or Curb and therefore not part of the sample.

included in both the predator and prey portfolios. That approach would tend to understate any differences in the behavior of the predators and prey because the returns on six firms would be included in both portfolios.

Using standard event-study technique (Brown and Warner 1985), I estimate a market model for each of the three portfolios using 250 days of return data ending on October 31, 1934. I select that period because in

TABLE 7.2. **Description of legislative events**

Date	Description	Effect
2/6/1935	Rayburn-Wheeler bill introduced	↑
4/22/1935	Informal House subcommittee vote against §11	↓
6/11/1935	Senate passes bill with amended §11	↑
6/17/1935	House subcommittee votes to remove §11	↓
7/1/1935	House votes to remove §11	↓
8/1/1935	House rejects motion to reinstate §11 following lobbying revelations	↓
8/22/1935	House approves Barkley compromise	↑
8/23/1935	Conference committee approves Barkley compromise	↑
8/24/1935	House and Senate pass PUHCA	↑
8/26/1935	President signs PUHCA	↑
11/7/1935	District court declares PUHCA unconstitutional in entirety	↓

Note: Up or down arrow indicates whether the event would have increased or decreased assessments of the probability of a partial or total ban on utility holding companies.

mid-November the press first reported that the administration's bill might ban holding companies altogether. (I also run the tests described below around the dates of published press reports and speeches regarding the possible content of the bill during mid-November through mid-January and do not find abnormal returns on the utility portfolios. Those tests are not reported.) Because the portfolios are value-weighted, I use the CRSP value-weighted index as the market proxy. I then measure abnormal returns on the event date(s) and subsequent trading day for each event described in table 7.2.[5] For each event, day 0 is the day of the vote or other legislative action and day +1 is the day on which the legislative action was reported in the press. I assess statistical significance using the time series standard deviation of abnormal returns for each portfolio during the estimation period.

The null hypothesis is that the ban on holding companies has no valuation effect. In addition to the "death sentence" provision, however, PUHCA included registration and disclosure provisions and imposed SEC oversight over the financing of utility companies. These provisions could have a valuation effect independent of section 11's holding company ban. Fortunately, the "independent" companies in the sample provide a plausible baseline against which to measure the statute's marginal effects on predators and prey.

An alternative hypothesis is that the "predator" holding companies extracted value from their "prey." If true, we would expect positive abnormal returns on the prey portfolio and negative abnormal returns on the predator portfolio around the time of events favorable to passage of the death sentence provision. The death sentence provision would damage the predators by depriving them of the ability to tunnel value from their prey, and by the same logic would benefit the prey group.

A second alternative hypothesis is that holding companies added value to their subsidiaries and public shareholders of the subsidiaries shared in that value. The source of added value, as described above, might have been (financial or operational) efficiency or regulatory evasion. In either event, the net effect would be that public shareholders were better off than they would have been had the company not been part of a pyramid group. This would be true, however, only if the value the controlling shareholder created exceeded the amount it extracted from the subsidiary through intragroup transactions and transfers. In that event, all holding companies should decline in value around the time of events favorable to PUHCA's passage.

We might also observe across-the-board declines if investors feared disorderly liquidations and consequent loss of value, even if orderly liquidations would have made them better off. There is good reason, however, to doubt that this would have had a large effect. PUHCA's drafters were attuned to the danger of "fire sale" liquidations from the outset. Section 11 as enacted called for the SEC to begin the process of dissolving holding company systems only in 1938 and provided for extensions of time when necessary to protect investors. In the event, reorganization of the main holding company systems continued into the 1950s.

Results

EVENT STUDY EVIDENCE: PORTFOLIO LEVEL. Table 7.3 reports abnormal returns for each of the three portfolios around the time of the legislative events described above. Abnormal returns are frequently economically and statistically large on the day of or the day after key votes, suggesting that traders had not already predicted their outcomes. This is not surprising. The death sentence provision was highly controversial and many of the votes were close.

Abnormal returns for the predator portfolio are negative around the release of information suggesting a higher probability that holding companies would be abolished and positive around the release of information suggesting a lower probability. The same is generally true, however, of the prey portfolio. On each of the nine individual days on which the abnormal return on the predator portfolio is significantly different from zero, the

TABLE 7.3. **Abnormal returns (in percentages) around legislative events**

Date	Predators (7 Companies)	Prey (16 Companies)	Neither (9 Companies)	Predicted Sign If PUHCA Harmful
Feb. 6, 1935	.28	−.55	−.05	
	(.19)	(−.52)	(−.05)	
Feb. 7, 1935	−1.81	−1.40	.49	−
	(−1.21)	(−1.32)	(.42)	
Two-day window	−1.53	−1.95	.43	
	(−0.73)	(−1.30)	(.26)	
April 22, 1935	1.58	3.02**	2.66*	
	(1.06)	(2.85)	(2.29)	
April 23, 1935	3.59*	2.66*	2.10	+
	(2.41)	(2.51)	(1.81)	
Two-day window	5.17*	5.68**	4.76**	
	(2.46)	(3.79)	(2.90)	
June 11, 1935	−.99	−.33	3.24*	
	(−.66)	(−.31)	(2.79)	
June 12, 1935	−4.90**	−2.97**	−3.11**	−
	(−3.29)	(−2.81)	(−2.68)	
Two-day window	−5.88**	−3.31*	.13	
	(−2.79)	(−2.21)	(.08)	
June 17, 1935	1.96	2.78**	2.65*	
	(1.32)	(2.62)	(2.28)	
June 18, 1935	.51	.40	−.82	+
	(.34)	(.38)	(−.71)	
Two-day window	2.47	3.17*	1.83	
	(1.17)	(2.12)	(1.11)	
July 1, 1935	−.32	.44	.49	
	(−.21)	(.42)	(.42)	
July 2, 1935	7.10**	2.46*	1.53	+
	(4.76)	(2.32)	(1.32)	
Two-day window	6.78**	2.91	2.03	
	(3.22)	(1.94)	(1.23)	
Aug. 1, 1935	.33	−.77	−.76	
	(.22)	(−.73)	(−.66)	
Aug. 2, 1935	4.47**	2.27*	1.34	+
	(3.00)	(2.15)	(1.16)	
Two-day window	4.80*	1.50	.58	
	(2.28)	(1.00)	(.35)	
Aug. 22, 1935	−.08	−1.05	.51	
	(−.05)	(−.99)	(.44)	
Aug. 23, 1935	−7.45**	−2.92**	−3.30**	
	(−5.00)	(−2.75)	(−2.84)	
Aug 24, 1935	−8.41**	−3.78**	−2.91*	−
	(−5.64)	(−3.60)	(−2.51)	
Aug 26, 1935	6.60**	1.52	.36	
	(4.43)	(1.43)	(.31)	
Aug. 27, 1935	−4.55**	−3.32**	−3.86**	
	(−3.05)	(−3.13)	(−3.33)	
5-day window	−13.88**	−9.55**	−9.20**	
	(−4.17)	(−4.03)	(−3.55)	

TABLE 7.3. **(*Continued*)**

Date	Predators (7 Companies)	Prey (16 Companies)	Neither (9 Companies)	Predicted Sign If PUHCA Harmful
Nov. 7, 1935	−.07	.10	−.09	
	(−.05)	(.10)	(−.08)	
Nov. 8, 1935	5.82**	2.04	4.22**	+
	(3.90)	(1.93)	(3.63)	
Two-day window	5.74**	2.14	4.12*	
	(2.73)	(1.43)	(2.51)	

Note: The *t*-statistics are in parentheses.
*Significant at the 5% level
**Significant at the 1% level

abnormal return on the prey portfolio has the same sign, and on seven of those it is statistically significant. It is noteworthy that the April 22, July 1, and August 1 events were votes focused on the death sentence provision rather than the entire bill. Traders appeared to believe that passage of the "death sentence" provision would be bad for both predators and prey.[6]

The portfolio of companies that are neither predator nor prey has abnormal returns that are less reliably in line with the other two portfolios. On eight of the nine dates on which the predator portfolio has an abnormal return significantly different from zero, the point estimate for the third portfolio has the same sign, but it is statistically significant on only five. It seems plausible that the independent companies in the sample could comply with PUHCA at lower cost as they were already more geographically compact and had simpler corporate structures.

There is a potentially confounding event at the time of PUHCA's final enactment, which is a period of large abnormal returns. The Revenue Act of 1935, which passed the House and Senate in final form on August 24, contained a tax on intracorporate dividends. Prior law had exempted from taxation dividends from a subsidiary to a parent company. The Revenue Act of 1935 replaced this 100 percent exemption with an 85 percent exemption, thus subjecting 15 percent of intracorporate dividends to taxation at prevailing corporate tax rates. While this would mean a modest tax on companies with only one layer of holding company, the tax would multiply with each additional layer. The explicit purpose of the tax, as described in Roosevelt's message to Congress urging its enactment, was to discourage holding company systems.

Fortunately, this fact makes the distinction between PUHCA and the tax bill unimportant for present purposes. Both were explicitly designed to dismantle holding company systems. As Morck (2005) observes, creation of a layer of tax for every layer of holding companies was a deliberate attempt to discourage business groups rather than a revenue-raising measure. Indeed, the tax would become irrelevant once PUHCA's "death sentence" was enforced. At that point, there would be no pyramids and thus no multiple layers of tax.

The evidence from this simple time-series test is consistent with the hypothesis that the utility pyramids were beneficial to their members at all levels of the pyramid and that dissolution of the holding companies was expected to harm public shareholders. This is not a complete welfare analysis of PUHCA because it does not include effects on consumers (which I discuss later). However, it does imply that PUHCA's effect on the public shareholders of all companies—including subsidiaries—was negative on average. This in turn suggests that top-tier holding companies did not extract as much wealth as their voting power standing alone would have enabled them to extract. I discuss potential explanations for that restraint below.

IS THERE EVIDENCE OF TUNNELING? Although top-tier companies were apparently constrained from taking full advantage of the public shareholders of their subsidiaries, it would be surprising if they made no self-interested use of their control rights at all. To see whether the evidence from stock returns is consistent with some extraction of private benefits of control by controlling shareholders, I examine cross-sectional differences among the sample firms.

At the outset, we can observe that the absolute value of returns on the predator portfolio is generally higher than on the prey portfolio during legislative events, suggesting that the dissolution of the pyramids would be particularly bad for the top-tier holding companies. This could be because the top tier was generally highly leveraged and might be left with little or no value after dispositions of its subsidiaries. Alternatively, it might be because the top-tier companies kept a disproportionate share of the gains created by the group structure.

To test whether top-tier companies took some advantage of their voting power, I rely on Bertrand, Mehta, and Mullainathan's (2002) observation that tunneling is a means of shifting assets from firms in which the controller has low cash-flow rights to firms in which it has high cash-flow rights. Faccio, Lang, and Young (2001) find that noncontrolling shares are worth less in firms in which the controlling stockholder owns less than

20 percent of the outstanding shares. I accordingly ask whether "prey" in which the "predator" owned a small stake fared relatively better from PUHCA's enactment.

I estimate a market model for each company coded as "prey" using the same methodology as that described above. I then calculate average abnormal returns for each stock over each of the two- or five-day event windows identified in table 7.3 except for the February 6 event, which did not generate abnormal returns for any portfolio. The result is 154 observations of average abnormal returns over seven event windows for each of twenty-two sample firms coded as prey.

Because some of the firms have very low stock prices, small nominal price changes can produce substantial percentage changes. In the prior tests this is not an issue because the portfolios are value-weighted, but in the cross-sectional tests it could produce outlying observations that might heavily influence the results. I therefore winsorize the abnormal returns at the 95 percent and 5 percent levels. The cross-sectional tests are not very powerful because of the small number of firm-event observations, which is another disadvantage. Note also that we cannot assume that the error terms are independent across events for a particular firm, and I accordingly cluster standard errors on firms in the reported tests.

I measure, for each firm, the fraction of common stock owned by the immediate parent company and use a dummy variable to segment the sample into firms where the controller owns more than 20 percent and those in which the controller owns less than 20 percent. I estimate the following regression:

(1) $$AAR_{it} = \alpha + \beta_1 Neg_t + \beta_2 Less20_i + \beta_3 Less20_i * Neg_t + \varepsilon_{it}$$

where i indexes firms, t indexes event windows, *AAR* is average abnormal returns over an event window, *Neg* indicates a negative event (that is, one implying a higher probability that PUHCA would become law), and *Less20* equals one if firm i's parent owns less than 20 percent of its equity and zero otherwise. Ownership of less than 20 percent should make a firm coded as "prey" more vulnerable to tunneling. The coefficients β_2 and β_3 measure the sensitivity of average abnormal returns to less than 20 percent ownership for positive and negative events, respectively. If holding companies treated firms in which they had low cash-flow rights worse than those in which they had high cash-flow rights, we would expect $\beta_2 < 0$ and $\beta_3 > 0$.

TABLE 7.4. **Regression: Comparison of abnormal returns for companies with more and less than 20 percent ownership by parent company**

Parameter	Value
Constant	1.78**
	(.43)
Negative event	−5.44**
	(.76)
Ownership < 20%	−1.04
	(.56)
Ownership < 20% × negative event	3.39*
	(1.48)
Adjusted R^2	.44
N	154

Note: The dependent variable is average abnormal return (in %) for firm-event window units of observation, winsorized at the 95% and 5% levels. Standard errors (in parentheses) are clustered on firms.
*Significant at the 5% level
**Significant at the 1% level

The results are shown in table 7.4. Both coefficients of interest have the expected sign and one is significant at the 5 percent level. While the point estimate of the effect of a positive (negative) event is still positive (negative) for the prey companies, the magnitudes are smaller for those companies in which the parent has less than 20 percent ownership. In other words, the benefits of having a parent company are reduced but not eliminated if the parent owns less than 20 percent of the cash-flow rights. This is consistent with parent firms being constrained in the amount of wealth they can extract from subsidiaries, but within those constraints extracting where it is most beneficial to them.

DID PYRAMIDS EXIST TO INFLATE THE RATE BASE? Both portfolio-level and firm-level analysis consistently shows that the prospect of dissolving a pyramid structure was seen as bad news by both parent company and subsidiary shareholders. Was the reason financing and operating efficiencies, regulatory evasion, or both? Kandel et al. (2013) conclude that regulatory evasion was likely not a substantial purpose of holding companies because they provided only a modest amount of operating company inputs. A conclusive test of PUHCA's effects on utility customers would require analysis of low-frequency utility rate data rather than high-frequency stock price data.[7] However, we can exploit differences in the intensity of regulation among states to infer whether traders reacted negatively to PUHCA because they anticipated that it would make state rate regulation more effective. As Stigler and Friedland (1962) note, not every state regulated retail electricity and gas rates. If the pyramids enabled their subsidiaries to evade rate regulation, they would have added less value to subsidiaries located in states that did not regulate rates.

Using the maps of utility systems contained in the FTC report and the maps and narrative descriptions in Moody's public utility manuals, I identify the principal states in which my sample companies operate. I rely on Jones (1967) for a description of the regulatory systems of US states. Among the largest states, Florida, Texas, and Minnesota did not regulate electricity rates in 1935; Minnesota and Florida also did not regulate gas rates. Four of the sample companies operated largely in jurisdictions that did not regulate rates. Three of these, American Power & Light, Tampa Electric Corp., and Utilities Power & Light, operated primarily in Florida, Texas, and/or Minnesota. A fourth, American & Foreign Power, operated principally in Central and South America. From the descriptions in Moody's, it appears that those subsidiaries operated pursuant to franchise and concession agreements with individual municipalities rather than through a system of comprehensive rate regulation. Those four companies, therefore, likely had little ability to affect the rates that their subsidiaries could charge.

In order to compare average abnormal returns for the entire sample of utility holding companies and the subsample of the four lightly regulated holding companies, I calculate abnormal returns during event windows for all the sample firms as described in connection with equation (1) and table 7.4. I then estimate the following regression:

(2) $$AAR_{it} = \alpha + \beta_1 Neg_t + \beta_2 Light_i + \beta_3 Light_i * Neg_t + \varepsilon_{it}$$

where *Light* is an indicator variable for the four lightly regulated firms and other variables are defined as in equation (1) above. The coefficients β_2 and β_3 represent the marginal impact of being lightly regulated on abnormal returns around the time of positive (unfavorable to PUHCA's passage) and negative (favorable to passage) events, respectively. If regulatory evasion was an important part of the value added by holding companies, we should observe $\beta_2 < 0$ and $\beta_3 > 0$.

The estimated coefficients are shown in table 7.5. Neither β_2 nor β_3 is significantly different from zero. In short, the lightly regulated companies experience abnormal returns nearly identical to those of the more intensely regulated companies. This is inconsistent with the hypothesis that the holding companies added value by evading rate regulation.

TABLE 7.5. **Comparison of average abnormal returns for more and less regulated utility systems**

Parameter	Value
Constant	1.50**
	(.24)
Negative event	−4.23**
	(.57)
Lightly regulated	.21
	(1.22)
Lightly regulated × negative event	−.40
	(2.41)
Adjusted R^2	.35
N	266

Note: The dependent variable is average abnormal return (in %) for firm-event window units of observation, winsorized at the 95% and 5% levels. Standard errors (in parentheses) are clustered on firms.
**Significant at the 1% level

As an (unreported) check, I used an alternative strategy to capture the same phenomenon. Many of the companies in my sample belong to one of the "super" holding company systems such as the Electric Bond & Share system, the United Company system, or the North American system. A substantial part of the Electric Bond & Share system was located in Texas and Florida, which did not regulate rates, and in less-populated and urbanized states that we might expect to have less well-funded and less effective regulatory commissions.[8] By contrast, the United Company system held substantial assets in New York and New Jersey, while the North American system was concentrated in large industrial states such as Ohio, Illinois, and Michigan. All of these states regulated utility rates.

I therefore compared abnormal returns on the eight sample companies that were part of the Electric Bond & Share system with those of the eight sample companies that were part either of the United Company or North American systems. Average abnormal returns do not differ in a statistically or economically significant way between the two systems. Once again, I fail to find evidence in favor of the proposition that the holding companies added value only, or primarily, by helping subsidiaries artificially inflate their rate base.

This analysis does not rule out the possibility that holding companies helped their subsidiaries exploit their monopoly positions in ways other than regulatory evasion. For example, holding company managers may have been more sophisticated than local utility executives at pricing and political strategy. If true, however, there would be ways other than pyramid structures for those managers to sell their expertise to local public utilities and PUHCA should therefore have had only a modest impact.

Implications

Like the Securities Exchange Act but unlike the Securities Act, there is no evidence that the affected industry desired or supported PUHCA. However, like both of those statutes, PUHCA was based on a market failure narrative that was simply incorrect. The statute's supporters viewed it as appropriately part of the New Deal's securities reforms because they believed that pyramidal holding company structures were bad for shareholders as well as for utility customers. The latter issue is difficult to prove or disprove empirically, although my analysis tries and fails to find evidence that PUHCA made existing regulation more effective. But the first part of the claim—the notion that holding companies were bad for shareholders of the subsidiary companies—is more tractable. Across several specifications, the same picture emerges. Traders expected PUHCA to destroy value for publicly traded firms at all levels of the pyramid structures. This suggests that group membership was valuable to subsidiary companies and their shareholders. That would be so if the holding companies were able to create value by bringing a large number of operating companies under common control and the holding companies shared that value with the public shareholders of their listed subsidiaries.

The evidence in this section also calls into question another core belief of New Deal reformers. Some of them—William O. Douglas in particular—believed that state-level corporate law was ineffective and should be federalized. They believed that corporate law turned a blind eye to depredations by corporate managers and directors.

Were this belief true, it is considerably more likely that pyramidal holding company structures would have destroyed value. Under lax corporate law, controlling shareholders have ample opportunities to tunnel assets from subsidiaries to the top holding company. Under high-quality corporate law, by contrast, such activities, if detected, subject the top holding company to liability. My results suggest that tunneling was constrained, although not wholly absent, which suggests that corporate law was reasonably effective.

This is not a conclusive demonstration. It may be that holding companies were constrained by reputation and not law. The utility industry was hugely capital intensive. Because the holding company systems had to go back to the capital markets on a frequent basis to raise capital for companies at all levels of the pyramid, they could not afford a reputation for being excessively rapacious.

Morck (2009) synthesizes the literature on pyramid groups around the world. He argues that pyramids can be useful in developing countries with poor institutions. In that environment, the controlling shareholder at the top of the pyramid can enforce contracts among group companies and run internal capital and labor markets that substitute for poorly functioning external markets. Unfortunately, in a poor institutional environment controlling shareholders may also exploit the public shareholders of their subsidiary companies. The evidence suggests that they do so (Bertrand, Mehta, and Mullainathan 2002; Jiang, Lee, and Yue 2010). However, the prices of public shares reflect the expected exploitation and the value to the firm from being part of a group exceeds the losses from tunneling.

In a developed country, by contrast, both the benefits and costs of a pyramid structure are reduced. Capital and labor markets and courts all perform better, leaving less work for controlling shareholders. Moreover, family controlled pyramids can become sclerotic and focus more on maintaining the political power and social prestige of the controlling family than on creating value for public shareholders. The stronger institutional environment also constrains (but does not eliminate) tunneling. Thus Morck concludes that pyramids are likely inefficient in a developed country, although his analysis focuses principally on holding companies owned by families rather than by public shareholders.

If corporate law functioned effectively in the United States in the 1920s and 1930s, Morck's analysis suggests that the holding company pyramids were unnecessary—indeed, outlawing them might have been a positive development that helped to create the modern dispersed ownership pattern typical of Anglo-American corporate governance (Becht and DeLong 2005; Morck 2005). This chapter's findings that the pyramids added value would then be questionable.

The differences between the public utility pyramids and the typical business group, discussed above, may help reconcile my findings with Morck's analysis. The utility pyramids were not conglomerates, but focused on an industry that faced substantial regulatory barriers to realizing economies of scale. Moreover, unlike many business groups of today, the ultimate controlling shareholder was typically a publicly held firm or a private partnership, not a family. Thus the pool of managerial talent from which the controlling shareholders could draw was not artificially limited.

Most important for present purposes, however, the data suggest that the arguments made by Bonbright, Roosevelt, and other reformers were incorrect. Utility holding companies did not exploit public shareholders and there is no evidence that they exploited utility customers. The market failure narrative of utility holding companies was politically valuable to Roosevelt's 1932 campaign but its use to enact PUHCA harmed stockholders with no measurable offsetting benefits.

The ICA: Regulation on Demand

The Depression hit highly leveraged companies hard. As discussed in the prior section, utility holding companies borrowed heavily in the 1920s. By the early 1930s many were in financial distress and some in bankruptcy. Investment companies also performed badly. In the late 1920s, these companies were often highly leveraged, issuing multiple tranches of preferred stock and debt in addition to common stock. They were closed-end, meaning that their shares were not redeemable like those of a modern mutual fund. An investor who wished to liquidate the investment had to sell on a secondary market. In the deflationary environment of the Depression, leverage led to dramatic declines in the value of investment company shares.

In the 1930s investors lost their taste for highly leveraged investments and the investment company industry adapted to new preferences. As described by Morley (2012), three major investment company complexes headquartered in Boston developed the modern "open-end" mutual fund, which stands ready to sell or purchase its shares at the net asset value of the underlying portfolio at the end of each trading day. These new funds invested in diversified portfolios of securities, sold a single class of common stock, and did not use leverage. Like the closed-end funds popular in the 1920s and unlike public utility holding companies, they were passive investors that did not seek to influence the policies or management of their portfolio companies.

By the end of the 1930s, the new mutual fund complexes were well established and the passive, diversified, no-leverage model had brought retail investors back to investment companies. The major fund sponsors accordingly sought legislation to freeze that model into place and ensure that new entrants could not try to attract investors with alternative practices. Their efforts resulted in the ICA. Like PUHCA, the ICA is not simply a disclosure statute. It comprehensively regulates the structure and business practices of investment companies marketed to retail investors. In concert with tax rules first adopted in 1938, the ICA limits concentration in mutual fund portfolios. It also limits the use of leverage. In concert with the Investment Advisors Act of 1940, it limits the use of performance-based fees in retail mutual funds.

Morley (2012) describes in detail the creation of the ICA. The statute was enacted entirely at the behest of two actors—the SEC and the mutual fund industry. The SEC's interests were obvious. The statute expanded its authority over an important and growing segment of the retail securities market. The industry's interests were also straightforward. The memory of its near-demise during the Depression was fresh. The industry feared that new entrants might reintroduce leverage or other practices that could increase returns in good times at the risk of bringing the entire industry back into disrepute.

The ICA is thus a clear example of "best practices" regulation that serves primarily the interests of the leading firms in the regulated industry. The three major Boston-based mutual fund complexes had a common business model and could easily coordinate their lobbying efforts. They were willing to give up the flexibility to change their business model in return for stifling competition from new entrants who might experiment with different practices. Morley (2012) notes that there was entry into the mutual fund industry by the late 1930s and attributes part of the timing of the ICA to the leading firms' concerns about those new entrants.

Explanations for the ICA's enactment apart from industry self-interest are implausible. The New Deal itself was a dead letter by 1940, following the mini-Depression of 1937–38, Republican congressional gains in the 1938 elections, and the coming of war to Europe in 1939. Legislative activity in 1940 was dominated by preparation for possible armed conflict. Only the fact that the SEC and the mutual fund industry came to Congress with a bill with which all parties were in agreement overcame Congress's disinclination to wade back into financial market regulation.

The market failure story of investment company regulation, which holds that investment companies exploited unsophisticated investors until prevented from doing so by regulation, is exactly backward. The investment company industry was spared significant regulatory oversight during the height of the New Deal and accordingly its problems were not resolved by legislation but by market competition. Having brought itself back into investors' good graces, however, the industry decided to solidify its gains by proposing "best practices" legislation that also protected it against competition. Thus the market adapted to investors' interests while regulation served the industry's interests.

Although it aided the investment company industry, the ICA had an important and possibly deleterious effect on retail investors. By limiting leverage and performance-based fees in the retail sector of the investment management market, it created a strict separation between the investment vehicles available to retail investors and those available to institutional and high net-worth investors (Mahoney 2004). Institutions and the wealthy invest in hedge funds, unregulated investment companies that use leverage, sometimes pursue activist investment strategies, charge performance-based fees, and typically lock in investments for a period of time and permit withdrawal of funds only at specified times. Retail investors are therefore denied one of the best forms of protection—the ability to invest side by side with highly sophisticated investors who can effectively negotiate with and monitor their investment managers.

Conclusions

PUHCA was based on an inaccurate market failure narrative but, as with the Exchange Act, there is no evidence that the regulated industry sought out or benefited from the regulation. There were persistent rumblings during the legislative process, however, that the real beneficiaries would be government-owned utilities such as the Tennessee Valley Authority. The dismantling of the utility pyramids would make utility assets available to the government-owned systems at potentially attractive prices. FDR was likely not indifferent to the fact that PUHCA's enactment would lead to the breakup of the Commonwealth & Southern Company. C&S's president, Wendell Willkie, was a Democrat who contributed to Roosevelt's 1932 campaign but then became disaffected and was a vocal opponent of the TVA. After PUHCA's enactment, C&S sold some of its utility assets to the TVA. Shortly thereafter, Willkie switched parties and ran unsuccessfully against FDR in 1940. Had he won, PUHCA would presumably have been repealed. Instead it survived and C&S was dissolved in the late 1940s.

By contrast, the investment company industry publicly supported the ICA just as the major investment banks supported the Securities Act. Unlike the latter, however, the former were able to take near-complete control of the legislative process. The SEC and the major mutual fund complexes took the draft statute to Congress, which accommodated them by enacting it. It is clear, however, that the statute's primary beneficiary was the growing mutual fund industry.

CHAPTER EIGHT

The Old Is New Again

Securities Reform in the Twenty-First Century

The United States has already experienced two severe equity market downturns in the twenty-first century. In each case, the aftermath closely followed the 1930s script. Would-be reformers argued that misbehavior by securities issuers or financial institutions caused the downturn, that a lack of regulation facilitated the misbehavior, and that their proposed reforms were well-designed to prevent a recurrence. It is now harder to make the second of these arguments persuasively. Unlike in the 1930s, finance in the twenty-first century is overseen by an army of regulators working for dozens of regulatory agencies with budgets and powers that would have made the New Dealers gasp. As we will see, however, policy entrepreneurs were nevertheless up to the task of blaming both downturns on a lack of regulation.

The prior chapters show that political actors used the market failure narrative of the 1930s financial crisis to enact into law a longstanding progressive wish list, including mandatory disclosure of underwriting fees and federal supervision of the New York Stock Exchange. The wish list was almost entirely unrelated to the causes of the crisis. Recognizing the political inevitability of financial reform legislation, financial intermediaries shaped that legislation to enshrine "best practices" that were their preferred methods of doing business, raising their rivals' relative costs. Top-tier securities dealers and investment company sponsors accordingly benefited from the reforms; smaller securities dealers, regional exchanges, and new entrants to the investment company industry were the major losers. Investors had to bear higher costs and diminished competition. The same basic description holds true for the Sarbanes-Oxley Act of 2002 and the Dodd-Frank Act of 2010.

Sarbanes-Oxley: The Reform that Wasn't

From its September 1, 2000, level of 1520.77, the S&P 500 index plunged by 47 percent to 800.58 on October 4, 2002. On the latter date, the tech-heavy NASDAQ Composite index stood at 1139.90, nearly 80 percent below its peak value. During the downturn, Enron, the seventh-largest US corporation by revenues, collapsed and filed for bankruptcy in December 2001. In July 2002 Worldcom, the country's second-largest long distance telephone company, also filed for what was at the time the largest bankruptcy proceeding in US history.

By focusing on Enron and Worldcom rather than the many tech firms that simply failed to live up to investor expectations, it was straightforward to identify misbehavior. Enron used off-balance-sheet devices to hide the extent of its indebtedness and Worldcom improperly accounted for expenses, thereby inflating reported earnings.

No one could argue that these disclosure practices were unregulated. Instead, critics argued that the problem was insufficient federal regulation of auditing and corporate governance. These failings meant that compensation practices gave top corporate executives incentives to mislead investors. Lower-level employees were able to take extreme risks with corporate funds because of lax internal controls. The external accounting firms on whom investors relied to ensure accurate disclosure failed to audit with sufficient vigor because they hoped to sell lucrative consulting services to their audit clients. Insufficiently independent boards of directors were unwilling to challenge risk-taking CEOs or rein in their compensation. And even nominally independent investment analysts would not blow the whistle on questionable financial practices because they worked for investment banks that hoped to get underwriting business. Thus each of the "gatekeepers" shareholders counted on—managers, directors, auditors, and analysts—was subject to misaligned incentives. The argument was doubly useful because policy entrepreneurs had long advocated a greater federal role in corporate governance.

Congress accepted the market failure narrative and responded with the Sarbanes-Oxley Act of 2002, commonly abbreviated as SOX. At the time, SOX held the title of "the most sweeping legislation since the New Deal" (Murray 2002). It comprised:

Auditor independence rules, including a ban on specified nonaudit services.

A new regulatory agency, the Public Company Accounting Oversight Board, or PCAOB, to regulate the auditing function of the accounting profession.

Corporate governance provisions, including a requirement that audit committees be composed entirely of independent directors, certification of quarterly financial reports, forfeiture of certain forms of compensation by officers when a company restates its financial statements, and a ban on loans from a company to its executive officers.

Additional disclosures, including disclosures relating to internal controls and an auditor assessment and report on internal controls, additional disclosures about off-balance sheet transactions, and additional disclosures about officers' transactions in the company's stock. Companies are required to disclose whether they have a code of ethics for senior financial managers and to describe it and any changes or waivers.

A command to the SEC to adopt rules relating to securities analyst conflicts of interest.

A grab-bag of other provisions relating to corporate civil and criminal fraud, penalties for white-collar crimes, tax returns, and other matters.

SOX's enactment closely followed the standard pattern of post-crash reform legislation. As Romano (2005) observes, many SOX provisions were longstanding recommendations of "policy entrepreneurs"—mostly government officials and academics—repackaged as ways to prevent future Enrons. Arthur Levitt, the former SEC chair, championed SOX's ban on nonaudit services—not surprisingly, as he had attempted unsuccessfully to restrict nonaudit services during his time at the SEC. Another former SEC chair advocated a stricter version of the NYSE's requirement that audit committees consist of independent directors. A former SEC chief accountant proposed executive certification of financial statements.

Many of these provisions elevate symbolism over substance. Even SOX's academic supporters cheerfully acknowledge that its corporate governance reforms are largely "stunts" (Cunningham 2003). This is so for two reasons.

First, the corporate governance provisions work only modest changes to existing rules and practices. The executive certification of financial statements creates a slight reduction in the plaintiff's burden of proof in some securities fraud cases. The audit committee independence provision was already the subject of stock exchange rules. Other provisions, such as the ban on loans to corporate officers and the encouragement of a code of ethics, replicate widely followed practices. Commentators routinely describe SOX's corporate governance provisions as codifying "best practices" (Sorin, Pappa, and Ragosa 2002; Cunningham 2003). A frequently noted irony is that Enron was a faithful follower of these corporate best practices and widely considered a paragon of good governance before its collapse (Gordon 2002).

A second and more disheartening reason, described in detail in Romano (2005), is that policymakers had available ample evidence that many of SOX's most heralded corporate governance reforms would be ineffective. There was a large existing literature on independent directors that in general failed to find a positive impact on corporate performance. Most studies of auditor provision of nonaudit services fail to find an association with diminished audit quality.

One need not be a cynic, then, to conclude that Congress's primary objective was to enact something that would firmly assign blame for the equity downturn to accountants, CEOs, and other private-sector actors. How has the statute affected investors and the regulated industries? It is indisputable that SOX increased the accounting and compliance costs of being a public company. The costs associated with compliance give a clear advantage to larger companies, although the SEC has tried to moderate it with exemptions. The evidence suggests that the value of publicly traded firms declined upon SOX's enactment, as we would expect if those costs generally exceed the benefits (Litvak 2007). It is also clear that after its enactment, the number of firms becoming or remaining public companies fell below expectations. Debate continues over whether SOX was a cause of the decline.

Whether SOX was the culprit or not, concerns that US securities markets were losing out to foreign markets for IPOs brought Congress and the SEC in for criticism and spurred action. In 2005 the SEC adopted a series of regulatory reforms designed to simplify the public offering process.[1] These reforms relaxed the detailed regulations described in chapter 4, particularly for the largest issuers. Congress also responded to criticism by enacting the Jumpstart Our Business Startups (JOBS) Act of 2012. The JOBS Act exempts startup companies from the Securities Act's pre-offering secrecy rules and from some SOX provisions. It was prompted by the same concerns that motivated the SEC in 2005—the investment banking industry's fear that IPO volume was weak in part because of securities laws that the industry had previously supported.

On the surface, the accounting profession would appear to be a substantial loser in the legislative process and was certainly cast as a villain in the press and in policy discussions. Yet the accounting profession suffered less harm from SOX than it might appear. Note that the SEC had attempted to ban nonaudit services prior to Enron. The accounting profession effectively lobbied the SEC and Congress to derail the proposal. The strict limits on nonaudit services in SOX were a loss for the accounting profession. But unlike the SEC proposal, which offered no *quid pro quo* for the lost revenue from nonaudit services, SOX opened up a new and lucrative line of business for firms that audit public companies. Section 404(b) requires that a public company's auditors attest to and report on management's assessment of the adequacy of internal controls. This time-consuming work represents an entirely new line of audit business and the statute makes publicly traded companies captive clients who cannot decline to purchase the service. Not surprisingly, then, the American Institute of Certified Public Accountants has consistently argued against SEC and congressional attempts to reduce the social cost of section 404 by exempting smaller public companies.[2]

The creation of the PCAOB with its detailed regulatory and investigatory powers may also appear to be a loss for public company auditors. Nevertheless, history teaches that the creation of a dedicated regulator for an industry is often beneficial to the leading firms in that industry. The SEC itself came about largely because the securities industry wanted its own regulator rather than having the Federal Trade Commission administer the securities laws as it initially did under the Securities Act. At a minimum, the requirement that an accounting firm register with the PCAOB before it can audit a public company will raise the already high costs of entry into the business of auditing public companies. It will help ensure that public company auditing remains the province of the major accounting firms and avoid any reversal of the concentration that has reduced the profession from the "Big Eight" of forty years ago to today's Big Four.

Dodd-Frank: The Second Time as Farce

The financial crisis of 2007–8 and Dodd-Frank share important traits with the early 1930s financial crisis and the New Deal financial reforms, although not the precise characteristics on which commentators have focused. In both, reform legislation was born in a highly partisan atmosphere after a financial crisis and recession that helped bring about a change in the party controlling the White House. Both new administrations found it politically useful to blame their predecessors and Wall Street for the dismal state of the economy. In each case, the market failure narrative was shaped to fit the desired regulatory changes rather than the reforms being designed to solve objectively identified problems.

Deregulation as the Culprit

The crisis had many moving pieces. Assigning primary responsibility to one rather than another has important policy and political implications. One could choose to emphasize banks' decisions to make large numbers of subprime loans and treat them as low-risk for capital purposes. To do so, however, would not help make the case for broad new regulations. Banks are heavily regulated and a primary focus of regulation is safety and soundness. To say that banks made high-risk loans with insufficient capital because they aren't regulated enough doesn't pass the straight-face test. Moreover, banks did not get the idea to make subprime loans entirely on their own; government housing policies played a role (Wallison 2011). There is debate over whether housing policies were a primary driver of the "subprime crisis" or played only a supporting role, but it is clear they deserve partial blame.

Supporters of new regulation have therefore focused on securities and derivatives markets and on "shadow banks" that fell outside the reach of traditional bank regulation. The market failure narrative begins by noting that financial innovation enabled all types of financial institutions to make large and highly leveraged directional bets on mortgage- and real estate–related assets, often funded principally with short-term liabilities. The combination of large positions and small capital proved disastrous when real estate prices began to decline. This much is not in dispute.

The more complicated question is *why* financial institutions behaved this way. In order to follow the standard script, the answer must be insufficient regulation. By focusing on the role of securities and derivative instruments and shadow banks, critics told a tale of *deregulation* that left important segments of the market unsupervised despite the attention of the Federal Reserve, the Federal Deposit Insurance Corporation, the SEC, the Commodity Futures Trading Commission, and dozens of other regulators. They further claim that more regulation—such as that provided in Dodd-Frank—could have prevented the crisis. This is the conclusion of the Financial Crisis Inquiry Commission (2011, xviii), created by Congress in the hope that it would be as great a public relations success as the Pecora Hearings of the early 1930s (Perino 2012):

> More than 30 years of deregulation and reliance on self-regulation by financial institutions, championed by former Federal Reserve chairman Alan Greenspan and others, supported by successive administrations and Congresses, and actively pushed by the powerful financial industry at every turn, had stripped away key safeguards, which could have helped avoid catastrophe.

A naïve version of the deregulation hypothesis focuses on two legislative changes: the Gramm-Leach-Bliley Act of 1999 (GLB), which repealed prohibitions on affiliations between banks and securities firms from the Glass-Steagall Act, and the Commodity Futures Modernization Act of 2000 (CFMA), which clarified that most over-the-counter derivatives were not "futures" for purposes of federal commodity futures regulation. They were already for the most part carved out of the definition of "securities" for purposes of federal securities regulation. In the immediate aftermath of the crisis, several politicians and journalists identified GLB and CFMA as partially responsible. The causal mechanism is not clearly specified, but the argument appears to be that GLB permitted banks to engage in "risky" securities activities and CFMA facilitated the growth of credit default swaps.

This version of the deregulation argument is more rarely heard today, and for good reason. GLB and CFMA largely codified the status quo. The most important deregulatory changes took place during the 1980s. During that decade, bank regulators permitted banks to engage in securities activities, including underwriting debt and mortgage-backed securities (MBS). The swaps market also grew up during that decade, with regulatory acquiescence, as an over-the-counter supplement to exchange-traded futures and options contracts.

Were GLB to blame, moreover, one would have expected financial distress to be most acute among institutions that combined deposit-taking with securities underwriting and trading, while those that stuck principally to one or the other would have been safer. But financial institutions of all types—small community banks, large wholesale banks, mortgage bankers, stand-alone investment banks, and a large insurance company—experienced financial distress because of exposure to the real estate market either directly through lending or indirectly through investments in mortgage-related securities or derivatives. Nonbank financial institutions invested in mortgage-related securities funded with short-term liabilities, taking risks similar to those commercial banks take when making mortgage loans funded by demand deposits. Glass-Steagall would not have prevented banks from selling mortgage loans to securitizers or broker-dealers from underwriting and investing in the resulting securities.

More sophisticated critics make a broader version of the deregulation claim that does not single out specific statutory or regulatory changes. Blinder (2013, 5) argues that there was "far too little regulation" of the financial system. The markets were overseen by "a deregulation-minded bunch of regulators" (58). Consistent with the classic market failure narrative, Blinder views the failure of regulation as a deliberate choice by policymakers with a "free-market ideology" (59) who believed in "laissez-fairey tales" (64). Implicitly, policymakers and regulators could have controlled the risk taking had they not been ideologically committed to deregulation and laissez-faire.

This implication sits uneasily with Blinder's explanation for financial institutions' willingness to take outsized risks. He attributes it largely to ignorance. Financial institutions invested in derivatives that they did not understand (55). "Sophisticated portfolio managers . . . were essentially clueless. . . . If ignorance is bliss, there was a lot of bliss going around before the crash" (76). Quoting Will Rogers, Blinder says the crash taught us "how little our 'big men' knew" (86).

But many of these "big men" revolve between government service and the executive suites of commercial or investment banks. It is implausible that they are too clueless to understand the risks posed by derivatives and structured products when employed by the private sector, but upon entry to the public sector gain the wisdom and understanding to stop financial institutions from investing in these instruments and financing them with overnight repurchase agreements. But this, in effect, is what we would have to believe in order to think that the problem is ignorance and the cure is more regulation.

Bad Policy as the Culprit

I wish to suggest that moral hazard resulting from bad policy played a more substantial role than ignorance in the precrisis years. Although portfolio managers were using inadequate models, I nevertheless suspect that large financial institutions realized that if housing prices fell sharply, their positions would lose value rapidly. But they chose to take the risk.

Why would anyone behave this way? To begin, note that when interest rates are low and asset prices are rising, more financial leverage is always better. Citigroup's CEO Chuck Prince has been vilified for saying "as long as the music is playing, you've got to get up and dance," but the statement captures the dangerous truth of the competitive dynamics of a period of cheap financing and rapidly appreciating assets.[3] Of course, asset prices cannot rise indefinitely and so the winners must intend to "stop dancing," or de-risk, before it is too late. But the fact that they failed to do so, and even the fact that it is hard to do so, does not mean that the strategy is inherently irrational. If you begin with a small stake, leverage it fifty to one, and ultimately lose everything, from an ex ante perspective you've still only made a small bet. Your lenders have made the large bet. Theirs is the more puzzling behavior, to which we'll turn momentarily.

How can regulators stop excessive risk taking? The key is to limit leverage. Capital rules are an important tool. In my opinion, a simple capital rule requiring cushions of equity and subordinated debt as a percentage of total assets is preferable to a rule that uses complex risk weightings. The latter, in practice, gives banks and governments room to game the system to encourage investment in particular types of assets. Indeed, the low risk weights on real estate–related assets encouraged banks to invest in mortgage-related securities (Romano 2012). However, no capital rule is foolproof. In a low interest rate, high asset price appreciation environment, financial institutions will use off-balance-sheet financing and other tools to hide the extent of their leverage from regulators.

It is therefore essential that lenders discipline financial institutions by refusing to lend when risks become too great. The fact that short-term creditors run for the exits at the first sign of trouble is a feature rather than a bug because it encourages borrowers to maintain sufficient capital. Governments, for their part, must refrain from interfering with that disciplinary mechanism. They can undercut it either by driving interest rates too low or by protecting creditors from the consequences of poor lending decisions. Unfortunately, the US government did both in the run-up to the recent crisis.

As Taylor (2009) notes, from 2002 to 2006 the Federal Funds rate was as much as 300 basis points lower than it would have been had the Fed followed historical norms. This deviation, the largest since the 1970s, fed house-price inflation and reduced bond yields. It spurred a search for higher-yielding and therefore riskier loans.

Equally or perhaps more damaging, past government actions had protected creditors of certain financial institutions from loss, a phenomenon popularly called "too big to fail" (TBTF). Beginning in the 1980s, the Federal Deposit Insurance Corporation (FDIC) and other regulators and government agencies began to differentiate among financial institutions in distress based on their assessment of the "systemic" risks associated with the failure. By the time of the 2007–8 financial crisis, market participants assumed that the government would intervene to protect short-term creditors and counterparties of the largest or most interconnected financial institutions against loss or delay in accessing funds.

From 1945 through 1974, only 110 FDIC-insured banks with aggregate assets of $5.8 billion failed.[4] Banking during that era was less risky than it would later become for a number of reasons. State-level branching restrictions curtailed competition. Federal banking regulations capped the interest rate on deposits, giving banks access to cheap funding, particularly before 1971 when the first money-market fund began to compete for depositors' cash. The interest-rate and exchange-rate environments were benign.

By the early 1980s, all of these conditions had changed and yearly bank failures rose into the hundreds. Even large banks began to fail, beginning with the First Pennsylvania Bank of Philadelphia in 1980. While the FDIC sometimes liquidated small banks and allowed uninsured depositors and other general creditors to take losses, it worried that the same policy would create financial system instability if applied to large wholesale banks (Hanc 1997).

The issue came to a head with the failure of the nation's seventh-largest bank, Continental Illinois, in 1984 (Davidson 1997). As depositors fled the bank, the FDIC provided short-term financial assistance and promised that all depositors and general creditors would be made whole. Ultimately, the FDIC agreed to purchase a package of bad loans from Continental Illinois and infuse additional capital, making the government temporarily the owner of 80 percent of the bank's equity. "Too big to fail" entered the vernacular.

Was TBTF limited to banks and based solely on size, or would regulators apply it to any financial firm sufficiently interconnected that its failure could cause problems at other institutions? The answer came in 1998 when a hedge fund, Long-Term Capital Management, became insolvent and the Federal Reserve Bank of New York brokered a sale to other financial institutions. The government created the expectation that it would intervene to prevent a liquidation or bankruptcy proceeding for any financial institution if the result would be to expose the rest of the financial system to substantial losses.

This expectation creates perverse incentives for lenders and borrowers alike. It relieves short-term lenders of their critical informational role as an early warning system. Because the withdrawal of short-term lenders can bring down a highly leveraged institution, those lenders anticipated that any bailout would preserve the value and liquidity of their positions.

The incentives for borrowers are equally bad. TBTF encourages financial firms to become larger and more interconnected. The expectation of a bailout reduces the cost of short-term funding because the lenders are protected from losses. Ueda and Weder di Mauro (2012) estimate that the subsidy was worth 60 basis points as of 2007. Kroszner (2013) notes the conceptual and methodological challenges confronting such studies and concludes that they are not definitive. However, he notes that perceived risks for the largest banks, as measured by credit default swap spreads, were small and undifferentiated by institution as late as 2007, suggesting that TBTF had an effect. Prior to the crisis, moreover, rating agencies incorporated implicit government support into some bank holding company credit ratings. There is substantial reason to believe, then, that TBTF contributed to the financial crisis by reducing the perceived risk of the largest financial institutions and increasing their leverage.

In addition, TBTF has profound implications for the operation of the over-the-counter derivatives market. During the 1990s, influential economist/policymakers, including Alan Greenspan and Larry Summers, argued that derivatives would make the financial system more stable by shifting risks to those parties best able to bear them. This view is unassailable in principle. Over-the-counter derivatives reduce the cost of transferring risk. Thus they should facilitate the dispersion of risks; indeed, they make it easier for passive investors to hold an approximation of the Sharpe-Lintner market portfolio consisting of an infinitesimal portion of every risky asset in the economy.

But this logic does not hold in a world with TBTF institutions. There any device that reduces the cost of transferring risks facilitates greater concentration of risks in TBTF institutions. Those institutions have a natural advantage at bearing any type of risk because taxpayers are forced to backstop their losses. The underlying theory—that reducing transaction costs moves risks to those entities most able to bear them—remains valid. Unfortunately, however, the question "who can bear this risk at lowest cost?" has the same answer no matter what the risk—TBTF institutions can bear it at lowest cost to themselves, because taxpayers are on the hook for the tail risk.

Even Greenspan (2003) eventually expressed concern that derivatives were facilitating the concentration of risk in the largest institutions:

> One development that gives me and others some pause is the decline in the number of major derivatives dealers and its potential implications for market liquidity and for concentration of counterparty credit risks. . . . Concentration of market-making has the potential to create concentrations of credit risks between the dealers and the end-users of derivatives as well as between the dealers themselves.

In the run-up to the financial crisis, then, derivatives transactions had the effect of concentrating rather than dispersing risk. But this was not, as some critics argued, proof that over-the-counter derivatives are inherently destabilizing and in need of greater regulatory oversight. Instead, it was an unintended consequence of the government's growing tendency to step in and save the largest financial institutions from trading losses that threatened insolvency.

Dodd-Frank and TBTF

Policymakers can try to end TBTF or accept and accommodate it. Unfortunately, Dodd-Frank tries to occupy a middle ground, doing much less than it could to end perceived government backing. While it is difficult for the government credibly to commit to a no-bailout policy, Congress could at least limit Fed and Treasury authority and create burdensome internal rules for legislating bailouts to sow doubts in the minds of financial institutions' creditors and managers. Dodd-Frank takes steps in this direction by restricting the Fed's power under §13(3) of the Federal Reserve Act to lend in "unusual and exigent" circumstances, a power the Fed used during the financial crisis to assist troubled financial institutions (Mehra 2010), and by declaring that taxpayers shall bear no losses from "orderly liquidations," but such losses will be recovered from assessments against other financial firms.[5]

Despite its authors' protestations to the contrary, however, Dodd-Frank also takes several steps in the direction of accepting bailouts as inevitable and simply trying to ameliorate the moral hazard and competitive distortions they cause. This approach fits much more comfortably with the market failure narrative because it treats TBTF as a problem of systemic risk and interconnectedness—that is to say, a problem inherent in a complex financial system—rather than as a problem created by past government interventions that undermined the monitoring function of creditors.

Title I of the statute empowers a Financial Stability Oversight Council to identify "systemically important" financial institutions, or SIFIs—TBTF institutions in all but name. By in effect preclearing the TBTF institutions, the statute attempts to bring regularity and predictability to the bailout process. The statute also imposes higher capital requirements and greater regulatory oversight on SIFIs under the theory that this will raise costs and thereby reduce the competitive advantage of TBTF status while enabling the government to prevent excessive risk taking and therefore failures.

Title I's system of identifying SIFIs in advance rests on inconsistent premises. If TBTF is really an *economic* fact rather than a political fact, then it should be possible to set rules to distinguish SIFIs from non-SIFIs. Dodd-Frank does not do so. Instead, it gives essentially unfettered discretion to the FSOC. This fact seems more consistent with the view that the real determination of which institutions are TBTF is political. The key question is whether government agents fear that they will be blamed for any problems that result from the failure to bail out a given institution. But this, in turn, undermines the proposition that SIFIs, and only SIFIs, will be bailed out. Before the crisis, no one would have identified General Motors as a company whose failure would threaten the *financial* stability of the United States. But GM received a bailout nevertheless. This suggests that when the next crisis occurs, companies that are not designated as SIFIs can successfully lobby for bailouts if they tell a plausible story that their failure will cause great harm and the government will be blamed.

Both the lack of a clear definition of a SIFI and the fact that some potential SIFIs have objected to their inclusion is evidence against the theory on which Title I is based. Some financial institutions have concluded that they can have the best of both worlds—they can argue for a bailout when the time comes but in the meantime can avoid SIFI status and the increased costs that go with it (Peirce and Broughel 2012).

Dodd-Frank also operates on the principle that in a world of interconnected financial institutions, it is better to accept concentrated risk and rely on the government to pay close attention to the areas of concentration than to attempt to disperse risk. As discussed above, securitization and derivatives transactions brought apparently dispersed risks onto the books of the TBTF financial institutions and in turn exposed far-flung commercial and investment banks, mutual and hedge funds, and others to the credit of the TBTF institutions. Dodd-Frank chooses to encourage concentration but focus heavy regulatory attention on it. Thus, in addition to the greater regulatory oversight of SIFIs, Dodd-Frank requires that some previously over-the-counter derivatives transactions be cleared by a centralized counterparty. The clearinghouses will inevitably become SIFIs and TBTF institutions. Indeed, the statute anticipates this by giving the FSOC the ability to declare a "financial market utility" a SIFI.[6]

There are two theoretical problems with this approach. The first is that it has cause and effect backward. Derivatives markets don't create TBTF institutions. Rather, financial institutions that know they are TBTF have every incentive to take risks off the books of non-TBTF institutions. The transferors of risk find the price attractive because it is taxpayer-subsidized. But the fact that risks become concentrated *given* the existence of TBTF institutions is a poor argument for creating still more TBTF institutions and accepting the resulting moral hazard.

The second and larger problem is that it is implausible that regulatory oversight will control these concentrated risks and thereby render them harmless to the financial system and economy as a whole. Dodd-Frank will not end financial crises any more than did its dozens of predecessor reforms. But by encouraging the buildup of massive interest-rate, exchange-rate, and credit risk in a small number of entities, it takes an enormous gamble with taxpayer money.

Dodd-Frank and securities regulation

Dodd-Frank's securities law provisions share several traits with SOX. They include symbolic provisions, such as the "say on pay" requirement of periodic advisory shareholder votes on management compensation; mandated disclose of the gap between CEO and employee pay; mandated disclosure of the company's use of conflict minerals; and the requirement that hedge fund advisers register with the SEC. They continue the encroachment of the federal securities laws into corporate governance. They extend the requirements for director independence, still lacking empirical support, to compensation committees. Prior to Dodd-Frank, the SEC had a "wish list" of provisions that it hoped to see added to omnibus legislation at some point.[7] Several made it into Dodd-Frank.

Dodd-Frank also shows that industries blamed for a crisis can benefit from the ensuing reforms. Rating agencies played the role in Dodd-Frank that accounting firms did in SOX. They were identified as villains in the market failure narrative and the statute accordingly orders the SEC to remove references to their ratings from its rules. However, at the same time it layers on additional SEC oversight that creates substantial barriers to entry (White 2012). Rating agencies' reputations were in tatters after the crisis, providing an opportunity for new entrants, but the statute makes new entry more difficult. Interest groups shaped Dodd-Frank at every turn. Kaiser (2013) provides a useful summary.

Dodd-Frank's possible consequences

One of the purposes of my study of the New Deal–era securities statutes was to allow us to assess how Dodd-Frank will affect the markets. The statute may do some good. In particular, the requirement that financial firms boost their capital may enhance the stability of the financial system. This comes with caveats; if interested parties influence the details of the system as much as they did in the Basel process, there will be many perverse incentives.

Like prior financial reforms, Dodd-Frank will likely decrease competition and increase concentration, in this case among financial institutions and rating agencies. Dodd-Frank's mixed approach to TBTF has the merit of increasing uncertainty about which institutions will receive government assistance in the next crisis. Consistent with this view, as this chapter went to press, the US Government Accountability Office (2014) released a study applying multiple approaches to modeling the funding cost advantage of potentially TBTF banks. It finds that the funding advantage declined beginning in 2010. By contrast, the Bank for International Settlements finds that worldwide, the largest banks have a long-term funding advantage that widened substantially from 2007 to 2011 following US and European government interventions.[8] By adopting a mixed approach, Dodd-Frank ensures that the extent of implicit government support for large financial firms, like so many other issues, will depend on how regulators exercise their increased discretion in the future. Regardless of the extent of implicit government support, however, the dramatically increased regulatory costs for the banking sector will give a structural advantage to the largest financial institutions, just as the 1930s reforms advantaged the largest investment banks, mutual fund complexes, and stock exchanges.

Because part of this book's target audience is lawyers, I will also offer a prediction about Dodd-Frank's impact on the market for legal services. Contrary to the conventional wisdom, I suspect the impact will be detrimental to lawyers, or at least to the traditional Wall Street financial practice.

It is commonplace to say that Dodd-Frank, like other federal regulatory statutes, will produce more work for lawyers.[9] Certainly that was true of past financial reforms, particularly the New Deal securities statutes. The Securities Act of 1933 created demand for lawyers to assist in the preparation of registration statements and to guide issuers and underwriters through the rules that shape the public offering process. The Securities Exchange Act forced exchanges, broker-dealers, and exchange-traded companies to hire more in-house legal staff and consume more advisory services from outside counsel. After enactment of the Investment Company Act, the creation and flotation of a new mutual fund required substantial assistance from lawyers. Wall Street lawyers existed before the federal securities laws, but their numbers and importance increased substantially afterward.

Why won't Dodd-Frank do the same? Compare Dodd-Frank with the Securities Act of 1933, which produces substantial bread-and-butter work for major law firms. The Securities Act contains meticulous and complex rules governing the public offering process. It gives the administering agency, now the SEC, broad rulemaking authority, but the statute itself regulates the offering process in detail and thereby shapes the content of the SEC's regulations. On the spectrum of rules versus administrative discretion, the Securities Act is highly rule-like. Moreover, while the statute departed from prior law, it drew heavily from existing legal concepts and terminology. As a consequence, the Securities Act is in the lawyer's sweet spot. To avoid violating the statute, anyone making a securities offering needs advice on the interpretation of the rules and application of those rules to facts. This is the principal focus of legal education and lawyers therefore have a substantial advantage over non-lawyers in performing these functions. Even relatively new lawyers can provide many of the basic services an issuer or underwriter needs to engage in a registered or exempt offering.

Dodd-Frank is entirely different. It creates new institutions such as the Financial Stability Oversight Council (FSOC) and the Consumer Financial Protection Bureau (CFPB). It gives these new agencies and existing ones such as the Fed, the FDIC, the SEC, and the CFTC new powers. But its 848 single-spaced pages include surprisingly few rules of conduct. Instead, the statute consists principally of grants of authority and instructions to undertake studies or engage in rulemaking. Many of the grants of authority convey extraordinary levels of discretion untethered to recognized legal principles or categories. The FSOC may subject certain nonbank entities to enhanced regulation, the content of which is largely within the discretion of the FSOC and the existing financial regulators, if it concludes their activities "could pose a threat to the financial stability of the United States."[10] When the Secretary of the Treasury finds that a financial company is in "danger" of a default that would have "serious adverse effects on financial stability in the United States," it can appoint the FDIC as receiver of the company with broad discretion to determine the payouts to creditors.[11] The SEC's new Investor Advocate may identify "problems that investors have with financial service providers and investment products" and propose changes to SEC rules "that may be appropriate to mitigate [such] problems."[12] The CFPB is authorized to prohibit "abusive" contract terms.[13]

As a result, Skeel (2011, 9) argues that Dodd-Frank creates "a system of ad hoc interventions by regulators that are divorced from basic rule-of-law constraints." This is necessarily a subjective judgment, but one I share. If correct, it should be of great concern to lawyers. There is empirical support for the proposition that constraints on executive discretion contribute to economic prosperity (DeLong and Shleifer 1993, La Porta et al. 2004).

Putting aside societal concerns, however, lawyers have self-interested reasons to fear the consequences of Dodd-Frank. Representing financial firms under Dodd-Frank will largely involve persuading regulators and other agencies to exercise their discretion in a particular way—to designate or not designate a particular firm as systemically important, to pay a particular class of creditors before others on the theory that financial catastrophe will otherwise ensue, or to treat a contract term as nonabusive (while of course treating a competitor's term as abusive).

These are effectively lobbying activities, not the practice of law as normally understood. They do not involve statutory interpretation, strictly speaking, because statutory language like "could pose a threat to the financial stability of the United States" is too vague and disconnected from legal concepts to bring into play the lawyer's normal toolbox of interpretive canons. They do not require persuading a government agent that the language of the statute mandates a particular result in a particular factual setting. Instead, they involve persuading the agent that the requested use of the agent's discretion will produce desirable political or economic consequences. The needed skill set is the lobbyist's ability to appeal to the agent's policy preferences or self-interest, to network, and to keep close track of the credits and debits accrued from prior interactions.

Dodd-Frank retains existing administrative procedures. It will generate rulemaking proposals, administrative hearings, and judicial review, all of which will involve lawyers. It will be a boon to those lawyers whose practice straddles law and lobbying. But the statute's keystone is almost limitless administrative discretion. The rule-heavy New Deal securities reforms substantially enhanced the role of the Wall Street lawyer, and the discretion-heavy Dodd-Frank Act will likely diminish it.

Can We Do Better?

Both the Great Depression and the subprime crisis involved debt-fueled asset price inflation followed by an equity market crash, deleveraging, and an economic downturn. The pattern will recur. When it does, politicians who want to avoid blame and policy entrepreneurs who want to gain influence will propose sweeping regulatory overhauls. How can we better avoid unintended consequences the next time? I conclude with a few suggestions.

Back to Basics

The two most effective features of the New Deal securities reforms were the mandatory disclosure of sellers' conflicts of interest in the Securities Act and the creation of federal causes of action for financial fraud and materially misleading disclosures. This observation is not unique to the United States. La Porta, Lopez-de-Silanes, and Shleifer (2006) conclude that rules mandating disclosure and providing for civil liability dominate other forms of securities regulation as means of fostering large and liquid equity markets. Not coincidentally, both measures facilitate private ordering by market participants rather than substituting policymakers' judgments for their own.

The farther Congress and the SEC have strayed from contract-enhancing regulation, the greater the tendency to reduce competition and increase industry concentration by eliminating diverse market practices in favor of the "best" practice, which is often the preferred practice of leading firms. Unfortunately, since the 1930s, Congress and the SEC have increasingly switched from contract-enhancing regulation and toward command-and-control regulation of the markets. Reversing the trend would benefit investors while imposing less cost on market participants.

It's Not about the Quantity of Regulation

After a crisis, legislators and the press, and even many academics, frame the issue as whether there should be "more" or "less" regulation. This framing is profoundly unhelpful. As Calomiris and Haber (2013, 100) observe with respect to bank regulation, a more useful question is how we got the regulations that failed to perform adequately in the crisis. Asking that question may help uncover the prior interest-group bargains that led to legislation that produced perverse incentives or unintended consequences. This is no guarantee that the same interest groups will not prevail again, but at least it focuses attention on the relevant issues.

Don't Lock In Bad Regulation

My findings show the wisdom in Romano's (2012) proposal that financial legislation include sunset provisions. Because financial reforms are adopted in haste in the wake of a crisis, the probability of unintended consequences is unusually high. There is ample evidence that policymakers are suffering buyers' remorse over parts of both SOX and Dodd-Frank. Indeed, a substantial reason for the JOBS Act was concern that SOX's mandates were contributing to the downturn in IPOs in the United States. The fact that many of Dodd-Frank's implementing regulations remain unwritten four years after enactment is not just a function of the number of required regulations; regulators are finding it hard to write the rules in part because they are finding it difficult to avoid adverse consequences. An automatic sunset provision would ameliorate these problems.

Do More by Doing Less

Finally, Congress should admit to itself, even if it cannot admit to its constituents, that post-crisis financial reform legislation is an exercise in blame avoidance. If it does so, it can resolve to do less the next time it responds to a crisis. Congressional hearings followed by largely symbolic changes to existing law should suffice to satisfy the public that Congress is doing something. Above all, Congress should say "never again" to the incoherent bundling of hundreds of unrelated lobbyist-provided provisions into omnibus legislation as in SOX and Dodd-Frank. Of course regulations need to be updated as market conditions change, but this should be done thoughtfully during noncrisis periods.

The government's response to the 2007–8 crisis went far beyond new regulations. The government provided loans and equity infusions to a variety of financial and nonfinancial firms and undertook unprecedented experiments in monetary policy with the objective of avoiding harm to the financial system and the economy. It would have been logically possible for the government to do much less in fall 2008. It could have provided liquidity in the form of secured loans to solvent financial institutions and allowed insolvent ones to proceed to bankruptcy. Policymakers and commentators were certain that doing so would return the United States to a financial Stone Age. We do not have any empirical basis for that conclusion—largely because we do not have an example of a financial crisis in which the government declined to "do something" since the 1907 crisis described in detail by Bruner (2007).

I concede that it is easy to disagree after the fact but it would have been hard to act differently at the time. That is all the more reason to cast a critical eye today on the response to the crisis in order to prepare to do better next time. The conventional understanding of the acute phase of the crisis is that Lehman Brothers' failure demonstrated that interconnection was indeed a serious problem. The Treasury Department and the Fed had no choice but to respond with extraordinary measures. An alternative worth considering is that the markets believed that there was a rule—an unwritten one, but a rule nevertheless—that said "no significant financial institution will be allowed to go through the traditional bankruptcy process; the government will do whatever it takes to arrange a purchase and assumption or similar transaction." The Lehman bankruptcy made it clear that there was no such rule—in fact, there were no rules at all. Officials in the Treasury, the Fed, and the FDIC were making it up on the fly. Boundless discretion and therefore boundless unpredictability, not Lehman's interconnectedness, may have made the crisis acute. Going forward, commitment to a set of rules, even a rule that says "all large financial institutions, except banks holding insured deposits, are subject to bankruptcy proceedings just like everyone else," would bring more stability.

This is not to say that the bankruptcy rules that apply to industrial companies are perfect for bank holding companies, broker-dealers, and hedge funds. It makes sense to have a separate chapter of the bankruptcy code for financial institutions. But any such chapter should embody the fundamental principle that prebankruptcy entitlements are respected. "Resolution" should not be a process of allocating losses to one creditor rather than another based on the FDIC's ad hoc assessment of what is best from a systemic perspective. Unfortunately, the resolution authority in Dodd-Frank fails this critical test.

Is it realistic to ask the government to show more restraint in a crisis? The federal government's limited role in resolving the 1907 crisis was less a matter of choice than of capacity. Lacking a central bank and with a total federal budget of roughly $600 million, President Theodore Roosevelt's administration took a back seat to J. P. Morgan in the resolution of insolvent banks and trust companies. The latter fact alarmed progressives, who concluded that the federal government must be in a position to control what they called a "money trust" led by Morgan. That conclusion led ultimately to the birth of the Federal Reserve System. More generally, it contributed to the view that the government must be large and powerful enough to manage the financial system.

The 1907 crisis thus paved the way for the triumph of one of two opposing strands in American political thought about the best way to prevent the financial sector from becoming too concentrated and powerful. The New Dealers and their modern successors believe that only a strong and intrusive central government can hold finance in check and force it to earn its profits by serving the public. The men who shaped the federal securities laws—Franklin Roosevelt, James Landis, and William O. Douglas, among others—subscribed to the progressive creed that large concentrations of economic power are dangerous. However, they did not follow Brandeis's prescription of favoring smaller economic units. Instead, they believed in encouraging larger economic units while creating a larger and more powerful government to check their power (Brand 2002; Milkis 2002). Inspired by that view, they did not stop at remedying the undoubted limitations of state-level corporate, contract, agency, and fraud law as applied to a national securities market. Instead, they concluded that the market and all its significant actors should be subject to licensing and oversight by a dedicated regulatory agency.

A much older view, associated with Thomas Jefferson, holds that private finance will be smaller and less powerful only if the government is smaller and less powerful. Government inevitably becomes the partner and enabler of major financial institutions. Government's attempts at oversight serve primarily to facilitate rent-seeking, which offers greater profit without greater productivity.

Whatever else one might say about the history of securities regulation in the United States, it should cause us to give Jefferson's opinion a renewed and serious hearing.

APPENDIX A

All variables, except as noted below, were downloaded from Price V. Fishback's website in December 2000. The current URL, as of June 2014, is http://econ.arizona.edu/faculty/fishback.asp.

Number of securities fraud cases. LEXIS/NEXIS state securities law database.

Average bank assets. Board of Governors of the Federal Reserve System, All-Bank Statistics, United States 1896–1955 (1959).

Investment banks per million employed. Number of investment bank offices from Investment Bankers Association of America, Proceedings of the Annual Convention (1912–30), extrapolated for 1910–11. Total employment from Fishback dataset.

Stockbrokers as percentage of employed. Number of stockbrokers from census data for 1910, 1920, and 1930, interpolated for other years. Total employment from Fishback dataset.

APPENDIX B

Earnings Announcement Dates

Company	Announcement Date 1935	1936
Affiliated Prods Inc	2/23	2/24
Air Way Elec Appliance Corp	2/28	2/25
Allegheny Stl Co	2/16	2/20
Allis Chalmers Corp	2/8	3/13
American Brake Shoe & Fdry	2/4	2/10
American Chain Inc	3/15	3/6
American Chicle Co	2/2	2/1
American Colortype Co	3/13	3/12
American Hawaiian Ss Co	2/5	2/27
American Ice Co	3/6	3/4
American Mach & Metals Inc	3/13	3/3
American Metal Ltd	2/20	3/4
American Safety Razor Corp	2/28	2/27
American Smlt & Refng Co	3/11	3/9
American Snuff Co	2/13	2/11
American Steel Foundries	2/8	2/7
American Stores Co	3/6	3/3
American Sugar Refng Co	3/14	3/12
American Tob Co	3/5	3/3
American Zinc Lead & Smlt Co	3/7	3/10
Artloom Corp	3/4	2/1
Atlantic Gulf & West Indies Ss	2/28	2/27
Atlantic Refng Co	1/25	1/27
Atlas Powder Co	1/29	1/29
Barker Bros Corp	2/15	2/20
Barnsdall Corp	3/4	2/28
Bayuk Cigars Inc	2/26	2/19
Belding Heminway Inc	2/18	2/6
Beneficial Indl Ln Corp	3/11	2/28
Bethlehem Steel Corp	2/1	1/31
Bigelow Sanford Carpet Corp	2/15	2/5
Blaw Knox Co	2/20	2/24
Bohn Alum & Brass Corp	2/26	3/9

Company	Announcement Date 1935	1936
Borden Co	3/13	3/11
Borg Warner Corp	3/4	3/3
Briggs & Stratton Corp	2/20	2/25
Bristol Myers Co	3/6	1/23
Brooklyn Union Gas Co	2/21	2/19
Bucyrus Erie Co	3/5	3/3
Burroughs Adding Mach Co	3/6	3/6
Butte Copper & Zinc Co	2/26	3/7
Calumet & Hecla Cons Copper Co	2/18	3/2
Campbell Wyant & Cannon Fdry Co	2/28	2/21
Case J I Co	3/6	3/11
Caterpillar Tractor Inc	1/22	1/23
Celanese Corp Amer	3/5	3/3
Certain Teed Prods Corp	3/6	3/2
Childs Co	2/21	2/10
City Ice & Fuel Co	2/23	3/7
Cluett Peabody & Co Inc	2/1	2/15
Coca Cola Co	3/5	3/2
Commercial Cr Co	2/14	2/5
Commercial Solvents Corp	2/26	2/26
Commonwealth & Southern Corp	1/23	1/29
Congoleum Nairn Inc	2/26	2/17
Consolidated Cigar Corp	2/4	2/3
Consolidated Laundries Corp	2/23	2/24
Continental Baking Corp	2/7	2/5
Continental Can Inc	2/8	2/13
Corn Products Refining Co	3/8	3/9
Cream Of Wheat Corp	2/13	2/17
Crucible Stl Co Amer	3/1	2/5
Curtis Publishing Co	2/7	2/14
Detroit Edison Co	2/1	1/20
Diamond Match Co	3/2	3/3
Du Pont E I De Nemours & Co	1/23	2/4
Eastern Rolling Ml Co	3/9	3/11
Electric Autolite Co	3/11	2/5
Electric Storage Battery Co	3/4	3/4
Eureka Vacuum Cleaner Co	2/8	2/14
Evans Products Co	2/28	2/26
Fairbanks Morse & Co Inc	3/12	3/7
Federal Mng & Smlt Co	3/15	3/12
Federal Screw Wks	3/6	2/24
Gabriel Co	3/6	3/14
General Amern Transn Corp	3/13	2/15
General Baking Co	2/2	2/24
General Bronze Corp	3/4	2/28
General Cable Corp	3/5	2/18
General Cigar Inc	1/31	1/31
General Foods Corp	3/15	3/12
General Printing Ink Corp	2/9	2/20
General Ry Signal Co	2/5	2/6
Gillette Safety Razor Co	2/6	2/28
Goodyear Tire & Rubr Co	2/19	2/18

Company	Announcement Date 1935	1936
Great Northern Iron Ore Pptys	1/22	1/30
Hamilton Watch Co	3/13	3/14
Harbison Walker Refractories Co	2/7	2/4
Helme G W Co	2/16	2/17
Hershey Chocolate Corp	3/7	3/7
Hollander A & Son Inc	2/1	1/30
Homestake Mining Co	3/7	3/4
Houdaille Hershey Corp	2/19	2/14
Houston Oil Co Tex	2/25	2/25
Industrial Rayon Corp	1/25	1/30
Inland Steel Co	1/30	1/29
International Business Machs Corp	3/14	3/7
International Harvester Co	3/14	3/14
International Silver Co	3/12	3/10
Intertype Corp	2/27	2/28
Jewel Tea Inc	2/4	2/3
Johns Manville Corp	2/27	2/29
Kresge S S Co	2/4	2/8
Kroger Grocery & Baking Co	2/13	2/10
Lambert Co	3/13	3/7
Lehigh Portland Cem Co	2/21	2/24
Liggett & Myers Tob Co	1/24	1/23
Lima Locomotive Wks Inc	2/13	2/25
Lorillard P Co	2/9	2/8
Ludlum Steel Co	3/1	2/28
Mack Trucks Inc	3/1	2/27
Marshall Field & Co Ill	2/23	2/24
Mathieson Alkali Wks Inc	2/21	2/20
Maytag Co	3/11	3/9
Mc Call Corp	2/6	2/28
Mc Keesport Tin Plate Co	2/20	2/17
Melville Shoe Corp	2/19	2/24
Mesta Mach Co	3/1	2/28
Midland Stl Prods Co	2/26	2/25
Minneapolis Honeywell Regulator	1/31	2/14
Mohawk Carpet Mls Inc	2/14	2/6
Monsanto Chemical Co	2/21	3/9
Motor Wheel Corp	2/14	2/13
Mullins Mfg Corp	3/7	2/17
Munsingwear Inc	2/14	2/15
National Acme Co	2/26	2/25
National Biscuit Co	2/23	2/20
National Distillers Prods Corp	3/14	2/17
National Steel Corp	2/4	1/31
National Supply Co Del	3/14	3/11
National Tea Co	2/21	2/21
Neisner Brothers Inc	2/15	3/4
New York Air Brake Co	2/18	2/17
Newberry J J Co	3/1	3/3
Owens Illinois Glass Co	2/16	2/15
Pacific Ltg Corp	1/25	2/4
Pacific Mls Inc	2/6	2/19

Company	Announcement Date 1935	1936
Pacific Westn Oil Corp	3/4	3/3
Penick & Ford Ltd	2/21	2/24
Peoples Drug Stores Inc	3/12	3/16
Phillips Jones Corp	2/23	2/24
Phoenix Hosiery Co	2/20	2/20
Pittsburgh Coal Co	3/11	3/10
Pittsburgh Screw & Bolt Corp	2/16	3/16
Plymouth Oil Co	1/23	2/18
Purity Bakeries Corp	2/13	2/6
Radio Corp Amer	2/27	2/21
Raybestos Manhattan Inc	2/21	2/20
Real Silk Hosiery Mls Inc	1/31	2/1
Reynolds Metals Co	3/6	3/3
Reynolds R J Tob Co	1/10	1/11
Reynolds R J Tobacco Co	1/10	1/11
Reynolds Spring Co	2/23	2/21
Safeway Stores Inc	2/23	2/5
Savage Arms Corp Old	1/30	1/29
Scott Paper Co	2/1	2/5
Seagrave Corp	3/5	2/25
Sharon Steel Hoop Co	3/4	2/27
Sharp & Dohme Inc	2/19	2/17
Shattuck Frank G Co	3/8	3/7
Silver King Coalition Mines Co	2/9	3/2
Simmons Company	3/15	2/28
Spear & Co	3/4	2/24
Spiegel May Stern Inc	3/14	2/27
Standard Brands Inc	3/8	2/1
Standard Oil Co Kans Del	3/5	3/3
Sterling Prods Inc	2/25	2/24
Stewart Warner Corp	3/7	2/5
Sun Oil Co	1/29	2/1
Superheater Co	3/6	3/7
Superior Stl Corp	2/1	2/21
Telautograph Corp	3/2	2/7
Texas Pacific Land Trust	2/19	2/26
Thatcher Mfg Co	2/13	2/13
Twin City Rapid Transit Co	2/1	1/31
Ulen & Co	2/23	2/24
Underwood Elliot Fisher Co	2/21	2/24
Union Oil Co Calif	2/18	2/15
Union Tank Car Co	3/13	3/11
United Carbon Co	2/21	2/17
United Drug Inc	3/11	3/10
United Fruit Co	2/5	1/16
United States Freight Co	3/1	2/13
United States Gypsum Co	2/20	2/19
United States Pipe & Fdry Co	1/25	3/16
United States Rubber Co	3/9	3/7
United States Steel Corp	1/30	1/29
United Sts Hoffman Machy Corp	2/14	2/13
United Sts Tob Co	2/13	2/11

Company	Announcement Date	
	1935	1936
Van Raalte Co	3/2	3/3
Virginia Iron Coal & Coke Co	1/22	1/25
Waldorf System Inc	3/2	3/2
Warren Fdry & Pipe Corp	2/1	1/30
Webster Eisenlohr Inc	2/26	2/24
Western Un Teleg Co	2/16	2/14
Westinghouse Electric & Mfg Co	3/11	3/10
Westvaco Chlorine Prods Corp	3/2	3/3
Woolworth F W Co	1/29	1/30
Worthington Pump & Machy Co	3/5	3/3

Notes

Introduction

1. The Davis Polk law firm's website reports that as of the fourth anniversary of Dodd-Frank's enactment, July 18, 2014, 45.4 percent of the rulemaking deadlines set by the statute have been missed.

2. "Investor Education: Disclosure for the 1990s," remarks by Chairman Arthur Levitt, US Securities and Exchange Commission, University of Virginia, Charlottesville, November 1, 1995. Available at http://www.sec.gov/news/speech/speecharchive/1995/spch063.txt.

Chapter One

1. *House of Commons Journal*, vol. 11, *1693–1697* (1803), 569–72.

2. Ibid., 593–95.

3. 8&9 Will. 3, ch. 32, 7 *Statutes of the Realm* 285 (1697).

Chapter Three

1. Brandeis (1914). See Seligman (2003, 41): "Rarely did Roosevelt speak about the stock market without invoking" Brandeis's book.

2. "Political Party Platforms, Democratic Party Platform of 1932, June 27, 1932," American Presidency Project of the University of California, Santa Barbara, http://www.presidency.ucsb.edu/ws/index.php?pid=29595.

3. *Gluckstein v Barnes,* App Cas 240, 248 (HL 1900) (Macnaghten, J.)

4. For example, *Lydney & Wigpool Iron Ore Co. v Bird,* 33 Chanc Div 85, 86–88 (Ct App 1886).

5. *Erlanger v New Sombrero Phosphate Co.,* 3 App Cas 1218 (HL 1878), 1229–30 (Penzance opinion), 1236 (Cairns opinion).

6. *Erlanger,* 1236 (Cairns opinion) (disclosure to independent directors); *Salomon v Salomon,* App Cas 22, 33 (HL 1897) (disclosure to shareholders as valid alternative to disclosure to directors).

7. For example, *Lomita Land & Water Co. v Robinson,* 154 Cal 36, 97 P 10, 11–13 (1908); *Wills v Nehalem Coal Co.,* 52 Or 70, 96 P 528, 530 (1908); *Yale Gas-Stove Co. v Wilcox,* 64 Conn 101, 29 A 303, 304 (1894).

8. *Old Dominion Copper Mining & Smelting Co. v Lewisohn,* 210 US 206, 209, 212 (1908) (Holmes opinion).

9. Business plan, for example: Ark Stat § 8418k (1921 & Supp 1927); Idaho Code Ann § 25–1602 (1932).

Schedule of the issuer's assets with an appraisal, for example: Ill Rev Stat ch 32, paras. 262(6), 263 (Cahill 1933); Comp Stat Neb § 81–5405 (1930).

Abstracts of title to real estate and a schedule of insurance policies: US Department of Commerce, A Study of the Economic and Legal Aspects of the Proposed Federal Securities Act, in *Securities Act, Hearings on S 875 before the Senate Committee on Banking and Currency,* 73d Cong., 1st Sess. 312, 321 (1933).

A statement of "all material facts, for example: Va Code § 3848(51)(f) (1930). See also Rev Stat Kan § 17–1228(6) (1923 & Supp 1933) ("all knowledge or information . . . relative to the character or value of such securities or of the property or earning power" of the issuer).

Chapter Four

1. The district court's opinion is reported at *US v Morgan*, 118 F Supp 621 (SDNY 1953).

2. *Stock Exchange Practices: Hearings Before the Senate Banking and Currency Comm.*, 73rd Cong., 1st Sess., Part 1, 168–69 (1933) ("Pecora Hearings") (testimony of George Whitney).

3. See Brief on General Points in Support of Defendants' Motion to Dismiss at 47, *US v Morgan.*

4. *US v Morgan*, 642–43.

5. *Proceedings of the Ninth Annual Convention of the Investment Bankers Association of America*, 1920 (hereafter "1920 Proceedings"), 38.

6. The market share figures provided later in this chapter include foreign as well as domestic issues. The *Federal Reserve Bulletin*, my source for foreign issues in the United States, does not provide information going back to 1912, so foreign issues are omitted from table 4.2.

7. For example, *Proceedings of the Sixteenth Annual Convention of the Investment Bankers Association of America* (1927) ("1927 Proceedings"), 45 (address of IBAA President noting "diminishing margins of profit"); *Proceedings of the Seventeenth Annual Convention of the Investment Bankers Association of America*

(1928) ("1928 Proceedings"), 8 (address of IBAA President arguing that a return to "the condition of wholesome competition enjoyed in former years" was necessary in order to "have happier conditions and better net profits").

8. 1927 Proceedings, 206.

9. Ibid., 187–93.

10. *Proceedings of the Eighteenth Annual Convention of the Investment Bankers Association of America* 170 (1929).

11. 1927 Proceedings, 240.

12. 1928 Proceedings, 174.

13. Ibid., 186.

14. 1927 Proceedings, 195.

15. Ibid., 236.

16. Ibid., 206.

17. "Wall Street at Close Range: II–The Bond Salesman's Problems," *World's Work*, January 1931, 98.

18. Senate Banking and Currency Committee, 73rd Congress, Minutes for May 23, 26, 30 and 31, and June 5, 1933 (housed at the National Archives).

19. "Halsey Develops New Form of Summary," *Wall Street Journal*, May 25, 1936, 1; "New Issue Bulletins May be Circulated in 20-day Period," same issue, 3.

20. Securities Act, Schedule A, paragraph 16, 15 U.S.C. §§ 77aa.

21. Investment Bankers Code Committee, *Code of Fair Competition for Investment Bankers* (Washington, DC: GPO, 1934).

22. Code of Fair Competition, Art. V, § 4(a).

23. Code of Fair Competition, Art. V, § 4(b); Art. IX, § 7; Art. X, §§ 1–3.

24. See Vincent Carosso, *Investment Banking in America: A History* (Cambridge: Harvard University Press, 1970), 389; "Investment Bankers Organize," *Business Week*, October 12, 1935, 23–24 (noting that SEC chairman James Landis "recommended that the work and ideas of the former code committee, as well as the personnel, be perpetuated in a voluntary group").

25. Section 15A(e)(1) of the Securities Exchange Act of 1934, 15 U.S.C. 78o-3(e)(1).

26. FINRA Manual, NASD Rule 2410.

Chapter Five

1. Parts of this section were previously published as Paul G. Mahoney, "The Exchange as Regulator," *Virginia Law Review* 83 (1997): 1453–1500. Reprinted with permission of the Virginia Law Review Association, which holds the copyright.

2. Form 10 and its instructions were published in full in the *Wall Street Journal*, December 26, 1934, 8.

3. The report is available online from the University of Pennsylvania Library's Corporate Records collection.

Chapter Seven

1. This section was first published in modified form as Paul G. Mahoney, "The Public Utility Pyramids," *Journal of Legal Studies* 41 (2012): 37–66. Reprinted with permission of the University of Chicago Press.

2. "Franklin Delano Roosevelt speech in Portland, Oregon, Sept. 21, 1932," http://newdeal.feri.org/speeches/1932a.htm, accessed December 31, 2013.

3. I am grateful to an anonymous referee for this observation.

4. I include US holding companies with foreign subsidiaries. PUHCA did not explicitly limit the SEC's ability to order a US company to divest itself of the shares of its non-US subsidiaries.

5. I do not include the May 7 and 8 events in table 7.2 or the tests because events favorable and unfavorable to the passage of the death sentence provision occurred on successive days, making it impossible to disentangle the responses to the two events.

6. The hypothesis that predators took advantage of prey does not generate any prediction about returns on the six companies that are both predator and prey. I created a portfolio of those companies and calculated returns on it, which are also similar to returns on the predator-only and prey-only portfolios. Those results are not reported.

7. In principle one could evaluate PUHCA's effect on industrial customers (although not households) by analyzing the returns of industrial companies that were heavy users of electricity, such as mining companies. Unfortunately, many of those companies had captive utility subsidiaries that would have to be divested under PUHCA, making the net effect indeterminate.

8. One subsidiary of Electric Bond & Share (American Gas & Electric) operated in Virginia, West Virginia, and Ohio, and another (American Water Works & Electric) operated in Pennsylvania and New Jersey. Omitting either or both from the "Electric Bond & Share system" sample does not change the result.

Chapter Eight

1. Securities Act Release 33-8591, *Federal Register* August 3, 2005, 44722.

2. Statement on the American Institute of CPA's website, http://www.aicpa.org/Advocacy/Issues/Pages/Section404bofSOX.aspx (accessed August 4, 2013).

3. Michiyo Nakamoto and David Wighton, "Citigroup Chief Stays Bullish on Buy-outs." *Financial Times* July 9, 2007.

4. Data from the website of the Federal Deposit Insurance Corporation, http://www2.fdic.gov/hsob/SelectRpt.asp?EntryTyp=30 (accessed August 4, 2013).

5. Dodd-Frank section 214.

6. Dodd-Frank section 804.

7. "SEC's 'Wish List' of 42 Changes It Seeks in the Federal Securities Laws," *Securities Docket*, July 16, 2009, http://www.securitiesdocket.com/2009/07/16/sec-s-wish-list-of-42-changes-it-seeks-in-the-federal-securities-laws/.

8. Bank for International Settlements, *BIS 82nd Annual Report 2011/12*, 75–76.

9. For example, SEC Commissioner Daniel M. Gallagher's remarks before the Corporate Directors Forum, January 29, 2013, https://www.sec.gov/News/Speech/Detail/Speech/1365171492142#.U6mkzctOV9A.

10. Dodd-Frank section 113(a).

11. Dodd-Frank sections 203(b), 210.

12. Dodd-Frank section 915.

13. Dodd-Frank section 1031.

Bibliography

Aggarwal, Rajesh K., and Guojun Wu. 2006. "Stock Market Manipulations." *Journal of Business* 79:1915–53.

Allen, F., and D. Gale. 1992. "Stock-Price Manipulation." *Review of Financial Studies* 5:503–29.

Allen, Franklin, and Gary Gorton. 1992. "Stock Price Manipulation, Market Microstructure and Asymmetric Information." *European Economic Review* 36:624–30.

Allison, Paul D. 1984. *Event History Analysis: Regression for Longitudinal Event Data.* Beverly Hills, CA: Sage.

Asthana, Sharad, and Steven Balsam. 2001. "The Effect of Edgar on the Market Reaction to 10-K Filings." *Journal of Accounting and Public Policy* 20:349–72.

Atiase, Rowland Kwame. 1985. "Predisclosure Information, Firm Capitalization, and Security Price Behavior Around Earnings Announcements." *Journal of Accounting Research* 23:21–36.

Attig, Najah, Wai-Ming Fong, Yoser Gadhoum, and Larry H. P. Lang. 2006. "Effects of Large Shareholding on Information Asymmetry and Stock Liquidity." *Journal of Banking and Finance* 30:2875–92.

Badger, Anthony. 2008. *FDR: The First Hundred Days.* New York: Hill and Wang, 2008.

Bailey, Warren, G. Andrew Karolyi, and Carolina Salva. 2006. "The Economic Consequences of Increased Disclosure: Evidence from International Cross-listings." *Journal of Financial Economics* 81:175–213.

Bamber, Linda Smith. 1986. "The Information Content of Annual Earnings Releases: A Trading Volume Approach." *Journal of Accounting Research* 24:40–56.

Bamber, Linda Smith, and Youngsoon Susan Cheon. 1995. "Differential Price and Volume Reactions to Accounting Earnings Announcements." *Accounting Review* 70:417–41.

Banner, Stuart. 1998. *Anglo-American Securities Regulation: Cultural and Political Roots, 1690–1860.* Cambridge: Cambridge University Press.

Bates, George E. 1937. "The Waiting Period under the Securities Act." *Harvard Business Review* 15:203–13.

Bauer, John. 1930. "New York Survey of Public Utility Regulation." *American Economic Review* 20:381–99.

Beaver, William H. 1968. "The Information Content of Annual Earnings Announcements." *Journal of Accounting Research* 6:67–92.

Becht, Marco, and J. Bradford DeLong. 2005. "Why Has There Been So Little Blockholding in America?" In *A History of Corporate Governance around the World: Family Business Groups to Professional Managers*, edited by Randall K. Morck, 613–66. Cambridge, MA: National Bureau of Economic Research.

Benston, George J. 1973. "Required Disclosure and the Stock Market: An Evaluation of the Securities Exchange Act of 1934." *American Economic Review* 63 (March): 132–55.

———. 1976. *Corporate Financial Disclosure in the UK and the USA*. Farnborough, UK: Saxon House.

———. 1977. "An Appraisal of the Costs and Benefits of Government-Required Disclosure: SEC and FTC Requirements." *Law and Contemporary Problems* 41:30–62.

Benveniste, Lawrence M., and Paul A. Spindt. 1989. "How Investment Bankers Determine the Offer Price and Allocation of New Issues." *Journal of Financial Economics* 24:343–61.

Berle, Adolf Augustus, and Gardiner C. Means. 1932. *The Modern Corporation and Private Property.* edited by Gardiner Colt Means. New York: Commerce Clearing House.

Bertrand, Marianne, Paras Mehta, and Sendhil Mullainathan. 2002. "Ferreting Out Tunneling: An Application to Indian Business Groups." *Quarterly Journal of Economics* 117:121–48.

Blackstone, William. 2001. *Commentaries on the Laws of England.* 4 vols. London: Cavendish.

Blinder, Alan S. 2013. *After the Music Stopped: The Financial Crisis, the Response, and the Work Ahead.* New York: Penguin Books.

Bonbright, James C., and Gardiner C. Means. 1932. *The Holding Company: Its Public Significance and Its Regulation.* New York: McGraw-Hill.

Brand, Donald R. 2002. "Competition and the New Deal Regulatory State." In *The New Deal and the Triumph of Liberalism*, edited by Sidney M. Milkis and Jerome M. Mileur, 166–92. Amherst: University of Massachusetts Press.

Brandeis, Louis D. 1914. *Other Peoples' Money and How the Bankers Use It.* New York: Frederick A. Stokes Company.

Brown, Stephen J., and Jerold B. Warner. 1985. "Using Daily Stock Returns: The Case of Event Studies." *Journal of Financial Economics* 14:3–31.

Bruner, Robert F. 2007. *The Panic of 1907: Lessons Learned from the Market's Perfect Storm.* Edited by Sean D. Carr. Hoboken, NJ: John Wiley and Sons.

Buchanan, N. S. 1933. "Service Contracts in the Electric Bond and Share Company." *Journal of Land and Public Utility Economics* 9:283–96.

Bushee, Brian J., and Christian Leuz. 2005. "Economic Consequences of SEC Disclosure Regulation: Evidence from the OTC Bulletin Board." *Journal of Accounting and Economics* 39:233–64.

Calomiris, Charles W., and Stephen H. Haber. 2013. "Why Banking Systems Succeed—and Fail." *Foreign Affairs* 92:97–110.

———. 2014. *Fragile by Design: The Political Origins of Banking Crises and Scarce Credit.* Princeton, NJ: Princeton University Press.

Carosso, Vincent P. 1970. *Investment Banking in America, a History.* Cambridge, MA: Harvard University Press.

Caudill, Steven B., and John B. Jackson. 1989. "Measuring Marginal Effects in Limited Dependent Variable Models." *Statistician* 38:203–6.

Chernow, Ron. 1991. *The House of Morgan: An American Banking Dynasty and the Rise of Modern Finance.* New York: Simon and Schuster.

Claessens, Stijn, Simeon Djankov, Joseph Fan, and Larry H. P. Lang. 2002. "Disentangling the Incentive and Entrenchment Effects of Large Shareholdings." *Journal of Finance* 57:2741–71.

Cottrell, P. L. 1980. *Industrial Finance, 1830–1914: The Finance and Organization of English Manufacturing Industry.* London: Methuen.

Cunningham, Lawrence A. 2003. "The Sarbanes-Oxley Yawn: Heavy Rhetoric, Light Reform (and It Just Might Work)." *Connecticut Law Review* 35:915–88.

Daines, Robert, and Charles M. Jones. 2005. "Mandatory Disclosure, Asymmetric Information and Liquidity: The Impact of the 1934 Act." Working Paper.

Dale, Richard. 2004. *The First Crash: Lessons from the South Sea Bubble.* Princeton, NJ: Princeton University Press.

Davidson, Lee. 1997. "Continental Illinois and 'Too Big to Fail.'" In *History of the 80s—Lessons for the Future*, edited by Federal Deposit Insurance Corp. Washington, DC: Government Printing Office.

DeLong, J. Bradford, and Andrei Shleifer. 1993. "European City Growth before the Industrial Revolution." *Journal of Law and Economics* 36:671–702.

Demsetz, Harold, and Kenneth Lehn. 1985. "The Structure of Corporate Ownership: Causes and Consequences." *Journal of Political Economy* 93:1155–77.

Dewing, Arthur S. 1931. *The Financial Policy of Corporations.* New York: Ronald Press Company.

Dickson, P.G.M. 1967. *The Financial Revolution in England: A Study in the Development of Public Credit, 1688–1756.* New York: St. Martin's Press.

Dillon, Gadis J. 1979. "Corporate Asset Revaluations: 1925–1934." *Accounting Historians Journal* 6:1–15.

Djankov, Simeon, Rafael La Porta, Florencio Lopez-De-Silanes, and Andrei Shleifer. 2008. "The Law and Economics of Self-Dealing." *Journal of Financial Economics* 88:430–65.

Eames, Francis L. 1968. *The New York Stock Exchange.* New York: Greenwood Press.

Easterbrook, Frank H. 1986. "Monopoly, Manipulation, and the Regulation of Futures Markets." *Journal of Business* 59:S103–S127.

Edwards, George W. 1967. *The Evolution of Finance Capitalism.* Library of Money and Banking History. New York: A. M. Kelley.

Edwards, Jeremy S. S., and Alfons J. Weichenrieder. 2004. "Ownership Concentration and Share Valuation." *German Economic Review* 5:143–71.

Fabricant, Solomon. 1936. "Revaluation of Fixed Assets, 1925–1934." *National Bureau of Economic Research Bulletin* 62:1–11.

Faccio, Mara, Larry H. P. Lang, and Leslie Young. 2001. "Dividends and Expropriation." *American Economic Review* 91:54–78.

Fietkiewicz, Kristina, and W. Trexler Proffitt Jr. 2010. "Local Stock Exchanges and Their Effect on Regional Economic Development, 1790 to 1930." Working Paper.

Financial Crisis Inquiry Commission. 2011. "The Financial Crisis Inquiry Report." Washington, DC: Government Printing Office.

Fischel, Daniel R., and D. J. Ross. 1991. "Should the Law Prohibit 'Manipulation' in Financial Markets?" *Harvard Law Review* 105:503–53.

Fishback, Price V., and Shawn Everett Kantor. 1998. "The Adoption of Workers' Compensation in the United States, 1900–1930." *Journal of Law and Economics* 41:305–42.

Flannery, Mark J. 1984. "The Social Costs of Unit Banking Restrictions." *Journal of Monetary Economics* 13:237–49.

Flynn, John Thomas. 1933. "The Wall Street Water Pump." *Harpers Magazine* 167: 404–13.

Foster, Taylor W., D. Randall Jenkins, and Don W. Vickrey. 1983. "Additional Evidence on the Incremental Information Content of the 10-K." *Journal of Business Finance and Accounting* 10:57–66.

Friedman, Milton, and Anna Jacobson Schwartz. 1965. *The Great Contraction, 1929–1933.* Princeton, NJ: Princeton University Press.

Friend, Irwin, et al. 1967. *Investment Banking and the New Issues Market.* New York: World Publishing.

Friend, Irwin, and Edward S. Herman. 1964. "The S.E.C. Through a Glass Darkly." *Journal of Business* 37:382–405.

Galbraith, John Kenneth. 1979. *The Great Crash, 1929.* Boston: Houghton Mifflin.

———. 1990. *A Short History of Financial Euphoria.* New York: Penguin Books.

Galston, Arthur. 1928. *Security Syndicate Operations; Organization, Management and Accounting.* New York: Ronald Press Company.

Garber, Peter M. 1990. "Famous First Bubbles." *Journal of Economic Perspectives* 4:35–54.

Gertner, Robert H., David S. Scharfstein, and Jeremy C. Stein. 1994. "Internal Versus External Capital Markets." *Quarterly Journal of Economics* 109:1211–30.

Gopalan, Rakhakrishnan, Vikram Nanda, and Amit Seru. 2007. "Affiliated Firms and Financial Support: Evidence from Indian Business Groups." *Journal of Financial Economics* 86:759–95.

Gordon, Jeffrey N. 2002. "What Enron Means for the Management and Control of the Modern Business Corporation: Some Initial Reflections." *University of Chicago Law Review* 69:1233–50.

Gordon, Robert J. 1986. *The American Business Cycle: Continuity and Change.* Chicago: University of Chicago Press.

Gourrich, Paul P. 1937. "Investment Banking Methods Prior to and Since the Securities Act of 1933." *Law and Contemporary Problems* 4:44–71.

Greenspan, Alan. 2003. "Corporate Governance: Remarks at the 2003 Conference on Bank Structure and Competition" (speech). Accessed July 31, 2013. http://www.federalreserve.gov/boarddocs/speeches/2003/20030508/.

Gul, Ferdinand A., Jeong-Bon Kim, and Annie A. Qiu. 2010. "Ownership Concentration, Foreign Shareholding, Audit Quality, and Stock Price Synchronicity: Evidence from China." *Journal of Financial Economics* 95:425–42.

Hanc, George. 1997. "The Banking Crises of the 1980s and Early 1990s: Summary and Implications." In *History of the 80s—Lessons for the Future*, edited by Federal Deposit Insurance Corp. Washington, DC: Government Printing Office.

Hannah, Leslie. 1983. *The Rise of the Corporate Economy.* London: Methuen.

Harris, Ron. 1994. "The Bubble Act: Its Passage and Its Effects on Business Organization." *Journal of Economic History* 54:610–27.

Hausman, William J., and John L. Neufeld. 2002. "The Market for Capital and the Origins of State Regulation of Electric Utilities in the United States." *Journal of Economic History* 62:1050–73.

Haven, T. Kenneth. 1940. *Investment Banking under the Securities and Exchange Commission.* Ann Arbor: University of Michigan Press.

Hawkins, David F. 1986. "The Development of Modern Financial Reporting Practices among American Manufacturing Corporations." In *Managing Big Business: Essays from the Business History Review*, edited by Richard S. Tedlow and Richard R. John Jr., 166–99. Boston, MA: Harvard Business School Press.

Hayes, Samuel L., III. 1979. "The Transformation of Investment Banking." *Harvard Business Review* 57:153–70.

Hayn, Carla. 1995. "The Information Content of Losses." *Journal of Accounting and Economics* 20:125–53.

Holderness, Clifford G., and Dennis P. Sheehan. 1988. "The Role of Majority Shareholders in Publicly Held Corporations: An Exploratory Analysis." *Journal of Financial Economics* 20:317–46.

Huebner, Solomon S. 1928. *The Stock Market.* New York: D. Appleton and Company.

Huertas, Thomas F., and Joan L. Silverman. 1986. "Charles E. Mitchell: Scapegoat of the Crash?" *Business History Review* 60:81–103.

Hyman, Leonard. 1985. *America's Electric Utilities: Past, Present and Future.* 2nd ed. Arlington, VA: Public Utilities Reports.

Jarrow, Robert A. 1992. "Market Manipulation, Bubbles, Corners, and Short Squeezes." *Journal of Financial and Quantitative Analysis* 27:311–36.

Jefferys, James B. 1977. *Business Organization in Great Britain, 1856–1914.* New York: Arno Press.

Jensen, Michael, and William Meckling. 1976. "Theory of the Firm: Managerial Behavior, Agency Costs, and Ownership Structure." *Journal of Financial Economics* 11:5–50.

Jiang, Guohua, Charles M. C. Lee, and Heng Yue. 2010. "Tunneling through Intercorporate Loans: The China Experience." *Journal of Financial Economics* 98:1–20.

Johnson, Simon, Rafael La Porta, Florencio Lopez-De-Silanes, and Andrei Shleifer. 2000. "Tunneling." *American Economic Review* 90 (May): 22–27.

Jones, William K. 1967. *Cases and Materials on Regulated Industries.* Brooklyn, NY: Foundation Press.

Kaiser, Robert G. 2013. *Act of Congress.* New York: Alfred A. Knopf.

Kandel, Eugene, Konstantin Kosenko, Randall Morck, and Yishay Yafeh. 2013. "Business Groups in the United States: A Revised History of Corporate Ownership, Pyramids and Regulation, 1930–1950." National Bureau of Economic Research Working Paper.

Kim, Oliver, and Robert E. Verrecchia. 1991. "Trading Volume and Price Reactions to Public Announcements." *Journal of Accounting Research* 29:302–21.

Kindleberger, Charles P., and Robert Aliber. 2005. *Manias, Panics, and Crashes: A History of Financial Crises.* Hoboken, NJ: John Wiley and Sons.

Kleer, Richard A. 2004. "'The Ruine of Their Diana': Lowndes, Locke, and the Bankers." *History of Political Economy* 36 (2004): 533–56.

Knight, John. 1930. *Report of Commission on Revision of the Public Service Commissions Law.* Albany, NY: J. B. Lyon Company.

Kroszner, Randall S. 2013. "A Review of Bank Funding Cost Differentials." Working paper.

Kroszner, Randall S., and Philip Strahan. 2001. "Obstacles to Optimal Policy: The Interplay of Politics and Economics in Shaping Bank Supervision and Regulation Reforms." In *Prudential Supervision: What Works and What Doesn't,* edited by Frederic S. Mishkin, 233–71. Chicago: University of Chicago Press.

Kuhn, C. John. 1937. "The Securities Act and Its Effect Upon the Institutional Investor." *Law and Contemporary Problems* 4:80–88.

La Porta, Rafael, Florencio Lopez-de-Silanes, Cristian Pop-Eleches, and Andrei Shleifer. 2004. "Judicial Checks and Balances." *Journal of Political Economy* 112:445–70.

La Porta, Rafael, Florencio Lopez-de-Silanes, and Andrei Shleifer. 2006. "What Works in Securities Laws?" *Journal of Finance* 61:1–32.

Landis, James M. 1966. *The Administrative Process.* New Haven, CT: Yale University Press.

Leffler, George Leland. 1963. *The Stock Market.* New York: Ronald Press.

Leuz, Christian. 2003. "IAS Versus U.S. Gaap: Information Asymmetry-Based Evidence from Germany's New Market." *Journal of Accounting Research* 41:445.

Leuz, Christian, and Robert E. Verrecchia. 2000. "The Economic Consequences of Increased Disclosure." *Journal of Accounting Research* 38:91–124.

Li, Ming-Hsun. 1963. *The Great Recoinage of 1696 to 1699.* London: Weidenfeld and Nicolson.

Lilienthal, David E. 1929. "The Regulation of Public Utility Holding Companies." *Columbia Law Review* 29:404–40.

Litvak, Katherine. 2007. "The Impact of the Sarbanes-Oxley Act on Non-US Companies Cross-Listed in the US." *Journal of Corporate Finance* 13:195–228.

Loss, Louis, and Edward M. Cowett. 1958. *Blue Sky Law.* Boston: Little, Brown.

Loss, Louis, and Joel Seligman. 1989. *Securities Regulation.* Boston: Little, Brown.

Loss, Louis, Joel Seligman, and Troy Paredes. 2014. *Securities Regulation.* New York: Wolters Kluwer Law and Business.

Macey, Jonathan R. 1984. "Special Interest Groups Legislation and the Judicial Function: The Dilemma of Glass-Steagall." *Emory Law Journal* 33:1–40.

Macey, Jonathan R., and Geoffrey P. Miller. 1991. "Origin of the Blue Sky Laws." *Texas Law Review* 70:347–98.

Mahoney, Paul G. 1995. "Mandatory Disclosure as a Solution to Agency Problems." *University of Chicago Law Review* 62:1047–1112.

———. 2000. "Contract or Concession? An Essay on the History of Corporate Law." *Georgia Law Review* 34:873–93.

———. 2004. "Manager-Investor Conflicts in Mutual Funds." *Journal of Economic Perspectives* 18:161–82.

Maitland, Frederick W. 2005. *State, Trust and Corporation.* Cambridge: Cambridge University Press.

Malkiel, Burton. 2002. "The Market Can Police Itself." *Wall Street Journal*, June 28, A10.

Manne, Henry G. 1974. "Economic Aspects of Required Disclosure under the Federal Securities Laws." In *Wall Street in Transition: The Emerging System and Its Impact on the Economy*, edited by Henry G. Manne and Ezra Solomon, 21–110. New York: New York University Press.

Maug, Ernst G. 2002. "Insider Trading Legislation and Corporate Governance." *European Economic Review* 46:1569–97.

McConnell, John J., and Henri Servaes. 1990. "Additional Evidence on Equity Ownership and Corporate Value." *Journal of Financial Economics* 27:595–612.

McCullagh, Peter. 1980. "Regression Models for Ordinal Data (with Discussion)." *Journal of the Royal Statistical Society, Series B* 42:109–42.

McFadden, Daniel. 1974. "Conditional Logit Analysis of Qualitative Choice Behavior." In *Frontiers in Econometrics*, edited by Paul Zarembka, 105–42. New York: Academic Press.

Mehra, Alexander. 2010. "Legal Authority in Unusual and Exigent Circumstances: The Federal Reserve and the Financial Crisis." *University of Pennsylvania Journal of Business Law* 13:221–74.

Milkis, Sidney M. 2002. "Franklin D. Roosevelt, the Economic Constitutional Order, and the New Politics of Presidential Leadership." In *The New Deal and the Triumph of Liberalism*, edited by Sidney M. Milkis and Jerome M. Mileur, 31–72. Amherst: University of Massachusetts Press.

Moody's Investors Service. 1935. *Moody's Manual of Investments: Public Utility Securities.* London: Moody's Investors Service.

Morck, Randall K. 2005. "How to Eliminate Pyramidal Business Groups: The Double Taxation of Inter-Corporate Dividends and Other Incisive Uses of Tax Policy." *Tax Policy and the Economy* 19:135–79.

———. 2009. "The Riddle of the Great Pyramids." Cambridge, MA: National Bureau of Economic Research.

Morck, Randall K., Andrei Shleifer, and Robert W. Vishny. 1988. "Management Ownership and Market Valuation: An Empirical Analysis." *Journal of Financial Economics* 20:293–315.

Morley, John. 2012. "Collective Branding and the Origins of Investment Fund Regulation." *Virginia Law and Business Review* 6:341–401.

Mulligan, Casey B., and Andrei Shleifer. 2005. "The Extent of the Market and the Supply of Regulation." *Quarterly Journal of Economics* 120:1445–73.

Murray, Shanon. 2002. "Is SEC Ready for Its Own Sweeping Changes?" *New York Law Journal*, August 29.

Neal, Larry. 1990. *The Rise of Financial Capitalism: International Capital Markets in the Age of Reason.* Cambridge: Cambridge University Press.

Neufeld, John L. 2008. "Corruption, Quasi-Rents, and the Regulation of Electric Utilities." *Journal of Economic History* 68:1059–97.

A New York Stock Exchange Broker. 1930. "Inside Pools, Bobtails and Jiggles." *North American Review* 229:295–304.

North, Douglass C., and Barry R. Weingast. 1989. "The Evolution of Institutions Governing Public Choice in 17th Century England." *Journal of Economic History* 49:803–32.

Palmer, Francis B. 1898. *Palmer's Company Law.* London: Stevens and Sons.

Parrish, Michael E. 1970. *Securities Regulation and the New Deal.* New Haven, CT: Yale University Press.

Pavalko, Eliza K. 1989. "State Timing of Policy Adoption: Workmen's Compensation in the United States, 1909–1929." *American Journal of Sociology* 95:592–615.

Pawson, E. 1979. *The Early Industrial Revolution: Britain in the Eighteenth Century.* New York: Barnes and Noble Books.

Peach, W. Nelson. 1983. *The Security Affiliates of National Banks.* New York: AMS Press.

Peirce, Hester, and James Broughel, eds. 2012. *Dodd-Frank: What It Does and Why It's Flawed.* Arlington, VA: Mercatus Center at George Mason University.

Perino, Michael. 2012. "The Financial Crisis Inquiry Commission and the Politics of Governmental Investigations." *UMKC Law Review* 80:1063–99.

Pirrong, S. Craig. 1995. "The Self-Regulation of Commodity Exchanges: The Case of Market Manipulation." *Journal of Law and Economics* 38:141–206.

Plumb, J. H. 1950. *England in the Eighteenth Century.* Baltimore, MD: Penguin Books.

Pratt, Sereno Stansbury. 1921. *The Work of Wall Street; an Account of the Functions, Methods and History of the New York Money and Stock Markets.* New York: D. Appleton and Company.

Priest, George L. 1993. "The Origins of Utility Regulation and the 'Theories of Regulation' Debate." *Journal of Law and Economics* 36:289–323.

Quinn, Stephen. 2008. "Securitization of Sovereign Debt: Corporations as a Sovereign Debt Restructuring Mechanism in Britain, 1694 to 1750." Department of Economics, Texas Christian University. Available at http://ssrn.com/abstract=991941.

Redlich, Fritz. 1968. *The Molding of American Banking; Men and Ideas.* History of American Economy: Studies and Materials for Study. New York: Johnson Reprint Corp.

Ripley, William Z. 1927. *Main Street and Wall Street.* Boston: Little, Brown.

Romano, Roberta. 2005. "The Sarbanes-Oxley Act and the Making of Quack Corporate Governance." *Yale Law Journal* 114:1521–1611.

———. 2012. "Regulating in the Dark." In *Regulatory Breakdown? The Crisis of Confidence in U.S. Regulation*, edited by Cary Coglianese, 86–117. Philadelphia: University of Pennsylvania Press.

Romer, Christina D. 1990. "The Great Crash and the Onset of the Great Depression." *Quarterly Journal of Economics* 105:597–624.

Roosevelt, Franklin Delano. 1972. *The Complete Press Conferences of Franklin D. Roosevelt.* Vol. 2. New York: Da Capo Press.

Schrade, William R., and W. David Walls. 2008. "Holding Companies, Market Liquidity, and the Development of the Electric Power Industry." *Journal of Energy and Development* 32:1–14.

Schwarzschild, Otto P., ed. 1925–35. *American Underwriting Houses and Their Issues.* New York: National Statistical Service.

Schwert, G. William. 1977. "Public Regulation of National Securities Exchanges: A Test of the Capture Hypothesis." *Bell Journal of Economics* 8:128–50.

Scott, William Robert. 1910. *The Constitution and Finance of English, Scottish and Irish Joint-Stock Companies to 1720.* Cambridge: Cambridge University Press.

Seligman, Joel. 1983. "The Historical Need for a Mandatory Corporate Disclosure System." *Journal of Corporate Law* 9:1–62.

———. 2003. *The Transformation of Wall Street: A History of the Securities and Exchange Commission and Modern Corporate Finance.* New York: Aspen.

Shannon, H. A. 1932. "The First Five Thousand Limited Companies and Their Duration." *Journal of Economic History* 7:396-424.

Shleifer, Andrei, and Robert Vishny. 1997. "A Survey of Corporate Governance." *Journal of Finance* 52:737–83.

Shughart, William F. 1988. "A Public Choice Perspective of the Banking Act of 1933." In *The Financial Services Revolution*, edited by Catherine England and Thomas F. Huertas, 87–105. Boston: Kluwer Academic Publishers.

Sissoko, Carolyn. 2013. "Taking Asymmetric Information Seriously: An Analysis of the London Stock Exchange." Working Paper.

Skeel, David. 2011. *The New Financial Deal: Understanding the Dodd-Frank Act and Its (Unintended) Consequences.* Hoboken, NJ: John Wiley and Sons.

Sorin, David J., Kristina K. Pappa, and Emilio Ragosa. 2002. "*Sarbanes-Oxley* Act: Politics or Reform?; Statute's Effects Are Not as Profound as Legislators Would Have Us Believe." *New Jersey Law Journal*, September 2.

Steiner, W. H., and Oscar Lasdon. 1934. "The Market Action of New Issues—A Test of Syndicate Price Pegging." *Harvard Business Review* 12:339.

Stigler, George J. 1971. "The Theory of Economic Regulation." *Bell Journal of Economics and Management* 2:3–21.

Stigler, George J., and Claire Friedland. 1962. "What Can Regulators Regulate? The Case of Electricity." *Journal of Law and Economics* 5:1–16.

Taylor, John B. 2009. *Getting Off Track: How Government Actions and Interventions Caused, Prolonged, and Worsened the Financial Crisis.* Stanford, CA: Hoover Institution Press.

Tkac, Paula. 1999. "A Trading Volume Benchmark: Theory and Evidence." *Journal of Financial and Quantitative Analysis* 34:89–114.

Telser, Lester G. 1960. "Why Should Manufacturers Want Fair Trade?" *Journal of Law and Economics* 3:86–105.

Temin, Peter. 1976. *Did Monetary Forces Cause the Great Depression?* New York: W. W. Norton.

———. 1992. *Lessons from the Great Depression.* Cambridge, MA: MIT Press.

Troesken, Walter. 2006. "Regime Change and Corruption: A History of Public Utility Regulation." In *Corruption and Reform: Lessons from America's Economic History*, edited by Edward L. Glaeser and Claudia Golden, 259–84. Chicago: University of Chicago Press.

Twentieth Century Fund. 1935. *The Security Markets: Findings and Recommendations of a Special Staff of the Twentieth Century Fund.* New York: Twentieth Century Fund.

Ueda, Kenichi, and Beatrice Weder di Mauro. 2012. "Quantifying Structural Subsidy Values for Systemically Important Financial Institutions." Working paper, International Monetary Fund.

US Government Accountability Office. 2014. *Large Bank Holding Companies: Expectations of Government Support.* Available at http://www.gao.gov/products/GAO-14-809T.

US Senate. 1932. *Stock Exchange Practices, Hearings Before the Committee on Banking and Currency.* Washington, DC: US Government Printing Office.

———. 1933. *Stock Exchange Practices, Hearings Before the Committee on Banking and Currency.* Washington, DC: US Government Printing Office.

———. 1934. *Stock Exchange Practices, Report No. 1455.* Washington, DC: US Government Printing Office.

Walker, R. G. 1992. "The Sec's Ban on Upward Asset Revaluation and the Disclosure of Current Values." *Abacus* 28:3–35.

Wallison, Peter J. 2011. "Dissent from the Majority Report of the Financial Crisis Inquiry Commission." American Enterprise Institute, Washington, DC.

Weaver, R. Kent. 1986. "The Politics of Blame Avoidance." *Journal of Public Policy* 6:371–98.

West, Richard. 1998. *Daniel Defoe: The Life and Strange, Surprising Adventures.* New York: Carroll and Graf.

White, Eugene Nelson. 1990. "The Stock Market Boom and Crash of 1929 Revisited." *Journal of Economic Perspectives* 4:67–83.

White, Lawrence J. 2012. "Dodd-Frank: The Good and the Not-So-Good." In *Dodd-Frank: What It Does and Why It's Flawed*, edited by Hester Peirce and James Broughel, 169–81. Arlington, VA: Mercatus Center at George Mason University.

Zeff, Stephen A. 1984. "Some Junctures in the Evolution of the Process of Establishing Accounting Principles in the USA: 1917–1972." *Accounting Review* 59:447–68.

———. 2007. "The SEC Rules Historical Cost Accounting: 1934 to the 1970s." Working paper, Rice University.

Index

accounting profession, 83, 150–51, 153, 163
"Act to restraine the Number and ill Practice of Brokers and Stock-Jobbers, An," (1697), 9, 13, 16

Bank of England, 11–13, 15, 17
banks, rural, 25, 34–36
Blackstone, William, 18–19
blame avoidance, by politicians, 2, 5, 13–14, 32, 152, 166–67
blue sky laws, 37; categories of issuers in, 29; competitive effects of, 21, 24, 32, 34–36; disclosure provisions of, 21, 46; fraud as motivation for, 9–10, 20–21, 23–24, 27–30, 32, 36; ideology as motivation for, 21, 28, 29–31; small bank lobby as motivation for, 21, 24–25, 28–29, 31–36; timing of adoption, 22, 24, 25, 26–31, 36; types of, 20, 22, 32–34, 35–36
Bonbright, John: *The Holding Company* (with Gardiner Means), 119, 120, 122–23, 129, 131; and utility regulation, 118–19, 120, 145
Brandeis, Louis, 45, 169; *Other People's Money and How the Bankers Use It*, 26, 42, 45
broker-dealers: bankruptcy code and, 168–69; competition among, 50, 60–64, 149; in-house legal staff, 164; participation in public offerings, 51, 53–54, 59, 65, 68–70, 98; participation in secondary distributions, 104; securitization by, 156; self-regulation of, 65, 69; single capacity rule, effect on, 98. *See also* market making
Bubble Act (1720), 9, 18–19
business groups, 124, 138. *See also* pyramid structures

capital requirements, 8, 25, 154, 157, 161, 163
Commodity Futures Modernization Act, 155
Commodity Futures Trading Commission, 154, 164
Companies Act (England), 38, 44–45, 47, 125
controlling shareholders: effects on other shareholders, 120–21, 124, 144; private benefits of, 78 (*see also* tunneling, by controlling shareholders); of utility companies, 123, 130–32
Cowles Index, 3
CRSP (Center for Research in Security Prices): daily price data, 8, 87, 92, 110–11, 129, 132; equally-weighted index, 87, 113–14; value-weighted index, 134

Defoe, Daniel, 14–15; *Robinson Crusoe*, 17
derivatives, 5, 154–55, 156, 159–60, 161, 162
Dillon, Read & Co., 52, 65–66, 73
Dodd-Frank Act: as "best practices" provision, 149; compared to New Deal reforms, 1, 8, 149, 153–54, 164–65; competitive effects of, 149, 162–163; as cure for deregulation, 154; implementation of, 1, 167; legislative process, 153–54, 168; orderly resolution authority, 165, 169; predicted consequences of, 163–66; registration of hedge fund advisers under, 162; and rule of law, 165; securities regulation provisions of, 162–63; and too big to fail, 160–62; treatment of rating agencies, 163

Douglas, William O., 143, 169
Dow Jones Industrial Average, 3–4, 40

earnings announcements: company practices, 84, 86–87, 97; traders' reactions to, effect of Exchange Act registration, 85–92, 96; traders' reactions to, general, 81, 85–86, 91
earnings management, 47, 82, 97, 106
electric utilities, rates and rate regulation, 26, 118, 141–43
Enron Corp., 150, 151, 152, 153
Exchange Act. *See* Securities Exchange Act of 1934
executive compensation, 83, 93, 97, 150–51, 162

Federal Deposit Insurance Corporation, 154, 158, 164–65, 168–69
Federal Reserve, 25, 154, 155; creation of, 169; and Dodd-Frank, 160, 164; and Great Depression, 39; and subprime crisis, 157, 160, 168; and too big to fail, 158
Federal Trade Commission, 46–47, 153; utility report of, 125, 131, 141
financial crises, 1–2, 7, 13, 161–63, 167–69; of 1696, 10–15, 39; of 1907, 168–69; of 1931–33 (*see* Great Depression); of 2007–8, 1–2, 5, 153–61, 163, 166, 168; as cause of regulation, 4–5, 7–8, 9, 15, 37, 118, 167 (*see also* market failure narrative); and monetary policy, 2, 13–14, 15, 39, 157; stock market blamed for, 1, 14, 41
Financial Stability Oversight Council (FSOC), 161, 162, 164, 165
Fletcher Report, 100, 103, 106, 109–10
floor traders, 96–97, 105–6, 109
FTC. *See* Federal Trade Commission

GAAP, US, 81
Glass-Steagall Act, 60, 70–71, 74, 155–56
Goldman, Sachs & Co., 52
government failure, 2, 13–14, 154, 156
government securities, 10–11, 17–18, 59, 157. *See also* Liberty Bond drives
Gramm-Leach-Bliley Act, 155–56
Great Crash, 37, 77, 103, 109–10, 166; as cause of Great Depression, 39–41; causes of, 4, 37, 39, 77; compared to 1987 market crash, 4; compared to subprime crisis, 1, 149, 153–54; as justification for regulation, 3, 37, 117, 149; magnitude of investor losses, 3–4, 39–41, 107, 125 (*see also under* market failure narrative)
Great Depression, 1–5, 34, 74, 77; causes of, 2–3, 37, 39–41, 103; compared to subprime crisis, 1, 153–54, 166; and corporate profits, 91; and new issue volume, 72; second wave, 41, 146; and stock price declines, 4, 39–41, 107, 145
Great Recoinage of 1696, 11–12, 15
Greenspan, Alan, 155, 159–60
gun-jumping, 60–62, 65, 67–68

Halsey, Stuart & Co., 52, 53, 65–66, 68, 74
Harris, Forbes & Co., 52, 53, 65–66, 71
Healy, Robert, 46–47, 82
holding companies. *See* pyramid structures
Hoover, Herbert, 120

insider trading, 105, 114
Insull, Samuel, 123, 125
Investment Advisors Act of 1940, 146
Investment Bankers Association of America: and blue sky laws, 24, 28, 31, 33, 66; and Code of Fair Competition, 68–69; concerns about discounts, 62–63, 66, 68; concerns about growth in membership, 55–57; concerns about gun-jumping, 61–62, 66–67; membership of, 28–31, 33, 55–57, 73–74; and Securities Act of 1933, 66; and syndicate system, 64–65
investment banks, 21, 104, 156, 162; commercial bank subsidiaries, 21, 63–64, 66, 70–71; compensation of 37–38, 41–42, 51, 66; competition among, 24, 38–39, 49–50, 55–59, 60–64, 149, 163; concentration, 58–59, 64, 72–74; concerns about IPO volume, 152; failures of, during subprime crisis, 155; industry structure, 52–55, 73–74; integrated, 65–66, 70; and Liberty Loan drives, 53; number of, 28–29, 33, 55–56; profitability of, 49, 56–58, 75; and public utility holding companies, 123, 131; retail, 51, 61, 70; security analysts, 150; trade group of (*see* Investment Bankers Association of America);

wholesale, 51, 61, 66–67, 70. *See also* broker-dealers
investment companies: closed-end, 145; financial leverage of, 145–46; open-end, 145; ownership of utility companies, 131
Investment Company Act of 1940: as "best practices" regulation, 146–47; competitive effects of, 145–46, 148; industry support for, 145–46, 147–48; lawyers and, 164; legislative process, 146; and market segmentation, 147
investor irrationality, 16–17, 77–78
IPOs, 45, 55; after SOX, 152, 167; in England, 43, 44; underpricing of, 64

Jefferson, Thomas, 3, 169–70
JOBS Act of 2012, 50, 152, 167
J. P. Morgan & Co., 75, 106; competitive position, 52, 66, 73; creation of United Corp., 131; and crisis of 1907, 169; Glass-Steagall Act, effect on, 71; legislative influence of, 66, 71. *See also* Morgan Stanley & Co.

Kennedy, Joseph P., 108, 127
Kuhn, Loeb & Co., 52, 66, 71, 73

Landis, James, 38, 45–48, 49, 169, 181n24
Liberty Bond drives, 53, 63
Levitt, Arthur, 3–4, 40, 77, 151

manipulation: Congressional misunderstanding of, 107–8; and fraud, contrasted, 101; and insider trading, contrasted, 105; as motivation for Exchange Act, 77, 100, 102, 116; price pattern as evidence of, 110, 114–15, 116; trade-based, 101–2, 106. *See also* stock pools
market failure narrative, 1–2, 9, 14, 103, 156; of 1696 financial crisis, 9–10, 12–13, 15; of 2001–2 stock market crash, 150, 163; of blue sky laws, 10, 20, 23–24, 30, 36; definition of, 1, 149; of Great Crash and Great Depression, 2, 38–41, 77, 81, 103, 117, 149, 154; of investment company regulation, 146; of public utility holding companies, 143–145, 147; of South Sea Bubble, 10, 18–19; of subprime crisis, 5, 154–56, 160–61, 163
market making, 53, 104–6, 109, 160
Mitchell, Charles E., 54
money trust, 26, 169
Morgan Stanley & Co., 73
mortgage-backed securities, 5, 12, 154, 155–57
mutual funds. *See* investment companies

NASDAQ, 150
National Association of Securities Dealers, 65, 69
National City Company, 53–54, 65–66, 71, 73–74
National Industrial Recovery Act (NIRA), 68–69
New Deal: 1–3, 98, 146, 149, 169; effects of, 7, 38, 66–68, 118, 164–66; ideology of, 2, 9, 38, 143, 169; modern comparisons to, 1, 8, 150, 153, 163; popular understanding of, 2–3, 9, 38, 76, 164; securities reforms, 37, 47, 77, 118, 143
New York Curb Exchange. *See under* stock exchanges
New York Times: coverage of PUHCA, 126–128; as data source, 8, 86–87, 91
NYSE: competition with regional exchanges, 81, 98–99; enforcement of own rules, 79–81, 102; FDR's and Congress's desire to regulate, 79, 106, 117, 125; listed companies, 79–80, 81–82, 96–98; listing standards, 79–81, 82–83, 84, 98, 130; manipulation on, 77, 103; member brokers, 79, 103, 105; opposition to Exchange Act, 98–99; receipt of SEC filings, 96–98; rules of, 77, 79, 84, 102, 104, 110, 151; value of listed stocks 3, 40–41. *See also under* Securities Exchange Act of 1934

off-balance-sheet transactions, 47, 150, 151, 157

Pecora, Ferdinand, 100, 109
Pecora Hearings, 103, 106, 112, 155; findings of market manipulation, 77, 100; purpose of, 103; testimony of Fiorello LaGuardia, 107; testimony of George Whitney, 106; testimony of pool operators, 106; testimony of Richard Whitney, 105, 107, 109
policy entrepreneurs, 9, 149, 150, 151, 166
populism, 21, 25, 28
private banks, 52, 71

progressive movement, 25–26; and blue sky laws, 20, 21, 25–34, 36; concerns about large financial institutions, 26, 169; and regulation of stock exchanges, 149; and Securities Act of 1933, 38, 42, 149
promoters, corporate, 9, 20, 42–45; compensation, 37, 43–45, 46; as fiduciaries, 44–45
prospectus, 43–44; advertisements as, 67; mandated disclosures in, 42, 45; preliminary, 68; in pre-SEC era, 3, 4, 79
Public Company Accounting Oversight Board, 151, 153
public utilities, state and local regulation of, 118, 122–23, 125, 140–42
Public Utility Holding Company Act of 1935 (PUHCA), 118, 129, 143, 182n4; Congressional opposition to, 126–28, 135; constitutionality of, 128–29, 134; "death sentence" provision, 120, 126–28, 134–35, 137–38; implementation of, 120, 129; industry opposition to, 126, 127–28, 143, 147; interconnection provisions of, 120, 128; legislative process, 121, 125–28, 134–35, 137; registration of holding companies under, 120, 134; SEC approval of utility financing under, 120, 126, 134; valuation effects of, 122, 129–38, 139–40
Pujo hearings, 26
pyramid structures: abolishment, under PUHCA, 120 (*see also* Public Utility Holding Company Act of 1935: "death sentence" provision); and business groups, compared, 123–24, 144; creation of, 123; evasion of rate regulation, 122, 125, 135, 138, 140–43, 145; financial leverage of, 125, 138, 145; and financing of subsidiaries, 121–22, 123–24, 135, 140, 143–44; and non-financial services to subsidiary companies, 122, 123–24, 135, 140, 142; separation of ownership and control in, 121, 123, 138; theories of, 121, 124; valuation effects of, 121, 125, 129–38, 143–45

Radio Corporation of America. *See* RCA
rating agencies, 5, 159, 163
RCA, 107–8
reallowances, 62–63, 66, 68–69
Revenue Act of 1935, 137–38
Roosevelt, Franklin D.: 1932 campaign of, 41–42, 45, 103, 119–20, 125, 145; criticism of NYSE, 79, 106; and Glass-Steagall, 71; governor of New York, 118, 119; invocation of Brandeis, 42, 45, 169; and market failure narrative of Depression, 2, 41; and NIRA, 68; and PUHCA, 118–20, 125–26, 127–28, 145, 147; relationship with Wendell Willkie, 147; and Revenue Act of 1935, 137; and Securities Act of 1933, 41–42, 45, 125; and Securities Exchange Act of 1934, 116, 125; support for larger federal government, 169
Roosevelt, Theodore, 26, 28, 29–31, 33, 169

S&P 500, 4, 150
Sarbanes-Oxley Act, 7, 149–53, 163; as "best practices" mandate, 149, 152; compared to New Deal reforms, 150; corporate governance provisions, 150–52, 162; effects of, 149, 152–53, 167; and IPO volume, 152, 167; legislative process, 151, 168
SEC, 3, 69, 154, 162; anti-manipulation rules of, 102–3; attempt to ban nonaudit services, 151, 153; borrowing of market practices, 4; borrowing of NYSE rules, 80–81, 82; confidentiality requests, 93; creation of, 80, 82, 86, 120, 153; desire to extend jurisdiction to investment companies, 146, 148; enforcement powers of, 86; exemptive authority, 50, 128, 152, 153; and financial accounting, 46–47, 81–84, 92–93, 97–98; and full disclosure philosophy, 41–42; public offering reforms of 2005, 50, 70, 152; records of, 92, 96; registration and disclosure forms of, 4, 45, 82–86, 92–97; rulemaking authority, 45, 86, 98, 102, 126, 151, 164–65; and self-regulation, 69; staff, 103, 165; studies by, 57–58, 99. *See also specific statutes*
Securities Act of 1933, 20, 37, 60; anti-fraud provisions of, 49, 85–86, 166; comparison to English law and practice, 38, 45–46, 70, 125; competitive effects of, 38, 49, 58–59, 65–76, 163; effects on market for lawyers, 164; gun-jumping provisions of, 62, 65, 67–68, 152; importance of, to FDR, 41; and investment bank profitability, 75–76; liability provisions of, 66, 166; mandatory disclosure provisions of, 8, 37–38, 41–42, 45–47, 68, 149, 166;

registration under, 45, 50, 67–68, 82; as secrecy statute, 38, 49–50, 70; support for, by major investment banks, 66, 143, 147, 152; and syndicate system, 65, 66, 70, 71–72; waiting period under, 50, 68, 69–70
Securities and Exchange Commission, US. *See* SEC
Securities Exchange Act of 1934: anti-fraud provisions of, 85–86; anti-manipulation provisions of, 100, 116–17; as best practices provision, 81, 149; creation of SEC, 80, 82; delegation of authority to SEC, 98; effects of, 81, 85–91, 92–97, 99; effects on market for lawyers, 164; enactment of, 118; initial implementation of, 81, 82–83, 84–86; mandatory disclosure provisions of, 80–84, 85, 89; opposition of stock exchanges to, 98, 143, 147; registration and regulation of stock exchanges under, 81, 84, 99, 149; registration of exchange-traded companies under, 81–82; registration form (Form 10), 82–84, 86, 92–97
securities regulation: adoption after crises, 4–5, 7–8, 9, 15, 37, 118, 167 (*see also* market failure narrative); and banker-populist coalition, 21, 118; and best practices 6, 81, 98, 146–47, 149, 152, 166; competitive effects of, 5–6, 15–16, 63, 65–66, 166–67; contract-enhancing versus command-and-control, 166–67; effects on quality of disclosures, 85–86; federal responsibility for, 118; fixed costs of; 24; market failure as justification for (*see* market failure narrative); mean reversion and illusion of success, 4–5, 10; New Deal reforms to (*see under* New Deal); regulation of corporate governance under, 150–52, 162. *See also specific statutes*
securitization, 5, 17, 161. *See also* mortgage-backed securities
selling concession, 62, 68, 69, 75
Senate Banking Committee: and Securities Act, 66; and Securities Exchange Act, 100, 102, 104, 107; Stock Exchange Practices, hearings (*see* Pecora Hearings); Stock Exchange Practices, report (*see* Fletcher Report)
Senate Commerce Committee, 126, 127, 128
shadow banks, 154
South Sea Company, 16–19
stabilization, 104
stockbrokers 10, 53, 98; on boards of public companies, 105; in England, 9, 10, 13, 16, 98; competition with banks, 21, 25, 36; disputes with customers, 27; influence on blue sky laws, 28, 31, 32, 34; number of, 28–31, 33, 56; as owners of exchanges, 78–79; participation in public offerings, 51–52, 68, 98; participation in stock pools, 103–5, 109; registration of, under blue sky laws, 23; sales of Liberty Bonds, 53. *See also* broker-dealers
stock exchanges: New York Curb Exchange, 129–30, 132–33; regional exchanges, 81, 98–99. *See also* NYSE
stock market crashes, 14, 151; of 1696, 12, 14–15, 39; of 1929 (*see* Great Crash); of 1987, 4; of 2001–2, 4, 149, 150; of 2008, 1, 5, 149, 156, 166. *See also* financial crises
stock pools: abnormal returns during, 113–15; abnormal turnover during, 115–16; as block trading, 104; as described by commentators 100–102, 106; as distribution of stock, 104; fictitious trades by, 101, 109; fraudulent statements by, 101–2, 116; list of stocks subject to, 112; as proprietary trading, 103; in Radio Corporation of America stock, 107–8; and rights offerings, 104; Senate investigation of (*see* Pecora Hearings); Senate's understanding of, 102, 106–10; tests of manipulative effect, 110–16; written agreements for, 103–4
systemically important financial institutions, 161–62. *See also* too big to fail
systemic risk, 158, 160–61, 165

too big to fail, 158–162, 163
trading, fictitious, 101–2, 109
tunneling, by controlling shareholders, 124, 135, 138–140, 144

underwriting: by commercial banks, 21, 63–64, 66, 70–71; growth of, after WWI, 45; managing or originating underwriter, 51, 61, 64; selling group, distinguished, 54; syndication of, 50–51, 59–60, 64–66, 71

United States v. Morgan litigation, 50, 53, 58–59

valuation, accounting: acquisitions, 119; current value versus historical cost, 47, 82, 97, 119–20, 124; of intangible assets 23, 47

Wall Street Journal, 8, 58
Washington Post, 126, 127
watered stock, 47, 119–20, 124
Whitney, George, 106
Whitney, Richard, 105, 107, 109